GENERAL INTRODUCTION

The BPP (I) Irish Business Law manual published in 1992 covered a wide range of topics. In a revised and updated text published in August 1995 coverage was confined to 4 subject areas, namely contract, agency, negligence and employment.

This Irish Business Law Supplement contains chapters on the following areas:

- The administration of justice
- Legal process and legal reasoning
- Sale of goods
- Negotiable instruments and cheques

- Intellectual property law
- Partnership law
- European Community law
- Competition law

The 1995 Irish Business Law text and this Supplement provide coverage of most of the business law topics examinable by ACCA, MII and IATI and in a number of college courses.

Your knowledge of the subject matter is tested by being asked quick revision type questions (Test Your Knowledge) and also more detailed questions indicated at the end of most chapters. For your assistance suggested solutions are given for the latter questions. Although multichoice questions are not always set in exams there are a number of multichoice questions at the back of the book as a further test of understanding and knowledge.

Cross references in the text to chapters in the Irish Business Law manual are prefixed with the letters IBL.

CASE LAW

There are references in the text to Irish, English and where appropriate, European Court of Justice decisions. Irish cases have been specifically distinguished in the text from decisions in other jurisdictions by the addition of (I). Decisions of the Courts of England, while not binding, are persuasive authority in the Republic of Ireland. Full case references are stated in the List of Cases.

BPP (I) Publishing,
March 1996

A note on pronouns

On occasions in this Study Text, 'he' is used for 'he or she', 'him' for 'him or her' and so forth. Whilst we try to avoid this practice it is sometimes necessary for reasons of style. No prejudice or stereotyping according to sex is intended or assumed.

CONTENTS

PART A
THE ADMINISTRATION OF
JUSTICE

Chapter 1

STRUCTURE OF THE LEGAL SYSTEM

Points covered in this chapter are:

- The Constitution
- Civil and criminal liability
- Structure of the legal system
- The courts
- The civil courts
- The criminal courts
- The European Court of Justice
- The European Court of Human Rights
- Administrative tribunals
- Tribunals of inquiry
- Arbitration
- Legal personnel
- The legal profession

Purpose of chapter

The practicalities of how the Irish legal system operates its structure and the procedures likely to operate if you have cause to resort to the system are outlined here.

Introduction

1. In the public mind the legal profession and the legal system tend to have an aura of mystique bolstered by archaic language and parlance and attired in wigs and gowns. Behind that facade, for the most part the system comprises practical and down-to-earth procedures designed to protect public security and resolve disputes.

2. Though the more spectacular and media-hyped cases tend to be heard in the High Court or Central Criminal Court, the vast majority of cases - both civil and criminal - are heard by the District Courts and Circuit Courts.

3. The Courts have a criminal law jurisdiction and a civil law jurisdiction. In Ireland the same Courts (eg District Court, Circuit Court) can and do administer both civil and criminal law. However, these dual jurisdictions will be considered separately here for convenience.

1: STRUCTURE OF THE LEGAL SYSTEM

● The Constitution

4. The Constitution of Ireland, 1937 has been the cornerstone of our legal system for over 50 years. Article 34 of the Constitution provides for the law to be administered in courts established by law and by judges appointed in accordance with the provisions of the Constitution. The Constitution is discussed in more detail in the next chapter.

● Civil and criminal liability

5. The central basis of the legal system is built on the distinction between criminal and civil liability.

Crime

6. A 'crime' is conduct forbidden by law that unjustifiably inflicts or threatens harm or injury to another individual, to public order or to property. Normally the State prosecutes the perpetrator of a crime since it is a wrong against the community as a whole which suffers as a result of the law being breached. Persons convicted are punished by various penalties such as imprisonment, community service, fines and the like.

7. Normally criminal proceedings are commenced by the State but in certain circumstances they may be brought by a private individual. The gardai take the initiative in deciding to prosecute. This may then be reviewed by the Director of Public Prosecutions and the Chief State Solicitor's Office which normally will subsequently conduct the prosecution of more serious criminal cases. Most crimes have a victim, however, beyond being called as a witness on behalf of the Prosecution the victim does not have any active part to play in decisions made regarding the prosecution of the charges. Normally there is no personal benefit or gain for the victim from a conviction - unless the Court specifically orders the convicted person to pay compensation - all fines are payable to the State.

8. In a criminal trial the burden of proof to convict the accused rests with the State (the Prosecution) to prove beyond reasonable doubt that the accused committed the offence alleged.

Civil proceedings

9. Civil law exists to regulate disputes over the rights and obligations of persons and companies dealing with each other. Normally, the State has no function in a private dispute of matters involving contracts or negligence and the like. If the parties involved cannot settle their dispute between themselves then they may resort to court to resolve the issues. The court will adjudicate on the issues after hearing evidence of both sides and make an order either directing one party to do certain acts or refrain from doing an act - an injunction - or may award damages to compensate the successful party. The court can also make an order for the costs of the action.

10. In civil proceedings the facts alleged must be proven on the balance of probabilities. The plaintiff sues the defendant and the burden of proof may shift from the plaintiff to the defendant depending on the nature of the claim.

11. The main area of civil liability in the syllabus is contract, although there are elements of tort. Both are forms of relationship between persons.

(a) A *contract* is a legally binding agreement, breach of which infringes one party's legal rights under the contract to have it performed.

(b) A *tort* is a wrong committed by one person against another, which infringes his general rights given to him by law. It is not necessary that there should have been any pre-existing personal relationship between the parties before the tort was committed.

Distinction between criminal and civil cases

12. Normally, it is the legal consequences of an act which give rise to the distinction between civil and criminal cases.

13. For instance in the case of a road traffic accident where a pedestrian is struck and injured by a drunken driver the accident may give rise to two separate actions:
     (a) a criminal action where the driver is prosecuted for drunk driving;
     (b) a civil action where the pedestrian sues the driver for damages and compensation for the injuries and loss sustained.

14. Such proceedings are clearly distinguishable and the court procedures and terminology used in each case are quite different.

• Structure of the legal system

15. Articles 34-36 and Article 38 of the Constitution of Ireland, 1937 contain the essential provisions relating to the courts. Article 34 provides for courts of first instance to include the High Court and also for a Court of Final Appeal. The Court of Final Appeal under the Constitution is the Supreme Court.

16. The detailed operation of the courts is governed by statute. The principal Acts are the Courts (Establishment and Constitution) Act, 1961 which established the District Court and the Circuit Court, which were new courts contemplated in the Constitution, and the Courts (Supplemental Provisions) Act, 1961 which regulated their several jurisdictions. Significant changes to the organisation of the courts have also been introduced by the Courts and Court Officers Act 1995, passed on 15 December 1995, which *inter alia* provides that the Supreme Court may sit in 2 or more divisions, for the abolition of the Court of Criminal Appeal and for the transfer of its jurisdiction to the Supreme Court.

17. The jurisdiction of the courts has been organised essentially by reference to the amount of compensation which is sought to be recovered by a plaintiff in a civil action or in a criminal case by reference to the gravity of the crime.

18. Most recently the structuring of the court business of the inferior courts was altered by the Courts Act, 1991.

• The courts

19. The Oireachtas is obliged by Article 34.3.4. of the Constitution to create courts of local and limited jurisdiction and these were created in 1961 as outlined at para 16 above.

20. The High Court is the only court of First Instance specifically mentioned in the Constitution.

21. The Supreme Court fulfils the functions of 'a Court of Final Appeal' as referred to in Article 34.2 of the Constitution.

The District Court

22. This is the lowest and most localised court in the legal system. For the conduct of legal business the country is divided up into two hundred District Court areas, which are grouped into District Court Districts, and the Dublin Metropolitan District. The maximum number of ordinary judges of the District Court is fixed by the Court and Court Officers Act, 1995 at 50 (previously 45) plus the President of the District Court who is also *ex officio* a judge of the Circuit Court.

    Judges are assigned on a permanent basis to particular Districts and to the Dublin Metropolitan District - a maximum of 12 judges are not permanently assigned to any District.

    Barristers and solicitors of 10 years standing are eligible for appointment as judges of the District Court.

23. Decisions of the District Court can be appealed to the Circuit Court where a complete re-hearing takes place. The Circuit Court may affirm the decision of the District Court or substitute its own decision.

    Where a case has been heard and decided by a District Judge, a party who is dissatisfied with such decision as being wrong on a point of law, can require the judge to 'state a case' for the High Court ie the judge seeks the opinion of the High Court as to the correctness of his decision on the point of law in question. This procedure is often referred to as 'an appeal by way of case stated'.

    A District Judge, before he gives a decision in a case, is also entitled to refer a question of law arising in the case to the High Court for determination - this procedure is referred to as a 'consultative case stated'. The District Judge may state a case on his own initiative or at the request of a party to the proceedings.

    The validity of proceedings in the District Court may be reviewed by the High Court by judicial review as outlined at paragraph 29 below.

The Circuit Court

24. This is the next court in the hierarchy of courts. For the conduct of legal business the country is divided into 6 circuits each consisting of 2 to 6 counties plus 2 circuits consisting of the county and city of Cork and the county and city of Dublin. In the case of all the circuits, except the Dublin circuit, the court sits at various towns in the circuit.

    The maximum number of judges of the Circuit Court is fixed by the Courts and Courts Officers Act 1995 at 24 (previously 17), including the President of the Circuit Court who is also *ex officio* an ordinary judge of the High Court. This Act provides for the permanent assignment of 10 judges to the Dublin Circuit and 3 to the Cork Circuit, the other circuits each have 1 judge permanently assigned to them.

    The 1995 Act provides that solicitors of 10 years standing are also now eligible for appointment as judges of the Circuit Court - heretofore only barristers of 10 years standing were eligible for appointment.

25. There is a right of appeal from the decision of the Circuit Court in civil proceedings to the High Court where a full rehearing of the case takes place and the High Court imposes its own findings and judgment. There is no appeal from the decision of the High Court. In the case of criminal proceedings there is at present a right of appeal in respect of conviction or sentence to the Court of Criminal Appeal but it should be observed that the Court and Court Officers Act 1995 provides for the abolition of that court and the transfer of its jurisdiction to the Supreme Court.

    The Circuit Court judge may, on the application of any party refer any question of law arising from the case before him to the Supreme Court by way of case stated as outlined in paragraph 23 above.

    The validity of proceedings in the Circuit Court may be reviewed by the High Court by way of judicial review as outlined in paragraph 29 below.

The High Court

26. According to Article 34.3.1 of the Constitution the High Court has full original and unlimited jurisdiction.

    The High Court can be constituted in three different ways, namely:
    (a) as a Divisional Court with three judges; or
    (b) when a judge sits with a jury. In civil matters this occurs only in limited cases such as actions for assault and defamation; or
    (c) as a judge sitting alone.

    When the court is exercising its criminal jurisdiction it sits with a judge and jury and is called the Central Criminal Court - discussed in paras 52 and 53 below.

    The High Court sits in Dublin permanently but twice a year one or more judges of the High Court sit in every county to hear appeals from the Circuit Court (civil matters only) and to hear personal injury actions.

    The Courts and Courts Officers Act, 1995, provides that the maximum number of ordinary judges of the High Court shall be 19 (previously 16) plus the President of the High Court (who *ex officio* is also a member of the Supreme Court and the second most senior judge in the State).

    Barristers of 12 years standing are eligible for appointment as a judge of the High Court. Solicitors are not eligible for direct appointment but with the passage of the Courts and Courts Officers Act, 1995, a solicitor who has served 4 years as a judge of the Circuit Court becomes eligible for appointment (as does a barrister in the same position). A judge of the European Court of Justice or the Court of First Instance or an Advocate-General of the Court of Justice is also eligible for appointment.

27. The original jurisdiction of the High Court extends to all manner of civil actions, wards of court applications and bankruptcy matters. As mentioned above, the court also hears, in a consultative role, cases stated from the District Court and appeals from the Circuit Court (in civil matters only).

28. One of the most important functions of the High Court is its power to decide whether any statute is or is not repugnant to the Constitution of 1937.

29. The High Court has had a traditional function which predates the Constitution of supervising the operation of inferior courts ie District and Circuit Courts, tribunals and administrative bodies and ensuring that their procedures are observed and hearings are conducted constitutionally and in accordance with natural law.

A dissatisfied party to a hearing of a tribunal or inferior court can seek a Judicial Review in the High Court of its proceedings in certain circumstances and the High Court will hear evidence and determine whether the proceedings were conducted fairly and in accordance with the Constitution.

The procedures for Judicial Review. These are set out in Order 84 of the Rules of the Superior Courts, 1986. A number of orders can be made upon a Judicial Review hearing, including:

   (a) **Habeas Corpus.** Article 40 of the Constitution provides for applications for an Order of Habeas Corpus to determine the legality or otherwise of an applicant's detention. Usually the applicant is either in prison or in a mental hospital. If the High Court decides that the detention is unlawful it will order his release.
   (b) **Certiorari.** This Order is used to quash the decision of a tribunal where it is found to have acted beyond its powers.
   (c) **Mandamus.** This is an Order directed to a public body or tribunal ordering it to fulfil a statutory obligation or do some act which it has an obligation to make or to do.
   (d) **Prohibition.** Normally this Order is used to prevent a tribunal or body exercising its powers until specific conditions are met.

30. Where a civil action commences in the High Court an appeal lies to the Supreme Court.

The Supreme Court

31. The Supreme Court is the highest court in the State. The Courts and Courts Officers Act, 1995, provides that it may sit in 2 or more divisions of 3 or 5 judges at the same time - however where the court has to consider references under Acticle 12 or Article 26 of the Constitution or where it has to consider the validity of any law having regard to the provisions of the Constitution, the court must sit with not less than 5 judges.

The Courts and Courts Officer Act, 1995, provides that the maximum number of ordinary judges of the Supreme Court shall be 7 (previously 4) plus the Chief Justice, as well as the President of the High Court, who is a member *ex officio*.

Eligibility for appointment as a judge of the Supreme Court is the same as that for the High Court.

32. The Supreme Court is a court of appeal so that an action will not commence in the Supreme Court except in two special situations specified in the Constitution, namely:
   (a) Under Article 12.3.1 it has power to determine the permanent incapacity of the President of Ireland. This power has never been used.
   (b) Under Article 26 of the Constitution the President can refer any Bill to the Supreme Court to determine its constitutionality. This power has been exercised on seven occasions.

Apart from these exceptions, no civil action can commence in the Supreme Court. It is possible to appeal from a decision of the High Court where it is alleged that damages awarded were excessive or that the High Court Judge erred in his interpretation or application of the law. If the Supreme Court accepts the grounds of appeal it can either set aside the judgment of the High Court and substitute its own or it can order a retrial.

It hears *cases stated* from the Circuit Court and appeals (on a point of law and with the leave of the High Court) from decisions of the High Court on *cases stated* to it by the District Court. Furthermore the High Court can state a case for the consideration of the Supreme Court.

33. At present the Supreme Court has only a limited criminal jurisdiction but there is provision in the Courts and Courts Officers Act, 1995, for the abolition of the Court of Criminal Appeal and the Courts-Martial Appeal Court and for the transfer of their jurisdictions to the Supreme Court. (This provision has not yet been brought into force.)

- **The Civil Courts**

34. Civil proceedings are dealt with by the District Court, the Circuit Court and the High Court. With the exceptions noted at para 32 above, no civil proceedings commence in the Supreme Court whose function in this area is purely an appellate one.

   Both the District and Circuit Courts are local and limited in their jurisdiction insofar as in their actual operation the courts only have power to hear cases brought against defendants who live in or where the events in dispute occurred in or where property in question is situate in the relevant District or Circuit. Furthermore they can only deal with claims and award damages or compensation up to certain monetary limits which vary from to time.

   As stated above the High Court has full original and unlimited jurisdiction and the Supreme Court has an appellate function.

   A diagram in the Appendix to this chapter gives a simplified overview of the civil court system.

The District Court

35. The District Court is empowered by the 1991 Courts Act to:
   (a) deal with claims for compensation or damages up to the sum of £5,000;
   (b) deal with the ejectment of a tenant for non-payment of rent where the annual rent does not exceed £5,000 per annum;
   (c) make Barring Orders and Protection Orders in family disputes;
   (d) make orders for the maintenance of a spouse and dependant children up to £200 per week and £60 per week respectively;
   (e) adjudicate on the recovery of rates by a local authority without limit to the amount recoverable;
   (f) grant renewals of liquor and dance hall licences.

36. Proceeding in the District Court are commenced by the issue of a Civil Process which sets out the plaintiff's claim. The defendant, against whom the claim is made, is served with the civil process. The defendant has the option of admitting the claim or indicating, within a prescribed period, of his intention to defend the action. In the latter case a date for the trial is given.

The Circuit Court

37. The Circuit Court can deal with claims where compensation or damages of up to £30,000 is sought.

   The Circuit Court has been given exclusive power to deal with:
   (a) applications for new leases under the Landlord and Tenant (Amendment) Act, 1980;
   (b) applications regarding the guardianship of infants (power given to Circuit Court by the Courts Act, 1981);
   (c) malicious injuries applications under the Malicious Injuries Act, 1981.

The court also has wide powers, conferred by the Judicial Separation and Family Law Reform Act, 1989, to grant Orders of Judicial Separation and make orders concerning family property and rights of access, custody and guardianship.

It also deals with:
(a) applications for new on-licences for premises selling alcohol and for restaurant liquor licences;
(b) claims concerning land where the rateable valuation is less than £200 per annum.

38. Proceedings in the Circuit Court are commenced by the issue of a Civil Bill which sets out the main points of the plaintiff's claim in an Endorsement of Claim contained in the Civil Bill. The defendant, against whom the claim is made, is served with the Civil Bill and then enters an Appearance and delivers a Defence to the claim. The action is then ready to go to trial.

The High Court

39. The High Court has full original and unlimited jurisdiction to hear, *inter alia*:

(a) claims for damages for breach of contract and tort (mostly personal injury cases) – such claims are usually taken in the High Court when they exceed £30,000, the Circuit Court limit, but the court can deal with claims under this amount;

(b) claims relating to land where the rateable valuation is over £200 – same comment as in (a) applies;

(c) petitions in relation to winding up of companies and examinerships;

(d) wards of court applications;

(e) bankruptcy applications;

(f) nullity and adoption cases;

(g) Constitutional actions;

(h) proceedings to have a solicitor struck off;

(i) petitions under the Referendum Act – when the court is required to sit as a divisional court of 3 judges.

40. Proceedings in the High Court are commenced in the majority of cases by the issue of a Plenary Summons but some proceedings are commenced by Summary Summons, Special Summons or Petition. The Plenary Summons sets out briefly and in general terms the nature of the plaintiff's claim. The defendant against whom the claim is made is served with the summons and if he intends to defend the action he must file an Appearance within a specified period – such Appearance will invariably state that the defendant requires the plaintiff to furnish him with a Statement of Claim. This is a document which sets out the plaintiff's claim in considerable detail. In due course the defendant will deliver a Defence to the action and the matter is then ready to go to trial.

● **The Criminal Courts**

41. For the purposes of exercise of jurisdiction by the criminal courts, offences are divided into minor offences triable summarily ie before a judge of the District Court sitting alone without a jury, and non-minor offences which are triable before a judge and jury.

The general law is that no person may be tried on a criminal charge except before a judge and jury but Article 38 of the Constitution recognises an exception in the case of minor offences triable in a court of summary jurisdiction (ie the District Court) and in cases tried before the Special Criminal Court. The power to try summarily in respect of an offence must be expressly conferred by statute.

42. In determining whether an offence is a minor offence the most important factor is the punishment which can be imposed. This matter has been considered in a number of cases and it would appear that the longest term of imprisonment which can be imposed by the District Court if the offence is to be considered as a minor offence is 12 months although this does not preclude the District Court from imposing consecutive sentences provided they do not exceed 24 months in total. As regards the level of fine which would take an offence out of the category of a minor offence, many common offences which are only triable summarily can attract fines of up to £1,000 eg driving without insurance, dangerous driving, drunk driving, common assault and there has been as yet no challenge to their categorisation as minor offences.

43. A diagram in the Appendix to this chapter gives a simplified overview of the criminal court system.

The District Court

44. The District Court deals with the vast majority of criminal cases tried before the courts. The court is precisely the same court as deals with civil matters as considered above and is dealt with separately here for convenience only.

    With rare exceptions all criminal prosecutions commence by the accused being brought before the District Court.

    If the offence is one which statute provides shall be triable summarily the District Judge has jurisdiction to hear the case and proceed to a conviction if he finds the accused guilty or if the accused has pleaded guilty.

45. If the accused is charged with an indictable offence ie one which is only triable before a judge and jury, then the District Judge must conduct a preliminary examination in order to satisfy himself that the accused has a case to answer. This procedure involves the service on the accused by the State of what is commonly called the 'Book of Evidence' which sets out, *inter alia*, a statement of the charges and statements of the evidence which each prosecution witness will give. It the District Judge is satisfied that the accused has a case to answer then he will send him forward for trial in the Circuit Court, Central Criminal Court or Special Criminal Court as appropriate.

    If the accused pleads guilty to an indictable offence, then in certain circumstances the District Judge may deal with the offence provided the Director of Public Prosecutions consents or he may send him forward for sentence if he feels the District Court's powers of sentencing are inadequate in the circumstances.

    The District Judge has jurisdiction to try certain indictable offences summarily provided the accused consents to summary trial and the court is of the opinion that the facts alleged or proved constitute a minor offence fit to be tried in the District Court. These indictable offences are set out in the Schedule to the Criminal Justice Act, 1951 (as amended) and include, *inter alia*, assault causing actual bodily harm and offences under the Larceny Act. 1916. In some cases the consent of the Director of Public Prosecutions to summary disposal is also required.

46. When hearing charges against a person under 17, the District Court proceedings are held in camera ie the public is excluded and the sittings are referred to as the 'Juvenile Court'. The

proceedings tend to be less formal than that in the ordinary District Courts.

The District Court's criminal jurisdiction also extends to the issuing of warrants for the arrest of persons for whom request has been made for their extradition and for the making of extradition orders.

The District Court has jurisdiction whether to grant bail to an accused person and to fix the terms of bail or to remand him in custody pending his trail. Where the District Court refuses to grant bail the accused is at liberty to apply to the High Court for bail – but this is in no sense an appeal from the decision of the District Court.

47. The District Court's decision as to conviction or sentence can be appealed by the accused to the Circuit Court where a full rehearing takes place and that Court imposes its own decision. The Circuit Court has power to increase sentence on appeal.

The validity of proceedings in the District Court may be reviewed by the High Court by judicial review as outlined at paragraph 29 above. The case stated procedures as outlined in paragraph 23 above are also available.

The Circuit Court

48. The Circuit Court, when sitting as a court of first instance, sits with a judge and jury. When it sits as a court of appeal from the District Court, it sits with a judge alone.

49. The 1981 Courts Act provides that all indictable offences, apart from a few exceptions (noted in para 52 below), are triable exclusively in the Circuit Court. Such cases include serious assaults, burglary and robbery.

50. The sentences which the Circuit Court can impose are in certain cases limited by statute and otherwise may be unlimited under the common law.

51. An accused can appeal either his conviction or sentence to the Court of Criminal Appeal.

The Courts and Courts Officers Act, 1995, provides for the abolition of the Court of Criminal Appeal. On its abolition appeals will lie to the Supreme Court. (This provision has yet to be brought into force.)

The Circuit Court Judge may, on the application of any party refer any question of law arising from the case before him to the Supreme Court by way of case stated as outlined in paragraph 25 above and the High Court has jurisdiction to review the validity of proceedings in the Circuit Court.

The Central Criminal Court

52. When acting as a criminal court the High Court is referred to as the Central Criminal Court. Only a limited number of very serious crimes are reserved for this Court including attempted murder, conspiracy to murder, murder, rape and other sexual offences, genocide, treason and offences under ss 6,7,8 of the Offences Against the State Act, 1939.

53. The decision of the Central Criminal Court to convict can be appealed either to the Court of Criminal Appeal or, since *People (AG) v Conmey (1975) (I)*, to the Supreme Court. It should be noted that when the Court of Criminal Appeal is abolished, there will be no right of appeal to the Supreme Court against an *acquittal* in the Central Criminal Court - this will overrule *People (DPP) v O'Shea (1982) (I)* which did allow such an appeal.

1: STRUCTURE OF THE LEGAL SYSTEM

The Court of Criminal Appeal

54. The Court of Criminal Appeal is the principal court of appeal in criminal matters where the offences are serious and ordinarily triable before a judge and jury. It convenes on occasion to hear appeals from the Circuit Criminal Court, the Central Criminal Court and the Special Criminal Court. Appeals are not by way of a full rehearing of the evidence. Instead the Court, of 3 Judges, being one Supreme Court Judge and two High Court Judges, reads a full transcript of the proceedings at the original trial and hears submissions on points of law. It has power to order a re-trial or to increase or reduce sentence or dismiss the appeal.

55. The decision of the Court of Criminal Appeal is final unless it or the Director of Public Prosecutions certifies that the decision involves a point of law of exceptional public importance such that it is desirable that an appeal should be taken to the Supreme Court.

56. The Courts and Courts Officers Act, 1995, provides for the abolition and for its jurisdiction to be transferred to the Supreme Court. (This provision has yet to be brought into force.)

The Supreme Court

57. The Supreme Court has a very limited criminal jurisdiction. It can:

   (a) hear appeals from the Court of Criminal Appeal where either the Court of Criminal Appeal, the Attorney General or the DPP certifies that the decision involves a point of law of exceptional public importance;
   (b) also hear appeals directly from the Central Criminal Court, since the decision of the Supreme Court itself in the case of *People v Conmey, 1975 (I)*;
   (c) consider a *case stated* for its opinion from the Circuit Court similar to a *case stated* in a civil action from the Circuit Court.

The criminal jurisdiction of the Supreme Court will be enlarged with the forthcoming abolition of the Court of Criminal Appeal.

The Special Criminal Court

58. The present Special Criminal Court came into being in 1972. It was established under Part V of the Offences Against the State Act, 1939. Its existence is continued by order of the government. The Constitution permits special courts when it is considered that the ordinary criminal courts are inadequate to secure the effective administration of justice and the preservation of order and public peace.

59. The Court is presided over by three judges and no jury. It deals primarily with terrorist-type offences called 'scheduled offences' as set out in The Offences Against the State Act, 1939. An appeal against conviction lies to the Court of Criminal Appeal.

• The European Court of Justice

60. This Court operates under the treaties of the European Communities which comprise: (1) the European Community, (2) the European Coal and Steel Community and (3) the European Atomic Energy Community. Ireland acceded to these in 1972 after an amendment to the Constitution.

Article 29.4(3) of the Constitution ensures that the Regulations and Directives and other laws of the three communities are carried over into Irish law and confirms the supremacy of the Community Law in the State since it provides that no provision in the Constitution prevents Community Law having effect in the State.

61. Irish citizens have a right to have a matter referred to the European Court of Justice in Luxemburg where an issue of Community Law arises in a case before a court in Ireland. The European Court will then give a 'consultative decision' to the Court hearing the case in Ireland and the national court will then decide the final outcome of the case in the light of that.

● **The European Court of Human Rights**

62. Ireland is a member of the Council of Europe and has ratified the European Convention for the Protection of Human Rights and Fundamental Freedoms. Both Irish citizens and the State itself can apply to the Court of Human Rights sitting at Strasbourg to interpret the Convention and any of its protocols and inquire into alleged violations of it by any member state.

● **Administrative tribunals**

63. Article 37 of the Constitution envisages that tribunals with limited powers can be created to determine matters of a non-criminal nature. In practice tribunals and administrative bodies have been created to regulate particular activities arising under statute.

64. The primary examples operating in Ireland today include:

   (a) The **Labour Court**. This is primarily a conciliation body established to carry out arbitration in the area of industrial relations. Its decisions can be appealed on a point of law to the High Court;

   (b) The **Employment Appeals Tribunal (EAT)** and **The Rights Commissioners** – which deal with unfair dismissals from employment, and claims regarding redundancy entitlements, rights to minimum notice and maternity leave entitlements of employees. The Tribunal's decision can be appealed to the Circuit Court;

   (c) **Social Welfare Tribunal** established under the Social Welfare (Consolidation) Act, 1981, considers appeals against decisions of the Deciding Officers as regards entitlement to social welfare payments.

   Other tribunals include **Bord Pleanála** which deals with appeals from a planning authority's decision to grant/refuse planning permission; the **Appeals Commissioner** who deals with disputes regarding tax liability and the **Fair Trade Commission** which reviews monopoly practices in industry and commerce.

65. Such tribunals must act within the powers conferred upon them and their procedures must not violate the Constitution and must be fair.

● **Tribunals of inquiry**

66. Sometimes, a special Tribunal may be set up to inquire into a major matter of public interest. See the Tribunals of Inquiry (Evidence) Acts 1921 and 1979. Recent examples include the Tribunal of Inquiry into the Kerry Babies Case and the Tribunal of Inquiry into the Beef Processing Industry.

● **Arbitration**

67. A dispute may be referred to arbitration:

   (a) by agreement out of court;

    (b) by statute;
    (c) by order of a court.

68.   It is common practice to include in commercial contracts (and also in partnership agreements) a clause providing that any dispute is to be settled by arbitration under the Arbitration Acts 1954 - 1980. The main advantage of this procedure is privacy since the public and the press have no right to attend a hearing before an arbitrator. It is also possible to appoint as arbitrator an expert in the matter in dispute and to simplify the rules of evidence and procedure. In some cases arbitration can be more expeditious and less expensive than court action.

69.   The parties may name their arbitrators or provide that some other person, say the President of the Law Society, shall appoint him. It is usual to appoint only one arbitrator; if two are appointed they jointly appoint a third as umpire.

70.   If either party institutes proceedings in a court in breach of the agreement which provides for arbitration, the other party may apply to the court to suspend the proceedings while the arbitration takes its course. The court will usually do so under s5 of the Arbitration Act, 1980 though the party seeking the referral to arbitration must have taken no step in the proceedings instituted.

71.   Unless otherwise agreed, a hearing before an arbitrator follows the same essential procedure as in a court of law. The right to appeal against an award made in arbitration is restricted, but the arbitrator is required in certain cases to state reasons for this awards. Further, if the arbitrator has been guilty of 'misconduct' his decision can be reviewed.

72.   The award of an arbitrator may be enforced in the same manner as a judgment of the High Court.

73.   In addition to voluntary arbitration as described above, compulsory arbitration may be enforced in certain circumstances.For example certain statutes provide for arbitration on disputes arising from the provisions of the statute, eg compulsory purchase of lands.

● **Legal personnel**

74.   We have already seen how the various courts are composed and the judge or judges who preside in each. Other personnel in the legal system are described below.

The Attorney General

75.   Article 30 of the Constitution of 1937 provides for the office of Attorney General. The Attorney General is appointed by the President on the nomination of the Taoiseach. He is normally a barrister of senior standing.

    The Attorney General's functions are as follows:
    (a) Under Article 30 of the Constitution, the Attorney General is the adviser of the Government in matters of law and legal opinion. He sits in on Government meetings, but is not a member of the Government. The Attorney General is involved if Ireland or the Government is suing or being sued in domestic courts or before European courts. He advises the Government on all Bills that come before the Government. He acts as a counsellor and legal adviser in the same way as a family solicitor.

    (b) Until 1975, the Attorney General was responsible for instituting all serious criminal prosecutions. But the Constitution allowed this function to be conferred on others (Article 30.3) and these powers were conferred on the Director of Public Prosecutions (DPP) in 1975. However, there are some powers of a criminal law nature which can be exercised either by the Attorney General or the DPP. For example, there can be an appeal from the Court of Criminal Appeal to the Supreme Court if the Attorney General or DPP certifies that a point of law of exceptional public importance is involved.

(c) The Attorney General can have additional powers conferred on him by law (Article 30.1). For examples, under the Extradition Act 1987, the Charities Act 1961 and the Law Reform Commission Act 1975.

(d) The Attorney General is guardian of the public interest (*parens patriae*). This is not mentioned in the Constitution or in legislation, but it has always been the function of the Attorney General and was carried over by s6 of the Ministers and Secretaries Act 1924, which states that there shall be vested in the Attorney General the functions formally vested in the Attorney General for Ireland and the Solicitor General for Ireland. Sometimes he will act under this power on being informed by somebody else that something should be done. If this occurs, it is known as a *relator proceeding* and the person who informs the Attorney General is known as the relator. This fourth function of the Attorney General has caused much controversy in recent times as a result of the following cases:

Case: Attorney General (at the relation of SPUC Ltd) v Open Door and Well Woman Centre 1988 (I)
The Society for the Protection of the Unborn Child Ltd informed the Attorney General that two counselling services were providing counselling which included information on abortion services available outside Ireland. The Attorney General brought relator proceedings, seeking an injunction to stop this activity, claiming that it infringed the constitutional right to life of the unborn (Article 40.3.3 of the Constitution).

Held: the Supreme Court granted the injunction. The court stated that the Attorney General was a particularly suitable person to take action in the case of protection of the life of the unborn, because the unborn cannot speak for themselves.

(There have been several other similar cases regarding abortion information since this case).

Case: Attorney General v X 1992 (I).
The Attorney General sought an injunction to prevent a fourteen year old girl from travelling to London for an abortion. He said he was acting as guardian of the public interest.

Held: the Attorney General was perfectly correct to bring the case, but in these particular circumstances, the injunction would not be granted. Two judges of the Supreme Court clearly stated that the Attorney General was actually *obliged* to take action in a case such as this.

Case: Attorney General v Tribunal of Enquiry into Beef Processing Industry 1992 (I)
The Attorney General sought a declaration that the Beef Tribunal could not enquire into discussions held at Government meetings.

Held: the Attorney General was entitled to the declaration.

The Director of Public Prosecutions

76. Since the coming into operation of the Prosecution of Offences Act 1974 the DPP carries out functions such as deciding whether to proceed with the prosecution of serious criminal offences. Prior to 1974 these functions were carried out by the Attorney General. The DPP is a civil servant completely independent of the government.

1: STRUCTURE OF THE LEGAL SYSTEM

The Chief State Solicitor

77. The Chief State Solicitor acts as solicitor for the DPP in the prosecution of criminal offences. He is a solicitor appointed by the government to act in relation to all matters - both criminal and civil - concerning the State.

• The legal profession

78. The legal profession is divided up into two mutually exclusive groups - barristers and solicitors. The two groups have different functions within the legal system and their professional training and the operation and administration of the two professions are entirely separate.

Barristers

79. A barrister specialises in advocacy and the presentation of a case in court on the instructions of a solicitor. Professional training courses are operated by the Honourable Society of the King's Inns and on successful completion and after satisfying certain conditions a student is conferred with the degree B.L. and thereafter he is 'called to the outer Bar' by the Chief Justice in the Supreme Court. He is then a junior counsel. His first year of practice is spent in professional training with a junior counsel ('devilling').

80. In addition to acting as an advocate a barrister will advise a solicitor on the strengths and weaknesses of a case and on points and areas of the law which may be unclear. To appear in court a barrister should be properly robed in wig (optional) and gown and bands.

    Junior barristers do a great deal of paperwork in addition to advocacy and they draft legal documents, court proceedings and opinions on legal issues on receiving instructions from a solicitor on behalf of his client.

    A Junior Counsel may seek membership of the 'inner Bar'. To do so he must apply to the government to be appointed as a Senior Counsel. This process is sometimes called 'taking silk' - Senior Counsel wear gowns of silk in court.

81. Generally speaking a barrister cannot accept instructions from a member of the public but only through a solicitor. A barrister cannot be sued for his in-court work or work closely connected with the court appearance. This is because if a barrister could be sued for negligence it would amount to a re-trial of the original case and dissatisfied clients might abuse this possibility in order to have their case reheard which could result in chaos and uncertainty. He can be sued for negligence arising otherwise. A barrister cannot sue for his fees. There are calls for changes in the operation of the profession, most recently the Report of the Restrictive Practices Commission, 1990 recommended changes.

82. Judges of the Circuit, High and Supreme Courts tend to be recruited from amongst Senior Counsel and some District Justices are barristers though the majority are solicitors, but note that the Courts and Courts Officers Act, 1995, makes solicitors eligible for appointment as judges of the Circuit Court.

Solicitors

83. Solicitors are the general practitioners, so to speak, of the legal profession. Solicitors engage in a lot of work which does not require court proceedings eg all aspects of conveyancing and the buying and selling of property, making wills.

84. Solicitors' training is controlled by the Incorporated Law Society and to gain admission to the professional training course applicants must be either a law graduate or have successfully attempted the solicitors entrance examination which is held annually in November. Rules for admission change from time to time. *Bloomer's Case (1995)* held that law graduates were not exempt from the solicitors' entrance examination. This decision was upheld on appeal to the Supreme Court (decision 6 February 1996).

85. Normally solicitors will appear for their clients as advocates in the District Court. Usually a solicitor will instruct a barrister to appear in the Circuit or higher courts where necessary though since 1971 solicitors have rights of audience in all courts.

86. A solicitor is an officer of the court and his conduct and business affairs are subject to supervision by the Incorporated Law Society and in case of complaints the Society investigates allegations and can refer certain breaches of discipline to the High Court.

Legal executives

87. Finally, mention should be made of the legal executives who are employed by firms of solicitors to do professional work. A legal executive is usually a specialist in one type of work only, such as litigation, conveyancing or trust administration. He may have greater practical experience in his own limited field than the solicitors who employ him but their general range and depth of legal knowledge and their professional responsibility is greater than his.

Summary of the chapter

88. There is a lot of detail to be learnt about the structure of the courts.

You should grasp the following main practical aspects.

(a) What type of case each court deals with - its 'jurisdiction'.

(b) In which court a litigant with a particular cause of action would commence his proceedings to obtain a remedy. Remember that, generally speaking, the victim of a crime has no control over any subsequent legal proceedings (criminal prosecution). The State, through the Director of Public Prosecutions, has the duty of prosecuting persons charged with criminal offences; private prosecutions when permitted at all are relatively infrequent - partly because of the expense.

(c) If either party is dissatisfied with the decision given by the court which tries his case, he usually has a right of appeal to a higher court. Appeals from the District Court to the Circuit Court are by way of complete re-hearing, appeals in civil matters from the Circuit Court to the High Court are by way of complete re-hearing but appeals from the Circuit Criminal Court to the Court of Criminal Appeal are by way of written transcript with some legal submissions but witnesses are not normally heard. Likewise appeals from the High Court to the Supreme Court are not full re-hearings but are normally against specific aspects of the case or on points of law.

(d) Arbitration on major disputes, where the amount at issue is large, is generally permitted only if both parties agree. But on small matters it is much more common as an alternative to formal civil proceedings in court. One of the practical considerations in favour of arbitration is that the hearing before an arbitrator is private. This can be valuable if either party anticipates that publicity, for example in a case alleging professional incompetence, could be damaging to him even if the case against him is dismissed.

TEST YOUR KNOWLEDGE

Numbers in brackets refer to paragraphs of this chapter

1.   What is the standard of proof of (i) criminal and (ii) civil proceedings?(8,10)

2.   In what circumstances does a person who has behaved in an unlawful fashion (i) pay a fine or (ii) pay compensation (damages)? (6,9)

3.   Explain the basis of liability in an action (i) in contract and (ii) in tort. (11)

4.   What is an appeal by 'case stated'? (23)

5.   Give examples of the kind of case tried (i) in a District Court, (ii) in a Circuit Court and (iii) in the Central Criminal Court.(35,44-46;37,49;52)

6.   What is the jurisdiction of the High Court? (28,29,39) What orders may it make by way of judicial review? (29)

7.   What matters does the Special Criminal Court deal with? (58,59)

8.   Give an example of an administrative tribunal. (64)

9.   What is the main advantage of submitting a dispute to arbitration instead of proceedings in a court of law? (68)

10. What are the functions of (i) the Attorney General (75), (ii) the Director of Public Prosecutions (76) and (iii) the Chief State Solicitor. (77)

11. Why are barristers immune from action as a result of their conduct of a case in court? (81)

Now try illustrative questions 1 and 2 at the end of the study text.

The civil court structure

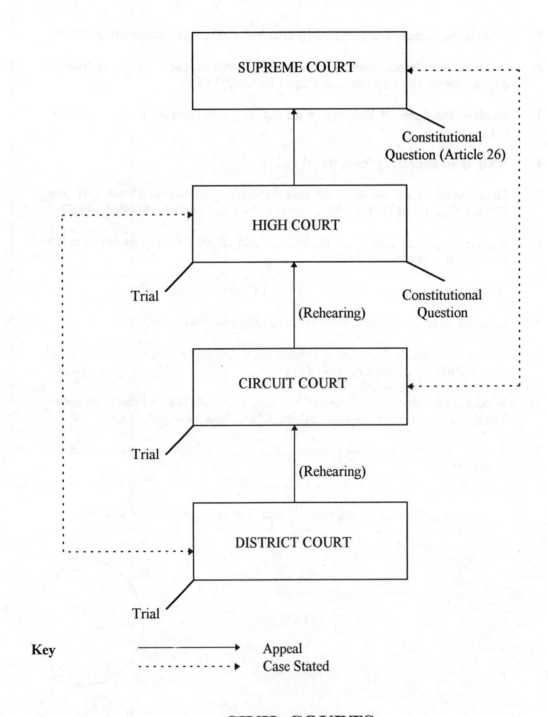

CIVIL COURTS

The criminal court structure

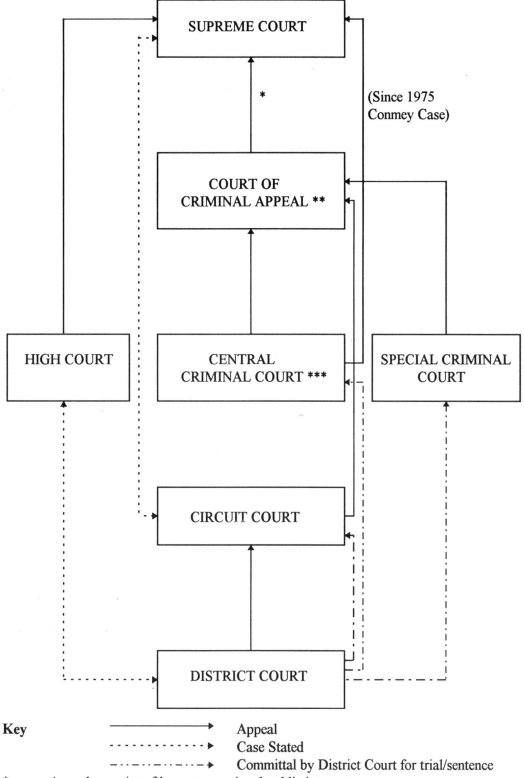

Key

→ Appeal

⋯⋯⋯► Case Stated

—··—··—► Committal by District Court for trial/sentence

* Appeal on point of law or exceptional public interest.

** This court is to be abolished and jurisdiction transferred to the Supreme Court.

*** This court is to be abolished and jurisdiction transferred to the High Court.

CRIMINAL COURTS

PART B
LEGAL PROCESS AND LEGAL REASONING

Chapter 2

SOURCES OF IRISH LAW

Points covered in this chapter are:

- The nature of law
- Sources of Irish law
- Historical sources
- Legal sources
- Subsidiary sources of law

Purpose of chapter

Having examined how the law is administered, it is necessary to examine how that law has come into being and what are its essential parts.

- **Nature of law**

1. Prior to the Norman invasion of Ireland in the 12th century Ireland had no central administrative system and the legal system was made up of a mixture of local customary law, and canon law known as the Brehon Laws. Written fragments and tracts from the Brehon Laws have survived from the 6th, 7th and 8th centuries.

   The Brehon laws were administered locally in each area or tuath by the ruling King or Assembly and provided the basis for the maintenance of the social order from century to century.

2. The Norman invasion led to the introduction of the Common Law system to Ireland though that system did not appear to have full force and effect throughout the whole country until about the middle of the 17th century. The common law was and is an unwritten system which over the centuries has evolved and developed by means of judicial decisions. One of the principal aspects of the common law is this reliance upon *precedent* whereby a court in administering justice can explain and justify its decision by reliance upon previous decisions of the Courts in similar cases.

   The common law system inherited from England continues to be an important feature of our legal system. This contrasts sharply with other European systems of law, in particular the Civil Law System, which are based on written codes derived from the Roman Law. Such systems do not attach such importance to precedents and prior judicial pronouncements. The Common Law system still operates in many Commonwealth states and also is the basis of the legal system in the United States.

2: SOURCES OF IRISH LAW

- **Sources of Irish law**

3. The term 'sources of law' is used in several different senses.

(a) **Historical sources** - generally regarded as common law and equity.

(b) **Legal sources** - the means by which the law is currently brought into existence. There are five legal sources:
   (i) the Constitution;
   (ii) judicial precedent;
   (iii) legislation (including pre-1922 legislation insofar as it applies to Ireland);
   (iv) EC law; and
   (v) custom.

(c) **Subsidiary sources** - not currently responsible for the direct creation of law. They include, for example, the earlier Constitution of 1922, legal texts and Canon Law.

The important elements will now be explained in greater detail.

- **Historical sources of law**

4. Law's historical sources are those procedures, rules and ways of thinking which have given rise to today's current sources of law. Hence a legal problem today may be decided on the rules of the legal sources, but these in themselves (particularly judicial precedent) have been derived from the historical sources of common law and equity.

Common law

what are (i) the historical and (ii) the legal sources of law?

5. The Brehon Law system was gradually superseded in Ireland over a period of 300 years. Initially the common law applied only in urban areas. Gradually the Court of King's Bench was established in 1395. The two systems of law co-existed for a time. In 1495 Poynings' Law provided that all statutes that had previously been passed in England should have full force and effect in Ireland. Judges, usually English, travelled around the country to apply the law in both civil and criminal cases. By the 1500's the Commissions of Assize convened at defined intervals in various towns and cities for the administration of justice.

These Commissioners convened in London from time to time to discuss developments in the law and varying local custom and sought to select from varying customs those that were most socially acceptable. The practices and customs selected became known as the common law and were applied uniformly in criminal and civil cases throughout England and Ireland.

6. The common law also developed through precedent whereby legal decisions were adopted from time to time to govern a particular point of issue. To commence an action before the court the plaintiff had to issue a writ. In the 14th century the office of Justice of the Peace was created whose function it was to assist the local Sheriff in the conduct of criminal trials and also to administer local affairs.

Explain how common law & equity developed as part of Irish Law?

7. By the 16th century there was a 3-tiered <u>criminal</u> system:
   <u>The Assize</u>: the main court for trials.
   <u>The Quarter Sessions</u>: convened four times per annum and dealt with very serious offences.
   <u>Petty Session</u>: which dealt with minor offences.

   The <u>Civil</u> Court has three main divisions:
   <u>Court of Exchequer</u>: which dealt with the collection and distribution of royal revenue.
   <u>The Court of Common Pleas</u>: this court dealt with actions which concerned the Crown and it could deal with land and financial matters.
   <u>King's Bench Division</u>: this dealt with a wide variety of civil matters, but excluding finance or taxes.

Equity

8. In time the common law system became inflexible and rigid and caused hardship in its strict application by the Courts. A plaintiff might lose his case owing to a minor technicality of wording or be frustrated by specious defences, deliberate delay or corruption, or find himself unable to enforce a judgment given in his favour because there was no suitable common law remedy. Unsuccessful litigants appealed to the Monarch directly to intervene and in time the King appointed his Lord Chancellor to deal with all such petitions. The Lord Chancellor's function was to investigate allegations of injustice and inequity under the common law. His court was called the <u>Court of Chancery.</u>

9. Because the principles on which the Chancellor decided points were based on fair dealing between two individuals as equals, it became known as equity.

10. The system of equity, developed and administered by the Court of Chancery, was not a complete alternative to the common law. It was a method of adding to and improving on the common law; it provided a gloss on the law. This interaction of equity and common law produced three major changes.

    (a) **New rights**: equity recognised and protected rights for which the common law gave no safeguards. If, for example, A transferred property to the legal ownership of B to pay the income of the property to C (in modern law B is a trustee for C) the common law simply recognised that B was the owner of the property at common law and gave no recognition of B's obligations to C. Equity recognised that B was the owner of the property at common law but insisted, as a matter of justice and good conscience, that B must comply with the terms of the trust imposed by A (the settlor) and pay the income to C (the beneficiary).

    (b) **Better procedure**: as explained above, equity could be more effective than common law in bringing a disputed matter to a decision.

    (c) **Better remedies**: the standard common law remedy for the successful plaintiff was the award of monetary compensation, damages, for his loss. Equity was able to order the defendant to do what he has agreed to do *(specific performance)* to abstain from wrongdoing *(injunction)*, to alter a document so that it reflects the parties' true intentions *(rectification)* or to restore the pre-contract status quo *(rescission)*.

11. The development of equity was based on a number of 'equitable maxims', or principles. These are still applied today if an equitable remedy is sought. The following are examples.

    (a) <u>He who comes to equity must come with clean hands</u>. To be fairly treated, the plaintiff must have acted fairly himself.

(b) Equality is equity. The law attempts to play fair and redress the balance; hence what is available to one person must be available to another.

(c) He who seeks equity must do equity. Similar to (a) above, this means that a person wanting equitable relief must be prepared to act fairly in future himself.

(d) Equity looks at the intent, not the form. However a person may try to pretend that he is doing something in the correct form, equity will look at what he is actually trying to achieve.

Common law and equity: later developments

12. In theory, equity accepted common law rights but insisted that they should be exercised in a just fashion. The practical effect was nonetheless that a decision of the Court of Chancery often reversed or conflicted with common law rules. At one stage, the Court of Chancery went so far as to issue orders by which litigants were forbidden to bring an action at common law to enforce strict common law rights. The rivalry between Chancery and common law courts was resolved in 1615 by a decision of the King (in the *Earl of Oxford's Case*) that where common law and equity conflict, equity must prevail.

13. Equity was not in its origins a consistent code of law: it was simply disconnected intervention in legal disputes. Each Chancellor (and the Chancery judges acting under his authority) applied a personal and sometimes arbitrary standard of what he considered fair. Equity, it was said, varied with the length of the individual Chancellor's foot. From the sixteenth century onwards, however, the Chancellor and his deputies were usually recruited from the legal profession trained in common law. (Sir Thomas More, appointed Chancellor by Henry VIII, was the first of these). Under common law influence, equity become a consistent body of doctrine and at least as technical as the common law.

14. By the 19th century the system had become ungainly and prohibitively expensive and a claimant might find that after pursuing his case through the common law courts for years, he might lose on a rigid or technical ground and would then have to commence proceedings all over again in the Chancery Courts. With the advent of the Industrial Revolution the system became largely unmanagable and the Supreme Court of Judicature (Ireland) Act, 1877, provided that the rules of equity could be applied in the common law courts. The Act also provided that in cases of conflict between the rules of the common law and those of equity, equity should prevail.

15. Although the courts have been amalgamated, common law and equity remain distinct. Where common law applies it tends to be automatic in its effect. Equity recognises the common law, as it always did; it sometimes offers an alternative solution but the court has discretion as to whether or not it will grant an equitable remedy in lieu of a common law one.

16. If, for example, breach of contract is proved, the plaintiff will at least get common law damages as compensation for his loss automatically; in certain circumstances the court may, at its discretion, provide an alternative remedy in equity. It may, for instance, order the defendant to perform the contract rather than allow him to buy his way out of his contractual obligations by paying damages. The discretionary nature of equitable remedies means that a person who wins an action may not necessarily get the remedy he wants.

Case: Miller v Jackson 1977
The Court of Appeal in England held that a cricket club had committed both negligence and nuisance by allowing cricket balls to be struck out of the ground into M's adjoining premises. However, the court refused to grant the injunction that M had sought. They awarded damages instead on the grounds that the interest of the public in being able to play and watch cricket on a ground where it had been played for over 70 years should prevail over the hardship of a few

individual householders who had only recently purchased their homes.

individual householders who had only recently purchased their homes.

- **Legal sources of law**

The Constitution

17. The single most important source of Irish law is the Constitution of 1937, Bunreacht na hEireann. This document sets out the basic legislative and judicial bodies and institutions of the State and provides comprehensive guarantees for the protection of fundamental rights of Irish citizens.

18. The Constitution established the Oireachtas or National Parliament which was granted the exclusive power to make laws. It also provided for the establishment of Courts and the administration of justice.

19. Article 6 provides that all powers of government, legislative and judicial, which are stated to derive from God, are vested in the people. While the people are the decision-makers ultimately the Constitution provides that these powers must be exercised 'in accordance with the requirements of the common good.' The Constitution effectively provides that certain rights cannot be interfered with or taken away or abrogated even by the people.

20. The Articles in the Constitution can be broadly divided into two parts:

    (a) those setting out fundamental personal rights which are guaranteed to every citizen and which the State is obliged to protect;
    (b) provisions directing the structure and establishment of the institutions of the State including the Oireachtas, the Government and the Judiciary.

21. The National Parliament is known as the Oireachtas (Article 15) and consists of the President, Dáil Eireann and Seanad Eireann. All legislative powers are vested in the Oireachtas and all executive powers are vested in the Government.

22. In relation to legislative functions the Dáil and Seanad have concurrent powers in certain respects:

    (a) either can, by resolution, remove from office the President, the Comptroller and Auditor General, or any judge;
    (b) either can declare the commencement, and cessation, of a state of emergency;
    (c) ordinary legislation can be introduced in either house;
    (d) each has the power to annul subordinate legislation.

23. However, both under the provisions of the Constitution and in practice, the Dáil is undoubtedly the more powerful house and its most critical powers include:

    (a) power to elect the Taoiseach and approve the other members of the Government;
    (b) the Dáil alone has power to initiate a Money Bill, ie legislation which proposes to levy taxes, appropriate public monies or raise and guarantee public loans.

24. Proposed legislation commences as a Bill. Every Bill, apart from one dealing with money matters, must be passed by the Dáil and is then sent to the Seanad. Normally the Seanad has 90 days to consider and debate the contents of the Bill. If it is passed without amendment it is sent to the President and upon signature the bill passes into law and becomes an Act. As mentioned before the President has power to refer any Bill to the Supreme Court to determine it's constitutional validity. The Seanad may initiate non-tax legislation in the same way as the Dáil

and a bill initiated and passed by Seanad goes to the Dáil. A 'Money Bill' is initiated in the Dáil and then sent to the Seanad for consideration only. The Seanad can neither reject nor amend such a bill.

25. All laws passed by the Oireachtas since 1937 are presumed to be in accordance with the Constitution. The Constitution provides that the Judiciary be independent both from the Legislature and the Government. The constitutionality of laws passed by the Oireachtas since 1937 can be challenged in the High Court under Article 34. They are declared 'invalid' and 'unconstitutional' if they are found to be inconsistent with the Constitution's provisions or a violation of rights guaranteed in the Constitution. All laws in force prior to the enactment of the Constitution were carried forward by Article 50 of the Constitution insofar as they were not repugnant to the Constitution and they do not enjoy the *presumption of constitutionality* as post 1937 legislation does.

26. The Supreme Court has held that the Constitution is a living document and in relation to its interpretation this means that the courts can take account of the fact that it's meaning and import can change from time to time. Where a long period of time has elapsed between an interpretation on a point of constitutionality of legislation, and a subsequent raising of a similar point, the Court may feel that because of changes in the meantime, a different interpretation is required later. This happened in the case of *Costelloe v Director of Public Prosecutions, 1984 (I)* where the Supreme Court held that the plaintiff's return for trial was invalid and that Section 62 of the Courts of Justice Act, 1936 was repugnant to the Constitution because it permitted interference by the Executive in the judicial domain. In arriving at this decision the Court expressly refused to follow the *ratio decidendi* in it's earlier decision of *The State (Shanahan) v The Attorney General, 1964 (I)*.

27. Articles 40-44 of the Constitution are entitled 'Fundamental Rights.' This section of the Constitution has received more judicial consideration than any other. Article 40, which provides for personal rights, is the most extensive and far-reaching of the Fundamental Rights Articles in the Constitution. Its guarantees include:

   (a) *Equality before the law* and this means that legislation must not invidiously discriminate between citizens. In *De Burca v The Attorney General, 1976 (I)* a statute was held to be repugnant to this provision because it restricted jury service to ratepayers and exempted women unless they applied to serve;
   (b) no citizen can be deprived of his liberty except in accordance with the law. This enshrines the Common Law remedy of *Habeas Corpus* in the Constitution;
   (c) the right to life, liberty, good name and property are specifically mentioned;
   (d) in a landmark decision of *Ryan v Attorney General, 1965 (I)* the Supreme Court held that the fundamental rights guaranteed by the Constitution were not confined to those rights specifically enumerated under Article 40, but also included a number of unspecified and unenumerated rights;
   (e) the inviolability of the dwelling of every citizen is protected and the dwelling cannot be entered forcibly except in accordance with law. *The People (Attorney General) v O'Brien, 1965 (I)* decided that this guarantee is only violated where there is a 'deliberate and conscious violation' of that right.

28. Article 40.6 (i) guarantees to citizens the liberty to exercise certain rights 'subject to Public Order and Morality.' These include:
   (a) freedom of expression - which cannot be used to undermine public order or morality or the authority of the State. This right has been restricted from time to time by legislation such as the Offences Against the State Act, 1939, the Censorship of Films Acts, 1923-1970 and the Official Secrets Act, 1963;
   (b) freedom to assemble peaceably and without arms. The State can regulate meetings and prevent a breach of the peace or a public nuisance;

(c) freedom of association; each citizen has the right to form associations and unions.

29. Articles 41 and 42 guarantee personal rights in relation to the family, to marriage and to education. The State cannot oblige parents to send their children to State schools or any particular type of school as this may be contrary to the parents' conscience and lawful preference. In the case of *The State (Nicolaou) v An Bord Uchtála, 1966 (I)* the Supreme Court held that 'the family' is based upon marriage only for the purposes of constitutional rights.

30. Article 43 deals specifically with the right to private property which is also protected by Article 40 (3) and Article 44(2) (v), (iv). It guarantees the individual's rights to private ownership of external goods. The State guarantees to pass no laws attempting to abolish the right to private ownership or the right of an owner to dispose of his property whether by will or transfer.

31. The State is given power to delimit property rights whenever the interest of the common good so require. In 1947 the Oireachtas attempted to prevent a dispute over monies bequeathed in a will of a testatrix of republican sympathies by passing the Sinn Féin Funds Act which purported to divert the money to a Board set up under the Act. The Supreme Court in the case of *Buckley & Others (Sinn Féin) v Attorney General, 1950 (I)* held that this act in attempting to appropriate the monies of the deceased breached the constitutional right to property and was repugnant to Article 43.

32. Article 44 provides elaborate provisions for the protection of freedom of conscience and of religion and forbids religious discrimination. These freedoms are subject to public order and morality. Article 44 was amended in 1972 to delete reference to the special position of the Catholic Church.

In *Quinn's Supermarket v Attorney General, 1972 (I)* a statutory instrument which controlled the opening and closing of meat shops was declared unconstitutional in that by permitting only kosher meat shops used by the Jewish community, to open on Sundays it discriminated on religious grounds, against the plaintiffs who served as butchers for the rest of the community.

33. The Constitution is the cornerstone upon which the legal system and laws are based. It has proved a powerful instrument in protecting the individual from oppressive interference with the rights it guarantees. In some cases an individual is entitled to damages against the State for violation of his constitutional rights.

Judicial precedent

34. Both common law and equity are the product of decisions in the courts. They are judge-made law but based on a principle of consistency. Once a matter of principle has been decided (by one of the higher courts) it becomes a **precedent**. In any later case to which that principle is relevant the same principle should (subject to certain exceptions) be applied. This doctrine of consistency, following precedent, is expressed in the maxim *stare decisis* - 'to stand by a decision'.

35. Judicial precedent is based on three elements.

    (a)   There must be adequate and reliable reports of earlier decisions.

    (b)   There must be rules for extracting from each earlier decision on a particular set of facts the legal principle to be applied in reaching a decision on a different set of facts.

    (c)   Precedents must be classified into those which are binding and those which are merely persuasive.

---

36. Point (a) - reporting of cases - is discussed immediately below. The points concerning legal reasoning and how binding precedents should be interpreted are clarified in Chapter 3.

37. Until the mid-nineteenth century law reports - reports of decided cases - were notes made by practising lawyers. Later on, reports were published without official authorisation by professional law reporters. In Ireland there are two series of law reports published. The Irish Reports (I.R.), published by the Incorporated Council of Law Reporting for Ireland and the commercially produced Irish Law Reports Monthly, (I.L.R.M.). In cases of conflict between the two, the Irish Reports takes precedence. In addition there are other special series of reports, eg. of tax cases, commercial cases, industrial relations cases etc. At a hearing in court, the barrister who cites a case as a precedent upon which he relies will read aloud from the reports the passage from the reported judgment.

38. Every case has a title, usually (in a civil case) in the form *Murphy v Kelly* ie. Murphy (plaintiff) versus (against) Kelly (defendant). Some cases are cited (for technical reasons of procedure) by reference to the subject matter. eg. *Re Clubman Shirts Limited* (company case) *Re Shannon's Settlement* (a trust case) ('re' means 'about'); or in shipping cases the name of the ship, eg *The Wagon Mound* . In a full citation the title of the case is followed by abbreviated particulars of the volume of the law reports in which the case is reported, eg. *Magee v The Attorney General 1974 I.R. 284* (the report is at page 284 of the Irish Reports for the year 1974). The same case may be reported in more than one series of law reports and sometimes under different names.

In this text reference to quoted cases is generally given by way of the year of the decision rather than the full report reference. Irish cases are distinguished in the text by the addition of (I) after the year.

39. As regards content:

    (a)   each report begins with a summary *(head note)* of the points of law established by the case and a list of the earlier cases cited as precedents at the hearing;

    (b)   the verbatim text of the judgment (or judgments if more than one) follows as given in court but with any minor corrections which the judge decides to make at the proof stage.

It is only decisions of the higher courts - the High Court, Court of Criminal Appeal and Central Criminal Court and Supreme Court - which are included in the general law reports. Only the important cases (in the effect on the law) are included in the law reports (though certain libraries hold a copy of the judgments in unreported cases also).

40. Students are often perplexed as to how much they are expected to memorise of cases referred to in textbooks, teaching manuals etc. The important aspect of a leading case is what it was about, - its essential facts and the point of law which it illustrates or establishes. It is always useful to preface the mention of a case (in a written answer) by citing the name of the case. But if you cannot remember the name you can say 'In a decided case...'.

Legislation

41. Statute Law or legislation consists of enactments by the Legislature passed in a manner set out in the Constitution. The enactment is called an Act or a Statute. After the Constitution, legislation is the most important source of law. It is possible to challenge any law in the Courts (as outlined above) on the grounds that it is repugnant to the Constitution and if the challenge is upheld the relevant Act or section of an Act will be struck down as void and unenforceable.

    It is important to note that pre-1922 legislation passed by the Houses of Parliament at Westminster, which were stated to apply in Ireland, are part of Irish statute law and still apply. Many important pieces of legislation fall into this category, eg Offences Against the Person Act 1861 and the Landlord and Tenant Act 1860 (Deasy's Act).

42. Proposals for legislation are put forward in draft form as a Bill. They can be introduced either in the Dáil or in the Seanad with the exception of Money/Taxation Bills which must be initiated in the Dáil. If a Bill initiated in the Seanad is subsequently amended in the Dáil, then it is deemed to be initiated in the Dáil (Article 21(1) of the Constitution).

43. All bills passed in the Dáil must be submitted to the Seanad. The power of the Seanad to amend a bill referred to it by the Dáil is limited in a number of ways by Articles 21-24 of the Constitution:

    (a) if, within 90 days of receiving the Bill, the Seanad does not pass it, the Dáil may resolve (at any time within a further one hundred and eighty days) that the Bill shall be deemed to have been passed by both Houses;
    (b) any rejection of the Bill by the Seanad, or any amendment by the Seanad which the Dáil does not agree with, is subject to the same provision;
    (c) the period of ninety days is reduced to twenty-one days in the case of a Money Bill, at the expiration of which the Bill is deemed to have been passed;
    (d) these periods of 90 days and 21 days may be abridged if the Government considers (and so certifies to the Chairman of each of the Houses and to the President) that the Bill is urgent and immediately necessary for the preservation of public peace and security, or by reason of the existence of the public emergency, whether domestic or international. The President must concur in such opinion. Such Bills, however, can only remain in force for 90 days unless both Houses agree that such a Bill should continue for a stated period.

44. In practice, the Oireachtas usually follows certain conventions which limit its freedom. It does not usually enact statutes which alter the law with retrospective effect or deprive citizens of their property without compensation. In addition to making new law and altering existing law, the Oireachtas may make the law clearer by passing a codifying statute to put case-law on a statutory basis, or a consolidating statute to incorporate an original statute and its successive amendments into a single statute (such as the Social Welfare (Consolidation) Act, 1981).

45. The power of the Oireachtas to legislate is unlimited except that it cannot enact legislation which offends any of the provisions contained in the Constitution. In considering the constitutionality of legislation passed by the Oireachtas, the Court will presume that it is in accordance with the Constitution unless and until the contrary is clearly established (post 1937 legislation).

46. Most Bills are Public Bills of general application, whether introduced by the government or by a private member. A Private Bill has a restricted application: for example, a local authority may promote a Private Bill to give it special powers within its own area. Private Bills undergo a different form of examination at the committee stage.

47. A Bill only becomes law when it is signed by the President. After signature the Bill becomes an 'Act'.

48. In each House of the Oireachtas the successive stages of dealing with a Bill are as follows:

(a) *First stage* - the Bill is published and introduced into the Order Paper or agenda of the House.

(b) *Second stage* - the general principles of the Bill are debated. No amendments to the contents of the Bill are permissible at this stage.

(c) *Committee stage* - the Bill is considered section by section in committee, amendments may be made, sections deleted and new sections inserted. The Bill is then reported, with or without amendments, back to the Dáil and an Order is made for its consideration on Report.

(d) *Report stage* - at this stage the Bill as reported from the committee is considered *in toto* and amendments are made.

(e) *Third reading* - a general debate on the contents of the Bill is permissible, but only verbal amendments may be made.

The President's role in legislation

49. When a Bill, other than a Bill to amend the Constitution is passed or deemed to have been passed by both Houses of the Oireachtas, it is then sent to the President for signature and promulgation into Law - Article 25 of the Constitution.

50. Unless a motion requesting earlier signature is agreed by the Seanad or unless the President decides to refer the Bill to the Supreme Court or to a Referendum, the President signs the Bill not earlier than the fifth day and not later than the seventh day after the date on which the Bill was presented - Articles 25,26,27 of the Constitution. A Bill to amend the Constitution must be passed by a majority of votes cast at a Referendum before it can be signed by the President.

Delegated legislation

51. The Constitution permits delegated legislation. This is legislation which though enacted under the authority of the Oireachtas, is not actually enacted by the Oireachtas itself. Delegated legislation consists mainly of statutory instruments prepared by Government Departments. These are laid before the Oireachtas for a specified number of days, usually 60, and in the absence of a negative ruling become law at the end of that period.

52. To save time in the Oireachtas it is usual to set out the main principles in the body of an Act as numbered sections and to relegate the details to schedules (at the end of the Act) which need not be debated though they are visible and take effect as part of an Act. But even with this device there is a great deal which cannot conveniently be included in the Act. It may for example be necessary, after the Act has been passed, for the government to consult interested parties and then produce regulations, having the force of the law, to implement the Act or to fix commencement dates to bring the Act into operation or to prescribe printed forms for use in connection with it. To provide for these and other matters a modern Act usually contains a section by which power is given to a minister, or public body such as a local authority, to make subordinate or delegated legislation for specified purposes only (often referred to as 'regulations').

53. This procedure is unavoidable and essential for various reasons.

    (a) The Oireachtas has not time to examine these matters of detail.

    (b) Much of the content of delegated legislation is technical and is better worked out in consultation with professional, commercial or industrial groups outside the Oireachtas.

    (c) If new or altered regulations are required later, they can be issued without referring back to the Oireachtas, and in a much shorter time than is needed to pass an amending Act.

54. The disadvantages of delegated legislation are that the Oireachtas to an extent loses control of the law-making process and a huge mass of detailed law appears piecemeal each year. It is difficult for persons who may be affected by it to keep abreast of the changes. Yet ignorance of the law is not accepted as an excuse for infringing it.

55. There are a number of types of delegated legislation.

    (a) Various statutes and acts confer on designated Ministers of the Government the power to make *statutory instruments*. This is referred to as ministerial delegated legislation.

    (b) Executive delegated legislation which gives to the Government the power to do certain things. An example of its operation is the power of the Government to bring Part V of the Offences Against the State Act, 1939 into operation establishing the Special Criminal Court. Normally, these Orders do not need to be confirmed by the Oireachtas.

    (c) Local authorities, harbour commissioners and borough councils are endowed by a variety of statutes with the limited power of enacting *bye-laws*.

    (d) Some statutes give limited powers to private bodies to make statutory regulations. The Solicitors' Act, 1954 empowers the Incorporated Law Society to make regulations for the governing of its own affairs.

56. The Oireachtas does exercise some control over delegated legislation by restricting and defining the power to make rules and by keeping the making of new delegated legislation under review as follows:

    (a) some statutory instruments do not take effect until approved by affirmative resolution of the Oireachtas;

    (b) most other statutory instruments must be laid before the Oireachtas for 40 days before they take effect. During that period members may propose a negative resolution to veto a statutory instrument to which they object.

There are standing committees of both Houses whose duty it is to examine statutory instruments with a view to raising objections if necessary, usually on the grounds that the instrument is obscure, expensive or retrospective.

57. As explained above, the power to make delegated legislation is defined by the Act which confers the power. A statutory instrument may be challenged in the courts on the grounds that it is repugnant to any provision of the Constitution or is *ultra vires* - exceeds the prescribed limits or has been made without due compliance with the correct procedure. If the objection is valid the court declares the statutory instrument to be void.

58. Both statutes and delegated legislation are expressed in general terms. It is not possible to provide in an Act for each eventuality of human endeavour which falls within its remit. It therefore often falls to judges to interpret Acts. The legal reasoning used to do this is covered in Chapter 3.

EC law

59. On becoming a member of the European Community in 1973, Ireland adhered to the Treaty of Rome (and the related treaties on coal, steel and atomic energy) and agreed to conform to EC law which is concerned with free trade in goods, agricultural support price policies, transport, company law and many other economic matters.

60. EC law is created in the following ways.

   (a) Regulations eg to implement Article 85 of the Treaty of Rome, may be issued. These are 'self-executing' - they have the force of law in every EC state without need of national legislation. In this sense regulations are described as 'directly applicable'. If they confer rights and impose obligations on individuals, regulations are also said to have 'direct effect'.

   (b) Decisions of an administrative nature are made by the EC Commission in Brussels mainly to implement the common agricultural policy. Such decisions are immediately binding on the persons to whom they are addressed.

   (c) Directives are issued to the governments of the EC member states requiring them within a specified period (usually two years) to alter the national laws of the state so that they conform to the directive. Thus the Companies (Amendment) Act, 1983 implemented the Second EEC Companies Directive 77/91 EEC.

61. Until a directive is given effect by an Irish statute it does not usually affect legal rights and obligations of individuals. In exceptional situations the wording of a directive may be cited in legal proceedings, but generally statutory interpretation is a matter for the Irish courts (see Chapter 3).

   In the Case of *McDermott & Cotter v The Minister for Social Welfare, 1987 (I)* it was held by the Court of Justice that where the provisions of a directive appear, as far as their subject matter is concerned, to be unconditional and precise, individuals may rely on those provisions in the absence of implementing measures adopted within the prescribed period as against a national provision incompatible with the directive or insofar as the directive defines rights assertable against the State.

62. Directives are the most significant and important means of importing continental law into the Irish legal system since the EC has a wide-ranging programme of assimilating the laws of member states to a common EC model. Recommendations and opinions may also be issued but these are merely persuasive and not binding.

63. Apart from the European Court, the principal institutions of the EC are the Council of Ministers, the Commission (the top layer of the Brussels bureaucracy) and the European Parliament. Proposals for EC legislation are initiated by the Commission, usually in the form of draft directives. These drafts are referred to member states for comments. In Ireland it is the normal practice for a committee of the Oireachtas to examine each draft and for the appropriate ministry to consult trade associations etc which would be affected by the proposals if implemented. These preliminary consultations between the commission and the member states may continue over a period of years and result in extensive alteration of the draft directive to meet national objections. The directives are also debated in the preparatory stage by the European Parliament to which every member state elects a number of representatives. The final stage is the consideration of a directive by the Council of Ministers. If the Council unanimously approves, it authorises the issue of the directive and the member states must then alter their law accordingly.

64. It is true that membership of the EC restricts the sovereignty of the Oireachtas (among other EC national legislatures). But the directives to which the Oireachtas must ultimately conform are issued as a result of negotiation and often agreement between the Irish government and the other governments of the EC. The Irish government in turn is dependent on the support of a majority of TDs to retain office. To that extent, the Oireachtas has indirect influence on the EC law-making process. It is certainly true to say, however, that since 1973 the EC has had considerable impact on the law, and this is set to increase.

Custom

65. In early mediaeval times the courts created law by enforcing selected customs. Custom is now of little importance as a source of law, but it is still classified as a legal source of law.

66. In determining what are the implied terms of a contract, the court may take account of local or trade customs which the parties intended should be part of their contract.

    Case: O'Conaill v The Gaelic Echo (1954) Limited, 1958, (I)
    A journalist recovered holiday pay on proof that it was a custom in Dublin that such payments were made to journalists.

67. In disputes over claims to customary rights, such as to use the land of another or to remove things from it, the alleged custom may be established subject to the following conditions.

    (a) It must have existed since *'time immemorial'*, in theory since 1189 AD. It usually suffices to show that the custom has existed without interruption from as far back as records (if any) exist.

    (b) It must have been enjoyed *openly as of right*. If it has only been enjoyed secretly, by force, or with permission of the landowner, it is not a custom which amounts to a right.

    (c) The custom must be reasonable, certain in its terms, consistent with other custom or law and exercised within a definite locality eg the Animals Act, 1985 at Section 2 recognises in introducing liability for animals straying upon the highway that it is customary in certain parts of the State that lands are not fenced along the highway.

• Subsidiary sources of law

68. The main sources of law as set out above are judicial precedent (derived from common law and equity), the Constitution and parliamentary and EC legislation. However, a number of subsidiary sources have had some influence on the law's development, and are recognised eg legal treatises.

A substantial number of authoritative texts have been written on Irish Law in recent years and such texts and articles have been cited with approval from time to time by the courts.

● **Summary of the chapter**

69. This chapter provides an introduction and a background to the more specific material in the later chapters. It is largely historical but it has its practical relevance to the current state of the law. It is particularly important to bear in mind the distinction between legal and equitable parts of law - we will see later on (particularly in contract law) that the different principles can lead to very significantly different results.

70. Questions on the sources of the law have quite often been set and it is worth your while to ensure that you have grasped both the differences between historical, legal and subsidiary sources, and the ways in which they interact.

TEST YOUR KNOWLEDGE

Numbers in brackets refer to paragraphs of this chapter

1. What are (i) the historical and (ii) the legal sources of law? (2)

2. Explain how common law and equity developed as part of Irish law. (5-16)

3. How does the idea of judicial precedent work? (34,35)

4. Discuss the categories of Articles in the Constitution (20)

5. Name the sequence of events through which a bill must go before it becomes an Act of the Oireachtas. (48-50)

6. What is meant by delegated legislation? (51,52)

7. Discuss Fundamental Rights under the Constitution (27-32)

8. How are the principles of EC law incorporated into Irish law? (60-61)

9. Discuss the relevance of Custom as a source of Law (65-67)

Now try illustrative questions 3 and 4 at the end of the study text.

Chapter 3

LEGAL REASONING

Points covered in this chapter are:

- Judicial precedent
- Avoidance of precedents
- Interpretation of statutes

Purpose of chapter

The legal framework is interpreted on a day-to-day basis by judges in the courts. This chapter sets out the rules used by them to determine how both case-law and statute should be applied.

- **Judicial precedent**

1. The chief source of Irish law is the Constitution of 1937 which lends validity to all rules and principles. Thereafter, the two major sources of Irish law are judge-made law (sometimes called judicial precedent or case-law) and legislation (or statutes). In order to apply these to the particular facts of a case, certain principles of legal reasoning have been evolved in order to ensure that the law's objectives of consistency and fairness are maintained.

2. In the early days of the common law there was very little legislation and therefore the chief source of law was the decisions of the Courts in particular cases. Sometimes an Act of Parliament will deliberately vest a wide discretion in the judiciary. In other cases there may be no statutory provision and no existing precedent relevant to the particular dispute. Even so, the doctrine of judicial precedent is based on the view that it is not the function of a judge to make law, but to decide cases in accordance with existing rules. The Latin for this idea is *stare decisis* - to stand by a decision.

3. The doctrine of judicial precedent is designed to provide consistency in the law. In order that this should be done in a coherent manner, three things must be considered when examining a precedent before it can be applied to a case:

   (a)   the *ratio decidendi*, which may be binding, must be identified;
   (b)   the material facts must be similar; and
   (c)   the preceding court must have had a superior (or in some cases, equal) status to the later court.

3: LEGAL REASONING

Ratio decidendi and obiter dicta

4. A judgment will start with a description of the facts of the case and probably a review of earlier precedents and possible alternative theories. The judge will then make statements of law applicable to the legal problems raised by the material facts. Provided these statements are the basis for the decision, they are known as the *ratio decidendi* of the case. The *ratio decidendi* (which literally means 'reason for deciding') is the vital element which binds future judges. If a judge's statements of legal principle do not form the basis of the decision (eg. a dissenting (minority) judgment) or if his statements are not based on the existing material facts, but on hypothetical facts, they are known as *obiter dicta* statements – something said 'by the way'. A later court may respect such statements, but it is not bound to follow them. They are only of *persuasive* authority.

5. It is not always easy to identify the *ratio decidendi*. The same judgment may appear to contain contradictory views of the law in different passages. In decisions of appeal courts, where there are three or even five separate judgements, the members of the court may reach the same conclusion but give different reasons. Most of all, the *ratio* will often be intermingled with *obiter* statements. To assist the process of legal reasoning, many judges indicate in their speeches which comments are *ratio* and which *obiter*.

Distinguishing the facts

6. Although there may arguably be a finite number of legal principles to consider when deciding a case, there are necessarily an infinite variety of facts which may be presented. Apart from identifying the *ratio decidendi* of an earlier case, it is also necessary to consider how far the facts of the previous and the latest case are similar. Facts are never identical. If the differences appear significant the court may 'distinguish' the earlier case on the facts and thereby avoid following it as a precedent.

Status of the court

7. Not every decision made in every court is binding as a judicial precedent. The court's status has a significant effect on whether its decisions are binding, persuasive or disregarded.

(a) The Supreme Court - until 1964 the Supreme Court had always followed its own previous decisions and also the decisions of those courts which had preceded it as the court of ultimate jurisdiction. It decided in *The State (Quinn) v Ryan, 1965 (I)* and in *The Attorney General v Ryan's Car Hire, 1965 (I)* that it is not absolutely bound by its own earlier decisions. It is free to depart from them for compelling reasons.

(b) The High Court must follow the decisions of the Supreme Court.

(c) The High Court is not considered to be bound by its own decisions.

(d) The Court of Criminal Appeal, in the case of *The People v Moore, 1964 (I)* has stated that it is not bound to follow its own previous decisions.

(e) Lower courts (Circuit Court, District Court) do not make precedents (their decisions are not usually reported) and they are bound by decisions of the higher courts.

---

8. Apart from binding precedents as described above, reported decisions of any court (even if lower in status) may be treated as *persuasive* precedents, ie they may be, but need not be followed in

a later case. For instance the High Court in *McCaffrey v Lundy, 1988* upheld an earlier decision of the District Court on the interpretation of s2 of the Animals Act, 1985. In addition Irish courts regularly follow decisions of courts which have a common law legal tradition such as the English courts, or on issues concerning the Constitution and its application and interpretation the decisions of the Supreme Court of the United States are frequently cited with approval.

9. A court of higher status is free to disregard the decision of a court of lower status and expressly overrule it. Remember that this does not reverse the previous decision; overruling a decision does not affect its outcome as regards the defendant and plaintiff in that earlier decision.

10. If, in a case before any court, there is a dispute about a point of European Community law it may be referred to the European Court for a preliminary ruling. Irish courts are also required to take account of principles laid down by the European Court in so far as these are relevant. The European court does not, however, create or follow precedents as such, and the provisions of EEC directives should not be used to interpret Irish legislation.

11. A case in the High Court may be taken on appeal to the Supreme Court. If the latter reverses the former decision, that first decision cannot be a precedent, and the reversed decision becomes a precedent. However, if the original decision had been reached by following precedent, then reversing that decision overrules the precedent which formed the *ratio*. Overruling a precedent does not affect the parties in that original precedent's case, but the parties in the reversed decision are affected by the new decision.

● **Avoidance of a binding precedent**

12. Even if a precedent appears to be binding, there are a number of grounds on which a court may decline to follow it:

(a)   by <u>distinguishing the facts</u> (see paragraph 6);

(b)   by declaring the *ratio decidendi* <u>obscure</u>, particularly when a Supreme Court decision by three or five judges gives as many *ratio decidendi;*

(c)   by declaring the previous decision made *per incuriam* - without taking account of some essential point of law, such as an important precedent;

(d)   by declaring it to be in conflict with a <u>fundamental principle of law;</u>

(e)   by declaring an earlier precedent to be <u>too wide</u> - for example, the duty of care to the parties found in *Donoghue v Stevenson 1932,* has since been considerably refined; or

(f)   because the earlier decision has been subsequently <u>overruled</u> by another court or by statute.

The advantages and disadvantages of precedent

13. Many of the strengths of judicial precedent as the cornerstone of Irish law also indicate some of its weaknesses. Generally the arguments revolve around the principles of consistency, clarity, flexibility and detail.

14. Consistency - the whole point of following binding precedent is that the law is decided fairly and predictably. In theory therefore it should be possible to avoid litigation because the result is a foregone conclusion. However, judges can be forced to make illogical distinctions to avoid an unfair result, which combined with the wealth of reported cases serves to complicate the law.

15. Clarity - following only the reasoning in *ratio* statements should lead to statements of principle for general application. In practice, however, the same judgment may be found to contain propositions which appear inconsistent with each other or with the precedent which the court purports to follow.

16. Flexibility - the real strength of the system lies in its ability to change with changing circumstances in society since it arises directly out of the actions of society. The counter-argument is that the doctrine limits judges' discretion and they may be unable to avoid deciding in line with a precedent which produces an unfair result. Often this may only be resolved by passing a statute to correct the law's failings.

17. Detail - precedents state how the law applies to facts, and it should be flexible enough to allow for details to be different, so that the law is all-encompassing. As had been noted above, however, judges often distinguish on facts to avoid a precedent. The wealth of detail is also a drawback in that it produces a vast body of reports which must be taken into account; again, though, statute can help by codifying rules developed in case-law - this, for instance, was the source of the Social Welfare (Consolidation) Act 1981.

18. The most famous (adverse) description of case-law is that made by Jeremy Bentham, when he called it 'dog's law'. Precedent follows the event, just as beating a dog follows the dog disobeying his master - before the dog transgressed, the offence did not exist. It can be answered, however, that it is in the nature of society that a thing can only be prevented when it is seen to be harmful, and that this is only usually seen when harm has already been done.

● **Interpretation of statutes**

19. Statutes, including delegated legislation, are expressed in general terms. For example, a Finance Act may impose a new tax on transactions described as a category; it does not expressly impose a tax of specified amount on the particular transaction of a particular person. If a dispute arises as to whether or how a statute applies to particular acts or events, the courts must interpret the statute, determine what it means and decide whether or not it applies to a given case.

20. In the interpretation of a statute the court is concerned with what the statute itself provides. It is never required to take account of what may have been said in parliamentary discussion, even by a government spokesman explaining the intended effect of the Bill. No opinion of an individual member is to be accepted as the collective intention of the Oireachtas. For the same reason the report of a committee or commission recommending legislation is not to be used as a guide to the interpretation of a statute. The objective of the court is to find the intention of the leglislation.

21. Unless the statute contains express words to the contrary it is presumed that the following 'canons of statutory interpretation' apply:

> (a)   a statute does not alter the existing law nor repeal other statutes;
>
> (b)   if a statute deprives a person of his property, say by nationalisation, he is to be compensated for its value;
>
> (c)   a statute does not have retrospective effect to a date earlier than its becoming law;
>
> (d)   any point on which the statute leaves a gap or omission is outside the scope of the statute.

In practice a statute usually deals expressly with these matters (other than (d)) to remove any possible doubt.

22.   Since judges are called upon to interpret statutes, a system has been developed to guide them. This consists of statutory assistance and a set of general principles.

23.   Statutory assistance consists of:

> (a)   the Interpretation Act 1937, which defines certain terms frequently found in legislation;
>
> (b)   interpretation sections in Acts - particularly long, complicated and wide-ranging Acts often contain definition sections; for instance, the Succession Act, 1965 s3 defines various words of relevance to succession law, eg 'property' includes all property both real and personal which belonged to the deceased;
>
> (c)   preambles or long titles to Acts often direct the judge as to its intentions and objects; private Acts must have a preamble, public ones recently have just contained long titles. But preambles may only be used to resolve an ambiguity - they may not be used when the enacted words are already clear: *Attorney General v Ernest Augustus (Prince) of Hanover 1957;*
>
> (d)   sidenotes - statutes often have summary notes in the margin - these may contain a reference to an earlier statute or common law rule affected by the section but marginal note is not part of the Act. This is provided for in the Interpretation Act, 1937.

24.   In interpreting the words of a statute the courts have the following well-established general principles.

(a)   The literal rule: words should be given their ordinary grammatical sense. Normally a word should be construed in the same literal sense wherever it appears throughout the statute. The courts will use standard dictionaries to aid them in their interpretation.

(b)   The golden rule: a statute should be construed to avoid a manifest absurdity or contradiction within itself.

Case: Re Sigsworth 1935
The golden rule was applied to prevent a murderer from inheriting on the intestacy of his victim although he was, as her son, her only heir on a literal interpretation of the Administration of Estates Act 1925 (English Act).

(c) The contextual rule: a word should be construed in its context - it is permissible to look at the statute as a whole to discover the meaning of a word in it.

(d) The mischief rule: if the words used are ambiguous and the statute discloses (say, in its preamble as explained above) the purpose of the statute, the court will adopt the meaning which is likely to give effect to the purpose or reform which the statute is intended to achieve (this is to take account of the mischief or weakness which the statute is explicitly intended to remedy).

Case: Gardiner v Sevenoaks RDC 1950
The purpose of an Act was to provide for the safe storage of inflammable cinematograph film wherever it might be stored on 'premises'. A notice was served on G who stored film in a cave, requiring him to comply with the safety rules. G argued that 'premises' did not include a cave and so the Act had no application to his case.

Held: the purpose of the Act was to protect the safety of persons working in all places where film was stored. Insofar as film was stored in a cave, the word 'premises' included the cave.

(e) The *eiusdem generis* rule: statutes often list a number of specific things and end the list with more general words. In that case the general words are to be limited in their meaning to other things of the same kind (Latin: *eiusdem generis*) as the specific items which precede them.

Case: Evans v Cross 1938
E was charged with driving his car in such a way as to 'ignore a traffic sign'. He had undoubtedly crossed to the wrong side of a white line painted down the middle of the road. 'Traffic sign' was defined in the Act as 'all signals, warning signposts, direction posts, signs or other devices'. Unless, therefore, a white line was an 'other device', E had not ignored a 'traffic sign' and had not committed the offence charged.

Held: 'other device' must be limited in its meaning to a category of signs in the list which preceded it. Thus restricted it did not include a painted line which was quite different from that category.

(f) *Expressio unius est exclusio alterius:* to express one thing is by implication to exclude anything else. For example, a statutory rule on 'sheep' does not include goats.

(g) *In pari materia:* if the statute forms part of a series which deals with similar subject matter, the court may look to the interpretation of previous statutes on the assumption that the legislature intended the same thing.

Presumption of constitutionality

25. There is a presumption that all statutes passed by the Oireachtas after 1937 are in accordance with the Constitution until the contrary is proven. In practice, where a court is faced with two reasonable interpretations of a legislative provision, one of which is constitutional and the other of which would render the legislation unconstitutional, the former must be adopted.

Case: Quinn v Ryan, 1985 (I)
In this case it was argued that the Extradition Act, 1965 was unconstitutional. The decision held that this presumption is a binding rule.

TEST YOUR KNOWLEDGE

(Numbers in brackets refer to paragraphs of this chapter)

1. What three elements of a previous case must be considered before it can be binding? (3)

2. Distinguish *ratio decidendi* from *obiter dicta*. (4)

3. (a) Which courts are bound by decisions of:

     (i) the Supreme Court;
     (ii) the High Court.
   (b) Is the Supreme Court bound by its own earlier decisions?
   (c) Is the High Court bound by its earlier decisions? (7)

4. On what grounds may a judge avoid a binding precedent? (12)

5. What are the main advantages of case-law? (14-17)

6. What presumptions are made about the effect of a statute? (21)

7. State 6 general principles used to interpret statutes. (24)

Now try illustrative question 5 at the end of the study text.

PART C
CONTRACT

48

Chapter 4

DURESS AND UNDUE INFLUENCE

Points covered in this chapter are:

- Duress
- Undue influence
- Statutory protection

Purpose of chapter

This topic may be covered fairly briefly since the effects of a person being pressurised to enter into a contract are clear-cut.

- **Duress**

1. A person who has been induced to enter into a contract by duress or undue influence is entitled to avoid it at common law - the contract is <u>voidable</u> at his option, because he has not given his genuine consent to its terms.

2. Duress is fundamentally a threat. This may be of physical violence, imprisonment, damage to goods or business, and even of breaching a contract. The threat may be translated to actual violence etc, but duress may still be implied merely from the threat.

    Case: Cumming v Ince 1847
    An elderly lady was induced to make a settlement of her property in favour of a relative by a threat of unlawful imprisonment in a mental home.

    Held: the settlement would be set aside on account of duress. (NB: the principles of duress and undue influence are applied to gifts (as in this case) as well as to contracts).

    See also *Williams v Bayley, 1866* at paragraph 6 below.

3. In older cases it has been held that threatened seizure of goods or property is not duress as it should be limited to threats of physical harm or imprisonment. But in some recent decisions the courts have set aside contracts made under 'economic duress'.

    Case: North Ocean Shipping v Hyundai Construction (The Atlantic Baron) 1979
    Shipbuilders demanded, without any legal justification, an increase in the contract sum to compensate them for a devaluation in the currency of the contract and threatened to terminate the contract if the plaintiffs did not agree to pay the extra sum demanded. The plaintiffs were at the time negotiating a very lucrative contract for the charter of the ship and, while stating that they were under no obligation to make the extra payment and were doing so without

prejudice to their rights, they did in fact agree to pay the extra sum and paid it without further protest.

Held: the threat to terminate the contract and discontinue amicable business relations amounted to economic duress and hence the agreement in respect of the extra payment was voidable. (In the event the plaintiffs' claim failed - by making the payments without further protest and by delaying their claim for the return of the extra payment until 8 months after the vessel had been delivered, the plaintiffs had by their conduct affirmed the contract for the extra payment.)

Case: Universe Tankships Inc of Monrovia v International Transport Workers' Federation, 1982
The defendants threatened to 'black' the plaintiffs' ship and prevent its sailing unless the plaintiffs paid a sum of money into a fund under the control of the defendants to help seamen serving in flag-of-convenience ships. The plaintiffs yielded to the demand and the vessel was allowed to sail. After the ship had sailed the plaintiffs' claimed the return of the money paid on the basis that it had been paid under duress.

Held: the plaintiffs were entitled to recover the money as having been paid under economic duress.

Case: Atlas Express v Kafco (Importers & Distributors), 1989
The defendants were a small company importing and distributing a particular line of goods to the retail trade. They contracted with the plaintiff carriers to deliver the goods to branches of a national retail chain on whose business the defendants were heavily dependent. Later the plaintiffs told the defendants they would not carry any more of their goods unless they were paid extra. In view of their dependence on their main customer and since they were unable to find an alternative carrier, the defendants agreed to the new terms but later refused to pay them and the plaintiffs sued to recover the amount owing under the new rate.

Held: that where a party to a contract is forced by the other party to renegotiate terms to his disadvantage and has no alternative but to accept the new terms, his apparent consent is vitiated by economic duress - and accordingly the plaintiffs were not entitled to recover.

It should be observed that the courts try to distinguish between economic duress (which is illegitimate) from the situation where one party to a contract uses its superior bargaining power to drive a 'hard bargain'.

A leading Irish case is:

Case: Smelter Corporation v O'Driscoll 1977 (I)
Mrs O'Driscoll contracted to sell her land to the plaintiffs and when she failed to complete the sale they sought specific performance of the contract. Evidence was that she had been reluctant to sell but was persuaded to do so by a statement of the plaintiffs' agent that if she did not agree to sell the local authority would compulsorily acquire the land for the development contemplated by the plaintiffs. Although the agent honestly believed his statement to be true there was no foundation for it as the local authority had no intention of acquiring the land compulsorily for the plainitffs. However, the defendant believed the statement to be true and was reinforced in her belief by a reference to compulsory purhcase in the course of a meeting with officials of the local authority and the plaintiffs' agent.

Held: there was a fundamental unfairness in the transaction in that the defendant agreed to sell believing she had no real option but to do so and the plaintiffs accepted her agreement to sell knowing this was not so. Specific performance refused.

Where a party has been compelled to pay money under a mistake of law, the courts have allowed recovery:

Case: Rogers v Louth County Council 1981 (I)
The plaintiff claimed for the return of money overpaid to the defendants in redeeming the annuity in respect of a cottage. The defendants had quoted a certain sum and it had been paid without question as to its correctness. The parties later agreed there had been an overpayment but the defendants argued that it had been paid voluntarily under a mistake of law and was therefore not recoverable.

Held: the payment had not been made 'voluntarily' in that the plaintiff could not have redeemed the annuity except on the terms quoted. The defendants were primarily responsible for the mistake. The plaintiff was entitled to recover.

The question of duress has also arisen in the context of petitions for nullity:

Case: MK (McC) v McC, 1982
A 21 year-old man and his 19 year-old pregnant girlfriend were put under intolerable pressure by both sets of parents to marry although neither wished to do so. Both sets of parents met and, in the absence of the parties and without consulting them at all, decided they should marry as soon as possible before the girl's pregnant condition became obvious.

Held: the will of both parties had been overborne by the pressure exerted by the parents and they had entered a marriage which neither desired and to which they had given no real consent and the duress exercised by the parents was of a character they were unable to withstand. Decree of nullity granted on ground of duress.

● Undue influence

4. A contract (or a gift) is voidable if the party who made the contract or gift did so under the undue influence of another person (usually the other party to the transaction). This is an equitable relief.

Presumption of undue influence

5. When the parties stand in certain relationships the law assumes that one has undue influence over the other. There must be a confidential relationship, and the contract must be clearly disadvantageous to the weaker party. These relationships include the following (the stronger party is mentioned first):

   (a) parent and minor child (*sometimes* even if the child is an adult);
   (b) guardian and ward;
   (c) trustee and beneficiary under the trust;
   (d) religious adviser and disciple;
   (e) doctor and patient.

   This is not an exhaustive list. It is possible to argue that any relationship in which one person places trust and confidence in another has given the latter undue influence if he appears to have obtained otherwise inexplicable benefits from the relationship. The courts will look at all the facts in ascertaining whether in a particular case undue influence has in fact been exercised. In the Northern Ireland case of re *Found's Estate 1979*, Jones LJ said sometimes the whole evidence, when meticulously considered, may disclose facts from which it should be inferred that a relationship is disclosed which justifies a finding that there is a presumption of undue influence. (This case was an action by the executors of Mrs F's estate to set aside legacies on the ground of undue influence having been exerted by a niece of the deceased.)

Case: O'Sullivan & Another v Management Agency & Music Ltd and Others, 1984
The now well-known entertainer Gilbert O'Sullivan, while young and unknown and inexperienced in business matters, entered into an exclusive managment contract with M (one of the defendants) and, in reliance on M and without the benefit of any independent advice, entered into publishing and recording contracts with various companies (the other defendants) with whom M was closely involved. The plaintiffs sought to have these contracts set aside on the ground, *inter alia*, that they had been obtained by undue influence.

Held: by the Court of Appeal, that there was a fiduciary relationship between the plaintiffs and all the defendants and that accordingly the agreements were to be presumed to have been obtained by undue influence.

It has been held that a marital and employment relationship are not confidential. Peripheral family relationships may give one party the opportunity to gain dominance over the other, eg brother and brother: *Armstrong v Armstrong 1873.*

The simple fact of marriage raises no automatic presumption of undue influence but a relationship of trust may be disclosed on the evidence: *Northern Banking Company v Carpenter 1931 (I).*

Case: Hodgson v Marks 1971
An elderly lady transferred her house to her lodger and allowed him to manage her affairs. He later sold the house.

Held: undue influence was to be presumed from the relationship and the benefits obtained by the lodger.

Undue influence as a matter of fact

6. Even where there is no apparent relationship of trust and confidence, it is possible to prove from the conduct of the parties in their dealings that one did in fact have undue influence.

   In *Glover v Glover 1951*, the court stated that certain matters are always regarded as relevant and sometimes conclusive amongst which the following receive special mention:
   - that the transaction in question was a voluntary gift or for manifestly inadequate consideration;
   - a marked disparity in age and position between the parties to the transaction.

   Case: Williams v Bayley 1866
   A bank official told an elderly man that the bank might prosecute his son for forgery and to avoid such action the father mortgaged property to the bank.

   Held: there is no presumption of undue influence in the relation of the bank and customer but it could be proved to exist (as it did in this case) by the relevant facts.

Upholding the contract

7. If it appears that there is undue influence, the party who is deemed to have the influence may resist the attempt to set aside the contract by showing that the weaker party did in fact exercise a free judgment in making the contract. A person who has undue influence is presumed to have used it but this is rebuttable. In rebuttal it is usually necessary to show that the person, otherwise subject to undue influence, was advised by an independent adviser to whom the material facts were fully disclosed and that adequate consideration was given: *Inche Noriah v*

Shaik Allie bin Omar 1929. Independent legal advice often suffices: *Horry v Tate & Lyle Ltd 1982*, or evidence that all relevant information about the transaction had been disclosed: *Midland Bank v Cornish 1985.*

Case: Lloyds Bank v Bundy 1975
On facts very like those of *Williams v Bayley* above (except that the son was in financial difficulty and the bank required additional security for its loan to him) a customer gave the bank a charge over his house.

Held: the bank could not itself give independent financial advice to a customer on a matter in which the bank was interested as a creditor. Since the bank had not arranged for the customer to have independent advice the charge in favour of the bank would be set aside.

8.   However, there may be undue influence even where the defendant tries to rebut the presumption by showing that the plaintiff has refused independent advice. The lack of independent advice does not automatically mean that there was undue influence.

Case: McCormack v Bennett 1973 (I)
An elderly man transferred his farm to his daughter. The daughter agreed in return to look after her parents for the rest of their lives. The father was advised by a solicitor, but the solicitor was not aware of the full facts. On the father's death, the transfer was challenged by other members of the family.

Held: while the transfer was *prima facie* improvident, it resulted from the free exercise of the donor's will. The father was a sufficiently astute man to know what he was doing.

Case: Goldsworthy v Brickell 1987
G, an 85 year old man entered into an agreement to give tenancy of a farm to B, who had been helping him run it. The terms were highly favourable to B, but G had rejected opportunities to consult a solicitor. G sought for the agreement to be rescinded.

Held: although there had been no domination (see *Morgan's* Case below), the fact that the agreement's terms were clearly unfair and that G placed trust in B meant that the presumption would not be rebutted by showing that free exercise of judgment was allowed. G could rescind.

Manifest disadvantage

9.   A transaction will not be set aside on the ground of undue influence unless it can be shown that the transaction is to the manifest disadvantage of the person subjected to undue influence. Also a presumption of undue influence will not arise merely because a confidential relationship exists, provided that the person in whom confidence is placed keeps within the boundaries of a normal business relationship.

Case: National Westminster Bank v Morgan 1985
A wife (W) signed a re-mortgage of the family home (owned jointly with her husband H) in favour of the bank, to prevent the original mortgagee from continuing with proceedings to repossess the home. The bank manager told her in good faith, but incorrectly, that the mortgage only secured liabilities in respect of the home. In fact, it covered all H's debts to the bank. W signed the mortgage at home, in the presence of the manager, and without taking independent advice. H and W fell into arrears with the payments and soon afterwards H died. At the time of his death, nothing was owed to the bank in respect of H's business liabilities. The bank sought possession, but W contended that she had only signed the mortgage because of undue influence from the bank and, therefore, it should be set aside.

Held: the House of Lords, reversing the Court of Appeal's decision, held that the manager had not crossed the line between explaining an ordinary business transaction and entering into a relationship in which he had a dominant influence. Furthermore, the transaction was not unfair to W. Therefore, the bank was not under a duty to ensure that W took independent advice. The order for possession was granted.

10. Despite the words 'dominant influence' in Lord Scarman's judgment in the *Morgan case*, the Court of Appeal has stated subsequently in *Goldsworthy v Brickell 1987* (see above), in an apparent move away from the House of Lords position, that an influence stopping short of a dominant one may be sufficient to allow the court to set the contract aside on the basis of undue influence. Once trust has been shown to have existed, it is then necessary to demonstrate manifest disadvantage rather than that the position of trust has been abused and exercised as a dominating influence: *Woodstead Finance Ltd v Petrou 1985*.

11. A recent case has identified what is and is not 'manifest disadvantage'.

Case: Bank of Credit and Commerce International v Aboody 1989
Mrs A purchased the family home in 1949 and it was registered in her sole name. Mr A ran a business in which his wife took no interest but in 1959 she became a director of his company on the understanding that she would have to do nothing. Between 1976 and 1980 she signed three guarantees and three mortgages over her house. Mr A deliberately concealed matters from his wife. The company collapsed due to Mr A's fraud and the bank sought to enforce the guarantees against Mr and Mrs A.

Held: there had been actual undue influence over his wife by Mr A but Mrs A had suffered no manifest disadvantage since, at the time she signed the documents, her husband's business was comfortably supporting her and there was no indication that it would not continue to do so. She had benefited from the business which she secured and could not be said to have suffered manifest disadvantage in that sense.

Unconscionable and improvident bargains

12. The courts may also intervene to set aside a contract which is clearly unfair to one party where advantage has been taken of his weakness or vulnerability. The situation is that if two persons stand in such a relationship to each other that one can take undue advantage of the other, whether by reason of distress or recklessness or wildness or lack of care and where the facts show that one party has taken undue advantage of the other by reason of such circumstances, a transaction resting on such unconscionable dealing will not be allowed to stand. (*Slator v Nolan, 1876*). The circumstances referred to can include illiteracy, old age and physical or mental infirmity. The following is a leading case.

Case: Grealish v Murphy 1946 (I)
G was a farmer who was deemed to be mentally deficient. He executed a deed after consulting his solicitor who had explained its effect to him. Under the deed G had assigned his farm to the defendant.

Held: setting aside the deed that although it was not a case of undue influence the transaction was improvident as G was not capable of properly understanding the legal advice and the solicitor was unaware of the full extent of G's mental deficiency.

Loss of right to rescind

13. The right to rescind the contract (or gift) for undue influence is lost if there is delay in taking action after the influence has ceased to have effect.

Case: Allcard v Skinner 1887
Under the influence of a clergyman, A entered a Protestant convent and in compliance with a vow of poverty transferred property worth about £7,000 to the order. After ten years A left the order and became a Roman Catholic. Six years later she demanded the return of the unexpended balance of her gift.

Held: it was a clear case of undue influence since, among other things, the rules of the order forbade its members to seek advice from any outsider. But A's delay of six years (after leaving the order) in making her claim, debarred her from setting aside the gift and recovering her property. (This is an example of the equitable doctrine of 'laches' or delay.)

14. The right to rescission is also lost if the party affirms the contract by performing obligations without protest, or if an innocent third party has acquired rights. A party who later approves and tries to take advantage of a contract will be bound by it, even if it was suspicious when it was concluded: *De Montmorency v Devereux 1840*.

● **Statutory protection**

15. Under the European Communities (Cancellation of Contracts Negotiated away from Business Premises) 1989 Regulations consumers are given a period of time within which they may cancel 'doorstep agreements' (See Chapter 6, Sale of Goods, para 116).

TEST YOUR KNOWLEDGE

Numbers in brackets refer to paragraphs of this chapter

1. Distinguish between duress and undue influence. (2,4)

2. How is undue influence established? (5,6)

3. What is the significance of ensuring that the other party to the contract has independent professional advice in deciding whether or not to enter into the contract? (7,8)

4. What is manifest disadvantage and when need it be shown? (9-11)

5. How may the right (based on undue influence) to rescind the contract be lost? (13,14)

Now try illustrative question 6 at the end of the study text.

Chapter 5

QUASI CONTRACT AND
SUMMARY OF CONTRACT LAW

Points covered in this chapter are:

- Quasi-contract
- Summary of contract law

Purpose of chapter

This is the last chapter in a very important part of your syllabus - contract law. It summarises the grey area of 'quasi-contract' and also notes the main points to be remembered when answering a question on the law of contract.

● **Quasi-contract**

1. In some circumstances where there is no contract the law seeks to achieve a just result by treating the persons concerned as if (*quasi* means 'as if') they had entered into a contract on the appropriate terms.

2. Quasi-contract relates only to the payment of money on the ground that retention of certain funds would be unjustified enrichment. No other sorts of obligations may be enforced by the law under this doctrine. Payment under quasi-contract may be categorised as:

> (a) plaintiff paying the defendant for the defendant's use;
> (b) plaintiff paying the defendant erroneously;
> (c) a third party paying the defendant erroneously on the plaintiff's behalf;
> (d) money paid in pursuance of an ineffective contract; and
> (e) *quantum meruit*.

Examples of each of these are set out in turn below.

3. When the plaintiff pays money to the defendant for the latter's use and at his request, then the plaintiff is entitled to its return. Alternatively, the plaintiff may recover money where:

(a) he has paid money for which he was liable to a third party, but the real liability was on the defendant - for example, where an employee pays an on-the-spot fine for a company vehicle he should be reimbursed by the employer; or

(b) he pays money, under compulsion, to the third party which was owed by the defendant.

4. If X pays money to Y under a mistake of fact, Y is treated as if he had agreed to repay it.

    Case: Norwich Union Fire Insurance Society v Price 1934
    Insurers paid a claim in respect of damage to a cargo of fruit under the mistaken belief that the damage had been caused by sea-water. In fact the cargo had begun to ripen so rapidly that it had been sold before it became rotten.

    Held: the insurers could recover the sum which they had erroneously paid.

5. There is no obligation to repay money which has been paid under a mistake of law but see *Rogers v Louth Co Co, 1981 (I)*, discussed in chapter 4. It is often difficult, however, to distinguish mistakes of fact and of law. Money paid under a contract which is void (unless it is also illegal) can usually be recovered.

6. An example of the third category would be where a third party pays money to the defendant, instructing that it be paid to the plaintiff, and the defendant promises to do so.

7. Where money has been paid over in pursuance of a contract which proves to be ineffective for some reason, it may have to be repaid. This would happen where:

    (a) the contract is void or illegal (see IBL Chapter 11);

    (b) there has been total failure of consideration (for example, where a deposit is paid for a car that never materialises - the deposit can be recovered and damages may also be sought for breach) (see IBL Chapter 12, paras 60 & 61).

    (c) the party in breach paid over some part of the contract price in part-payment (*not* if he paid a deposit and then failed to perform).

8. We saw in IBL Chapter 13 how *quantum meruit* may be claimed as an alternative to damages for breach of contract. The right to be paid on *quantum meruit* is based on an implied term that the person claiming would be paid at a reasonable rate for work done or goods supplied. If the contract expressly provides for payment on completion this is inconsistent with any term that the person may be paid pro-rata and it will be difficult to imply such a term into the contract. *Quantum meruit* may be claimed in quasi-contracts on the grounds that:

    (a) the plaintiff has performed obligations under a contract which is void (for instance, a managing director claiming remuneration for services performed under his service contract which was void since the directors who approved it were not qualified to do so: *Craven-Ellis v Canons Ltd 1936*);

    (b) at the defendant's request the plaintiff has performed tasks under a 'contract' which has not yet been finally agreed and which in the end falls through;

    (c) necessaries have been supplied to minors, drunks or mentally disordered persons.

● Summary of contract law

9. Most students find contract law interesting because it is of immediate relevance to everyone's lives - every day we enter into contracts to buy goods, or perform contracts of employment etc. It is also fascinating because of the abundance of case-law, and this element is probably the most important when it comes to answering exam questions.

10. Partly because of the case-law, a fair proportion of the questions set on the law of contract are in problem form. It is well worthwhile making oneself thoroughly familiar with the case-law, from which questions are often derived.

11. The narrative of a problem question usually takes one through a sequence of events or exchanges between the parties. This is particularly characteristic of questions on offer and acceptance. It is often a useful method of achieving a sound solution to follow a certain procedure.

   (a) Identify the main and subsidiary principles - postal acceptance, lapse of offer etc - which have to be applied to the facts. These can be stated as the opening passages of the answer.

   (b) Discuss each stage in the story, as it occurs, and offer a conclusion as to the legal position at that point. A preliminary conversation may be no more than an invitation to treat (to enter into negotiations) or it may be an offer open for acceptance etc.

   (c) If some key fact is missing - eg whether a letter of acceptance was posted before or after the offeree became aware of an act of revocation by the offeror - the answer should be developed in the alternative - if before then ..., if after then...

   (d) Reach a conclusion, even if it is that, without more information, it is impossible to state whether, for instance, an agreement has been reached.

12. This process applies to all the main areas of contract law.

13. It is possible to view contract law as a series of three matters for attention.

   (a) Formation of the contract

   To be valid at all, a contract must be formed under the rules relating to agreement, consideration and the intention to create legal relations. Some must observe certain formalities such as being evidenced in writing. It is also necessary to consider whether some other factor has vitiated the contract at its formation - remember misrepresentation, mistake, duress and undue influence, the capacity of the parties and illegality.

   (b) Contents of the contract

   The contract's terms are the reason for and the meat of its creation. Terms may be conditions, warranties or innominate. They may include exclusion clauses and clauses for liquidated damages. Some sorts of mistakes as to the contents of the contract may not invalidate it; likewise, terms which are illegal or contrary to public policy may be separated from the rest of a valid contract. The agreement may become impossible but again that does not necessarily mean it no longer carries legal obligations.

   (c) Termination of the contract

   Most contracts come to an end through performance of their terms. Parties may agree to bring it to an end, and a contract may also be frustrated or be breached. In the last case, a number of remedies are available, both under common law and under equity.

PART D
SPECIFIC CONTRACTS

Chapter 6

SALE OF GOODS

Points covered in this chapter are:

- Definition of 'sale of goods'
- Terms of the contract
- Express terms
- Types of goods
- The price
- Significance of the contract terms
- Implied conditions and warranties
- Implied terms
- Passing of property and risk
- Sale by a non-owner - *nemo dat quod non habet*
- Delivery
- Acceptance and rejection
- Remedies in sale of goods contracts
- Auction sales (s58 1893 Act)
- Export sales
- Product liability
- Summary of the chapter

Purpose of chapter

Sale of goods is one of the most common and important forms of contract. Like employment contracts, it is regulated by a number of important statutes, but this does not detract from a significant amount of case-law.

- **Definition of 'sale of goods'**

1. The main statute on sale of goods is the Sale of Goods Act 1893 (referred to herein as the '1893 Act'). The 1893 Act has been amended by the Sale of Goods and Supply of Services Act 1980 (referred to herein as the '1980 Act'). The 1980 Act for the first time introduces into Irish Law the legal concept of a person 'dealing as a consumer'.

   The 1980 Act also extends some degree of protection into areas which had hitherto been ignored by legislation such as contracts for the provision of a service and also commercial activities which had come in for criticism such as unsolicited goods.

These two statutes do not pretend to contain all the law governing the sale of goods - they are essentially a codification of the common law rules peculiar to contracts for the sale of goods and all other matters are governed by the ordinary rules of contract law. Parties to a sale of goods contract are not generally bound by the provisions of the Acts except as regards certain implied terms and are quite free to make their own agreement and to exclude most of the statutory provisions. The Acts for the most part set out rules which will apply where some aspect of the contract is not covered expressly.

The two Acts are read together and care should be exercised, particularly in referring to section numbers, because of the scheme adopted by the legislature whereby the 1980 Act heavily amends certain parts of the 1893 Act by insertions and substitutions, and can lead to confusion in the section numbering.

2. A contract for the sale of goods is defined in s1(1) of the 1893 Act as:

> 'a contract by which the seller transfers, or agrees to transfer, the property in goods to a buyer for a money consideration, called the price'

Section 1(3) divides contracts for the sale of goods into 2 types:

> where ownership (ie property in the goods) passes immediately under the contract, the transaction is called a *sale* eg purchase of goods in a shop; and
>
> where ownership is to pass at some future time or subject to some condition to be fulfilled, the transaction is called an *agreement to sell*.

If the sale of goods contract is a *sale* the transaction has two aspects - it is a contract and also a conveyance which operates to pass ownership of the goods from the seller to the buyer. If the contract is an *agreement to sell* then it is a contract only and the seller remains the owner of the goods for the time being. The distinction can sometimes be important as the rights of the buyer and the seller may depend on who is the owner of the goods at the relevant time, eg if goods are destroyed the loss is normally borne by whoever owns them at the time.

3. Contracts for the sale of goods should be distinguished from other types of transactions which may resemble sales of goods, such as:

(a)   a hire-purchase contract - eventual sale is the usual result, but such a contract is first a bailment, with an option to buy;

(b)   a gift - there is no contractual status in a gift unless it is under deed;

(c)   a contract of barter - much depends on the intention of the parties: for instance, an old car 'traded-in' for a new one is certainly part of a sale of goods;

(d)   a contract of bailment - property does not pass in such a transaction: the bailee is mere custodian;

(e)   an agency contract - this is discussed in IBL Chapter 14; and

(f) a loan, with goods as security - such a transaction may be where X 'sells' his car to Y who then lets it back to X on hire-purchase. If the intention of the parties is solely to provide security for the loan there is no sale of goods within the meaning of the Acts. If however they intend that there be a sale then there is a contract of sale followed by a hire-purchase contract.

● **Terms of the contract**

The terms of the contract will be determined by the normal principles of contract law subject to the effects of the statutory provisions.

● **Express terms**

Usually the parties will expressly agree on the basic terms which would be expected to cover such matters as: quantity of goods, quality - possibly by reference to specifications, price, time and method of delivery, and in the absence of express agreement some of these terms will be governed by the Acts.

● **Types of goods**

4. 'Goods' mean physical, tangible moveable articles such as merchandise, cattle, vehicles etc, money is not 'goods' unless it is a collector's item and not just currency.

Section 5 of the 1893 Act distinguishes between -

> *existing goods* which are those which exist and are owned by the seller at the time when the contract is made and,
> *future goods* which are those which do not exist or which the seller does not yet own when he contracts to sell them.

The 1893 Act further distinguishes between *specific goods* (defined in s62(1) as *goods identified and agreed upon at the time when a contract of sale is made*) and *unascertained goods*.

Specific goods are the unique goods which by the agreement between the parties are to be delivered by the seller to the buyer - there is no provision for further selection or substitution.

Goods which are not *specific* are *unascertained* and they fall into 3 categories: (a) generic goods, referred to as being of a particular type or description eg 100 tonnes of coal or one new Honda Civic; (b) goods not yet in existence ie future goods; and (c) a part, as yet unidentified, of a specified bulk eg 100 tonnes of coal out of the 1000 tonnes stored at the seller's yard.

Ascertained goods means goods originally unascertained which are selected and irrevocably appropriated to the contract after the contract of sale is made.

The main point of these distinctions is that property and ownership cannot usually pass from seller to buyer unless, or until, the goods exist as specific or ascertained goods.

The property in specific goods *may* pass when the contract is made but no property is transferred under a contract for the sale of unascertained goods unless and until they are ascertained ie selected and irrevocably appropriated to the contract. An interesting illustration is: *Flynn v Mackin & Mahon, 1974*. (see para 59 below).

Goods which have perished

5. In a contract for sale of specific goods there are rules laid down regarding the contract's status if the goods are perishable.

    (a) If, unknown to the seller, the goods have perished at the time when the contract is made, the contract is void: s6. Refer back to the case of *Couturier v Hastie 1852* in IBL Chapter 8 on mistake in contract and *res extincta*.

    (b) If the goods perish after the contract is made, without fault of either party and before the risk passes to the buyer, the contract is avoided: s7 1893 Act.

6. In addition to simple destruction, goods may 'perish' when they deteriorate to such an extent as to lose their commercial identity. The case-law is concerned mainly with rotting of produce; it is a question of degree as to when they perish.

    Case: H R & S Sainsbury v Street 1972
    S agreed to sell a 275 ton crop of barley to be grown on his farm to H. Due to general adverse conditions, his crop failed and only 140 tons were yielded. These he sold at a higher price to a third party.

    Held: although 135 tons of produce had perished so that the contract in that respect was frustrated, S should have offered the remainder to the plaintiff. Hence the contract as a whole had not been avoided.

• The price

7. The price may be fixed by the contract or in a manner agreed by the contract, such as the ruling market price on the day of delivery, or by the course of dealing between the parties. If there is no agreed price, a reasonable price must be paid: s 8 1893 Act.

    Case: Foley v Classique Coaches 1934
    A bus company agreed to purchase its petrol from F 'at a price to be agreed in writing from time to time'; any dispute between the parties was to be submitted to arbitration. For three years the bus company purchased its petrol from F at the current price but there was no formal agreement on price. The bus company then repudiated the agreement arguing that it was incomplete since it was an agreement to agree on the price.

    Held: in view of the course of dealing between the parties and the arbitration clause there was an agreement that a reasonable price (at any given time) should be paid. The agreement was therefore enforceable.

8. As with any contract, leaving an important term such as the price out of an agreement may mean that genuine agreement has not been reached - it is an 'agreement to agree' and not a contract. In some senses, s8 of the 1893 Act conflicts with the basic tenets of contract law that there should be full agreement. This problem is not resolved in case-law.

9. A reasonable price must be paid for goods delivered and accepted if a third party to whom the fixing of the price is delegated fails to do so.

- **Significance of the contract terms**

  This is governed by s11 of the 1893 Act as amended by s10 of the 1980 Act. The following summarises the position:

  (i)   If the parties intended (or are deemed by the court to have intended) themselves to be bound by a particular stipulation, then it will be a term of the contract.

  (ii) If the term is regarded as vital it will be a condition but otherwise a warranty.

  (iii) The terms implied into sale of goods contracts by the Acts are classified as conditions or warranties.

  (iv) Whether a non-statutory term is a condition or a warranty depends on the construction of the contract. A term may be a condition although called a warranty and vice versa.

  (v)   A breach of a condition gives the injured party the right to repudiate the contract, a breach of warranty gives a right to damages only.

  (vi) Where the seller is in breach of a condition the buyer may choose to treat the breach of condition as a breach of warranty and sue for damages while still treating the contract as subsisting.

  (vii) If there is a breach of condition but the party not at fault accepts the goods or part of them, then unless the contract is severable - it provides for delivery by instalments and separate payment for each instalment - he loses his right to treat the contract as discharged by breach and may only claim damages for breach of warranty.

10. Note that 'acceptance' has a peculiarly legal meaning which is discussed at paragraphs 78 - 80 below. The position has been altered in respect of a buyer who is dealing as a consumer by s53 of the 1893 Act as substituted by s21 of the 1980 Act.

- **Implied conditions and warranties**

11. A person is said to deal as a consumer who:

(a)   does not make the contract in the course of a business nor holds himself out as doing so;

(b)   the other party does make the contract in the course of business;

(c)   the goods or services supplied under or in pursuance of the contract are of a type ordinarily supplied for private use or consumption - s3(1) 1980 Act.

---

12. Where the buyer is dealing as a consumer and there is a breach of condition and the buyer promptly upon discovering the breach, makes a request to the seller that he either remedy the breach or replace any goods which are not in conformity with the condition, then if the seller refuses to comply with the request or fails to do so within a reasonable time the buyer is entitled to:

(a)   reject the goods and repudiate the contract; or

(b)   have the defect constituting the breach remedied elsewhere and bring an action against the seller for the cost incurred – see s53 of the 1893 Act as inserted by s21 of the 1980 Act.

● **Implied Terms**

13.   One of the main functions of the 1893 Act and the 1980 Act is to codify the terms implied into contracts of sale. As noted above, these have largely evolved from case-law. Much depends on whether an implied term is a condition or a warranty, and on whether one party to the contract is dealing as a *consumer*. The rules are set out below.

14.   A sale of goods may be subject to statutory rules on:

(a)   the effect of delay in performance (s10);

(b)   title; or the seller's right to sell the goods (s12);

(c)   contract description (s13);

(d)   quality of the goods (s14);

(e)   fitness of the goods for the purpose for which they are supplied (s14); and

(f)   sale by sample (s15).

Note: Ss 12, 13, 14 and 15 of the 1893 Act have been amended by s10 of the 1980 Act.

---

15.   Section 55 of the 1893 Act, as substituted by s22 of the 1980 Act, places restrictions on the seller's ability to contract out of the various implied conditions and warranties.

This section relates to the protection afforded to the buyer by section 12 of the 1893 Act, which deals with the seller's right to sell the goods and ss 13, 14 and 15 of the 1893 Act which imply terms as to the quality and fitness for purpose of the goods sold. The section has the following effects:

(a)   any term of the contract purporting to exclude the provisions of s12 1893 Act (as amended) (undertakings as to title etc) shall be void;

(b)   any term exempting the contract from the provisions of ss 13, 14 or 15 of the 1893 Act (as amended by the 1980 Act) shall, in the case of a consumer be void, and in any other case, not be enforceable until it is shown to be fair and reasonable. The Schedule to the 1980 Act sets out the criteria to determine what is 'fair and reasonable'.

Section 3 of the 1980 Act provides that a party to a contract is said to 'deal as a consumer' if:

(i)   he neither makes the contract in the course of a business nor holds himself out as doing so; and,

(ii)   the other party does make the contract in the course of a business; and,

(iii)   the goods or services supplied under or in pursuance of the contract are of a type ordinarily supplied for private use or consumption.

It is for those claiming that a party does *not* deal as a consumer to show that he does not.

Section 3 has been considered in *O'Callaghan v Hamilton Leasing (Ireland) 1984 (I)* and *Cunningham v Woodchester Investments 1984 (I)* which cases are authority for saying that where goods are purchased for use in a business as distinct from their purchase for the purposes of trade or for re-sale, the buyer deals not as a consumer. So that eg a shopkeeper who buys a heater to heat his shop does not deal as a consumer.

Section 11 of the 1980 Act outlaws statements purporting to restrict or exclude the rights of a buyer which are given him by s12-15 of the 1893 Act (as amended) except as may be permitted by s55 of the 1893 Act (as amended).

Time of performance (s 10)

16. It depends on the terms of the contract whether time of performance is of the essence. If it is, then breach of it is breach of a condition, which entitles the injured party to treat the contract as discharged.

17. In commercial contracts for the supply of goods for business or industrial use, it will readily be assumed that time is of the essence even where there is no express term to that effect (see IBL Chapter 12 on discharge of contract). Often one party is given a period of time within which to perform his obligation, say for delivery of goods. The deliverer is not in breach until the whole period has elapsed without performance.

18. The contract may stipulate that the party should use his 'best endeavours' to perform his side by a certain time. If he fails to make that date, he must perform his obligations within a reasonable time. Under s29 1893 Act, similar reasonableness is required if no date is set by the contract. In any case, time of performance stipulates a 'reasonable hour' for obligations to be performed - this is a question of fact. Hence it is not reasonable to offer delivery of perishable goods to a factory on the Friday night before a two-week shutdown of which the seller is aware.

19. Time for payment is not of the essence unless a different intention appears from the contract. For example A, a manufacturer, orders a supply of components from B and B fails to deliver by the agreed date. A can treat the contract as discharged and refuse to accept late delivery by B. But if B delivers a first instalment on time and A pays the price a week after the agreed date, B could not (under a continuing contract) refuse to make further deliveries, and treat the contract as discharged. If, however, A failed to pay altogether, that is not delay in payment but breach of an essential condition, that the obligations to deliver the goods and to pay the price are concurrent obligations (unless otherwise agreed).

Seller's title (s 12)

20. It is an implied *condition* that the seller has, or will have at the time when property in the goods is to be transferred, a right to sell the goods.

21. In the ordinary way the seller satisfies this condition if he has title to the goods at the moment when property is to pass to the buyer. (NB in this statutory code 'title' and 'property' are both used in different contexts to mean the same thing - ownership). But the condition is broken if the seller, although he owns the goods, can be stopped by a third party from selling them: the right to transfer is essential.

Case: Niblett v Confectioners Materials 1921
A seller sold condensed milk in tins labelled with the name 'Nissly' to the plaintiffs. The well-known company Nestle took legal action when the goods arrived in the UK to have them detained as infringing the Nestle trademark. The buyers were obliged to remove the labels from the tins in order to have them released from the customs warehouse in which they were held at the instance of Nestle and could only sell them at a loss.

Held: the buyers were entitled to damages for breach of condition implied by s12(1): '--if an owner can be stopped by process of law from selling, he has not got the right to sell'.

22. If the seller delivers goods to the buyer without having the right to sell, there is a total failure of consideration, and the buyer does not obtain the ownership of the goods which is the essential basis of the contract. If the buyer has then to give up the goods to the real owner he may recover the entire price from the seller, without any allowance for the use of the goods meanwhile.

Case: Rowland v Divall 1923
R, a motor dealer, bought from D a car which, unknown to D, had been stolen. R re-sold the car to a customer. Later the owner of the car recovered it from R's customer and R repaid to his customer the price received from him. R then sued D to recover the entire price paid by R to D. D argued that allowance should be made for two months use of the car before it was returned to the owner.

Held: no allowance should be made. The contract was for transfer of ownership and none had been transferred. Possession and use were in the circumstances immaterial.

23. The seller also gives implied *warranties* that the buyer shall have quiet possession of the goods and that the goods are free of any incumbrance or challenge by a third party (unless disclosed to the buyer when the contract is made): s 12(2). If the terms of s12(2) are complied with and the buyer's quiet possession is disturbed, the remedy is damages only.

Goods to correspond with contract description (s 13)

24. In a contract for sale of goods by description, a *condition* is implied that the goods will correspond with the description. If the sale is by sample as well as by description, the goods must correspond with description as well as sample.

25. If a description is applied to the goods by the contract, it is a sale by description even though the buyer may have inspected the goods. If he himself asked for the goods by stating his requirements and the seller then supplies them to those requirements that is also a sale by description.

Case: Beale v Taylor 1967
A car was advertised as a 1961 Triumph Herald 1200. The buyer came to inspect the car and noted on the rear of the car a metal disc showing '1200'. After buying the car he found that only the back half corresponded with the description. It had been welded to a front half which was part of an earlier Herald 948 model. The seller relied on the buyer's inspection and argued that it was not a sale by description.

Held: the advertisement and the metal disc described the car as a 1200. It was a sale by description in spite of the buyer's pre-contract inspection.

Case: O'Connor v Donnelly, 1944 (I)
Plaintiff was made sick by a bad can of salmon.

Held: by the high Court that there can be a sale of goods by description even if the goods are shown to the buyer.

26. But if a contract contains the phrase 'bought as seen' (as many auction sales do) then the sale is expressly not one by description: *Cavendish-Woodhouse Ltd v Manley 1984.*

27. 'Description' is widely and strictly interpreted to include ingredients, age, date of shipment, packing, quantity, etc.

Case: Varley v Whipp 1900
The seller advertised a secondhand reaping machine describing it as new in the previous year. The buyer bought it without seeing it. When it arrived he found that it was very much more than a year old and rejected it. The seller sued for the price.

Held: it was a sale by description and a breach of condition which entitled the buyer to reject. (See also *Moore v Landauer 1921* in IBL Chapter 12 on discharge of contract.)

If the seller uses a false description he may also infringe the Consumer Information Act 1978.

Implied undertakings as to qualify and fitness

28. The main protection for the buyer against faulty goods or goods whose quality falls below the expected standard is given by s14 of the 1893 Act as amended by s10 of the 1980 Act. (References are to the sub-sections of s14 as amended).

Note that s14(I) upholds the principle of *caveat emptor* but subject to the provisions of the Acts. The sub-sections to which particular attention must be paid are (2), (3) and (4).

Merchantable quality

29. Section 14(2) provided that where a seller sells goods in the course of business there is an implied condition that the goods are of merchantable quality.

This *condition* applies only to goods sold 'in the course of a business'; the seller must be carrying on a business or profession and make the sale in connection with that activity. If a grocer sells his delivery van that is within the rule; if he sells his domestic refrigerator it is not. The condition also applies to all sales by sample: s15.

30. The condition applies to all 'goods supplied under the contract' – not only to the goods themselves therefore but also to the packaging in which they were sold (such as a returnable lemonade bottle and not merely the lemonade - *Geddling v Marsh 1920*) and also to any instructions provided for the use of the goods.

Case: Wilson v Rickett Cockerell & Co 1954
Contract for the supply of patent fuel (Coalite). An unexploded detonator was mixed in with the fuel. It exploded in the fireplace causing damage.

Held: the detonator (goods supplied) rendered the contract goods (Coalite) unsuitable for their purpose and unmerchantable.

Case: Dillon Leetch v Maxwell Motors Ltd 1984 (I)
The plaintiff purchased a car from the defendant. The car had numerous defects over a period of time. The plaintiff sought to rescind the contract and claim damages.

Held: plaintiff was not entitled to rescission. Damages were awarded, including an amount for inconvenience. The defendant was in breach of an implied term as to merchantable quality.

31. The condition that the goods supplied under the contract are of merchantable quality is excluded if:

> (a) the buyer's attention is drawn to defects before the contract is made; or
>
> (b) the buyer examines the goods before the contract is made, and that examination ought to reveal the defects.

32. Section 14(3) provides that goods are of merchantable quality if they are as fit for the purpose for which goods of that description are commonly bought and as durable as it is reasonable to expect having regard to any description applied to them, the price (if relevant) and all other relevant circumstances.

Case: Cehave v Bremer, The Hansa Nord 1975
This case concerned a contract for the supply of 'citrus pulp pellets' (a raw material used in making animal feeding stuffs). On arrival at port of destination, part of the cargo had deteriorated and the buyers rejected the entire cargo. The cargo was offered for sale and was purchased (at a much lower price) by the same buyers who used it for its intended original purpose. The sellers denied that the buyers had been entitled to reject the cargo as not being of merchantable quality.

Held: the fact that the cargo could only be sold on the market at a lower price than the contract provided was not conclusive that it was not of merchantable quality. It could be - and was - used for its purpose, ie making cattle food, and so by that test it was of merchantable quality. On a different point (not referred to above) the Court of Appeal held that some contract terms cannot be treated as conditions until the consequences of breach of those circumstances can be seen. Such terms have come to be described as 'innominate' - see IBL Chapter 6 on contract terms.

33. If the goods can be used for only one purpose, such as a hotwater bottle (see *Priest v Last 1903)* or a pair of underpants *(Grant v Australian Knitting Mills 1936)*, and the goods are unsuitable for that purpose, they are of unmerchantable quality. On the other hand where goods are multi-purpose, the Court of Appeal held in *Aswan Engineering Establishment Co v Lupdine Ltd 1986* that the Act does not mean that the goods must be suitable for all of the purposes for which goods of that kind are commonly bought. They will still be merchantable providing they are suitable for at least one or more purposes for which they might reasonably be expected to be used.

34. If it is contemplated that the goods will be processed in some way before use, such as cooking or washing foodstuffs, and this treatment will remove a defect, the goods are merchantable in spite of the defect: *Heil v Hedges 1951* (plaintiff failed to cook pork chops properly).

35. Once goods are found not to be of merchantable quality the seller has no defence - there is strict liability, so showing that all reasonable care was taken will not succeed.

36. The goods must remain of merchantable quality for a reasonable time, eg during the time of transit between seller and buyer. One of the major areas of uncertainty in consumer protection law is how long the goods must remain in satisfactory condition after transfer to the buyer. But if a fault appears soon after the transfer it will readily be concluded that the goods were not of merchantable quality when sold.

Case: Bristol Tramways v Fiat Motors 1910
Sale of omnibuses intended for heavy use by a public transport company on hilly roads. The vehicles broke down soon after delivery.

Held: the buses were neither of merchantable quality nor fit for their purpose.

37. If the buyer examines the goods before agreeing to buy them he is treated as discovering any defects apparent on examination, whether or not he actually discovers them - but not defects which no examination could reveal, eg arsenic in beer.

Case: Thornett & Fehr v Beers & Son 1919
Contract for sale of glue in barrels. The buyer inspected the outside only of the barrels. The defect would have been discoverable if he had also looked inside.

Held: the defects which the buyer could have discovered should count when deciding whether the goods were of merchantable quality.

38. Merchantable quality has recently been extended in England to include not only the physical condition of the goods but also other qualities.

Case: Shine v General Guarantee Corporation 1988
S obtained an enthusiast's car under hire purchase. He had inspected it and assumed it had a rust warranty. He later discovered that the car had been totally submerged in water for 2 days, and so had been an insurance write-off. He stopped paying the instalments and sought to rescind the contract.

Held: although the car had no physical defects, S was entitled to rescind for breach since merchantable quality included such fundamentals as having been previously written off.

Fitness of goods for a disclosed purpose

39. Section 14(4) provides that where the buyer expressly or by implication makes known to the seller any particular purpose for which the goods are bought, it is an implied condition that the goods supplied under the contract are reasonably fit for that purpose (whether or not that is the common purpose of such goods), unless the circumstances show that either:

(a) the buyer does not rely, or
(b) it is unreasonable for him to rely

on the skill or judgment of the seller.

Case: Ashington Piggeries v Christopher Hill 1972
B gave S a recipe for mink-food and requested that S should mix the food in accordance with the recipe and supply it to B. S told B that they had never supplied mink-food before although they were manufacturers of animal foodstuffs. One of the ingredients was herring-meal which had been stored in a chemical which created a poisonous substance damaging to all animals but particularly damaging to mink. As a result many of the mink died.

Held: because the poison affected all animals the food was unfit for its disclosed purpose since B relied on S's skill and judgment to the extent that S was an animal-food manufacturer and should not have supplied a generally harmful food. If the poison had only affected mink then B's skill and judgment demonstrated by its supply of a recipe would have made it unreasonable to rely on S's.

Case: McCullough Sales v Chetham Timber Co 1983 (I)
The plaintiffs sold to the defendants some plastic skirting boards and some nails. The nails did not prove suitable for securing the boards to walls. Against the plaintiffs claim for price the defendants counterclaimed breach of implied terms as to merchantable quality and fitness for purpose.

Held: the provisions of s 14 of the 1893 Act applied. The defendant was relying upon the plaintiff's skill and judgment when the goods were sold.

40. The 'fitness for purpose' condition overlaps the 'merchantability' condition:

Case: Egan v McSweeney 1955

Held: that a detonator included in a bag of coal made the coal both unmerchantable and unfit for its purpose.

Foodstuffs which, unknown to the seller, are unsound at the time of sale are both unmerchantable and unfit for their purpose:

Case: Wallis v Russell 1902
The plaintiff sent her grand-daughter to the fishmonger (the defendant) to buy two crabs. She told the fishmonger she wanted 'two nice fresh crabs for tea'. The crabs were selected by the defendant and both plaintiff and her grand-daughter got food poisoning. The defendant said he had inspected the crabs himself and would normally have been able to detect if anything was wrong with them.

Held: by the Court of Appeal that:

(i)   section 14(I) (of the original 1893 Act, the equivalent of s14(4) of the amended Act) was not confined to manufactured goods;

(ii)   the intimation that the crabs were to be eaten was sufficient indication to the defendant of the particular purpose for which they were required; and,

(iii) it was no defence to say the defect was latent and could not be discovered by inspection.

Very often the particular purpose for which the goods are required is obvious and in such cases the courts have taken the view that the buyer, merely by asking for the goods is 'by implication' making known the purpose for which the goods are required as in *Wallis v Russell.*

41. If the goods have only one obvious purpose, the buyer by implication makes known his purpose merely by asking for the goods.

Case: Priest v Last 1903
A customer at a chemist's shop asked for a hot-water bottle and was told, in answer to a question, that it should not be filled with boiling water. It burst after only five days in use.

Held: if there is only one purpose that particular purpose is disclosed by buying the goods. Because it was not an effective hot-water bottle, it was in breach of s14(3). This was followed by *Frost v Aylesbury Dairy Co 1905* - in the purchase of milk supplied to a domestic address the buyer discloses his purpose, which is human consumption.

42. A buyer, however, has no remedy against a seller if the goods supplied are reasonably fit for their purpose even though, owing to some special factor affecting the buyer, they are not fit for him:

Case: Griffiths v Peter Conway 1939
The plaintiff purchased a Harris tweed coat which had been specially made for her and from which she contracted dermatitis. There was nothing in the material which would have affected a normal person but the plaintiff's skin was abnormally sensitive. This fact had not been mentioned to the defendants.

Held: the defendants were not liable as the coat was 'reasonably fit' for its purpose.

43. Even partial reliance of the buyer on the seller's skill etc makes the latter subject to the condition.

Case: Cammell Laird v Manganese Bronze & Brass Co 1934
Shipbuilders ordered a ship's propeller to be manufactured by a specialist contractor. The buyers specified the materials and certain dimensions but left other details to the seller's judgment.

Held: partial reliance on the seller's skill etc is sufficient to bring the condition into operation as regards matters left to the seller to determine.

If the seller wishes to avoid liability it is for him to show that the buyer did not rely on his (the seller's) skill and judgment or that it would have been unreasonable for him to have done so:

Case: Draper v Rubenstein 1925 (I)

Held: that a butcher with 17 years experience of buying cattle in the Dublin cattle market relied on his own skill and judgment and he could not rely on this section when the cattle proved unfit for human consumption.

The seller might also escape liability if the buyer tested the goods before buying: *Stokes & McKieran v Lixnaw Co-op 1937 (I)*.

44. If the goods can be used for more than one purpose or there are special circumstances which affect their suitability, there is no breach of this condition unless the buyer has made an express disclosure. But if the goods are multipurpose and the buyer has disclosed that he has one purpose only, it is no defence to the seller that his goods are suitable for other purposes. They may in such a case be of merchantable quality (as in the *Lupdine case* in paragraph 33), but they are not fit for the disclosed specific purpose. The one condition is a test of general suitability and the other (where it applies) of specific suitability.

Sale by sample (s 15)

45. In a sale by sample there are implied *conditions* that:

    (a) the bulk shall correspond in quality with the sample; and

    (b) the buyer shall have a reasonable opportunity of comparing bulk with sample; and

    (c) the goods shall be free of any defect rendering them unmerchantable which would not be apparent on a reasonable examination of the sample.

This section was not amended by the 1980 Act.

Sale of motor vehicle – s13 Sale of Goods and Supply of Services Act 1980

46. In addition to the other implied conditions and warranties, in a contract for the sale of a motor vehicle (except a contract in which the buyer is a person whose business it is to deal in motor vehicles) there is an implied condition that at the time of delivery the vehicle is free from any defect which would render it a danger to the public, including persons travelling in the vehicle.

    There is no such implied condition where:

    (a) it is agreed between the buyer and the seller that the vehicle is not intended to be used in the condition in which it is delivered; and

    (b) a document consisting of a statement to that effect is signed by the seller and buyer and given to the buyer prior to or at the time of delivery; and

    (c) the agreement at (a) is fair and reasonable.

    Similar terms are implied into contracts for the supply of motor vehicles on lease and by hire-purchase.

    Note that these provisions apply to private sales of motor vehicles so that the sale of a secondhand car by a person who is not in the motor trade to another person who is not in the motor trade is caught by the section.

47. There is a presumption that the defect existed at time of delivery.

48. The period within which such a claim can be brought under s13 of the 1980 Act is two years.

    Case: Glorney v O'Brien 1988 (I)
    The plaintiff purchased from the defendant an old car. Whilst driving the car one evening the car went out of control, hit a wall and telegraph pole, and the plaintiff was injured. The plaintiff claimed the defendant was in breach of s13(2) of the 1980 Act.

    Held: the defendant was in breach of s 13 of the 1980 Act. Further, it was pointed out that a seller could not be exempted from the provisions of s13(2) because of the provisions of s13(9). Damages for personal injuries were awarded to the plaintiff.

Liability of finance houses

49. Under s 14 of the 1980 Act where goods are sold to a buyer dealing as consumer and in relation to the sale an agreement is entered into by the buyer with another person acting in the course of a business, being a finance house, for the repayment of money paid by the finance house to the seller in respect of the price of the goods, the finance house shall be deemed to be a party to the contract of sale and will be jointly and severally liable for breach of contract of sale and any misrepresentations made by the seller with respect to the goods.

    Case: Cunningham v Woodchester Investments 1984 (I)
    C purchased a telephone system for a non profit making agricultural college of which he was Bursar. The phone system was incomplete and unsatisfactory. Woodchester Investments Ltd financed the purchase. The plaintiff claimed to be dealing as a consumer and sued relying on s14 of the 1980 Act.

    Held: the plaintiff did not come within the definition of consumer in s3 of the 1980 Act and could not rely on s14 of the 1980 Act.

• Passing of property and risk

50. Determining at what stage property passes is important for two reasons.

    (a) Risk of accidental loss or damage is, as a general rule, borne by the owner, so risk passes with ownership (or 'property') in a sale of goods: s20 1893 Act.

      However the parties can agree that risk in the goods is to pass at any time either before or after the passing of the property in the goods.

    (b) The rights of parties against each other, and the rights of either party's creditors if he becomes insolvent, are also affected. Thus the seller can sue the buyer for the price if the property in the goods has passed and the buyer's right to claim goods if the seller becomes bankrupt and the right of the buyer's creditors to the goods if the buyer becomes bankrupt will generally depend on whether or not the property in the goods has passed to the buyer.

51. No inference is drawn merely because the seller is still in possession - the goods may now be owned by the buyer. Similarly, even though the buyer is in possession the seller may still be the owner of them eg if the seller has delivered the goods subject to reservation of title until they are paid for in full.

52. The rules for determining when the property in goods passes are essentially governed by sections 16 to 18 of the 1893 Act and depend on whether the goods are specific, ascertained or unascertained.

Specific goods

53. Section 17 provides that property in specific goods is transferred at such time as it appears the parties intended it to be transferred having regard to the terms of the contract, the conduct of the parties and the circumstances of the case.

    Many contracts for the supply of goods contain a clause stating that title to the goods remains with the seller until the contract price is paid. Such 'retention of title' clauses are a common example of the s17 rule that title to specific goods passes when the parties so intend. These clauses are discussed later in this chapter in the context of an unpaid seller's remedies against goods.

    If however the intention of the parties is not clear then it will be presumed they intended the property to pass in accordance with section 18, Rules 1 to 4.

54. <u>Rule 1</u>: Where there is an unconditional contract for the sale of specific goods, in a deliverable state, the property in the goods passes to the buyer when the contract is made.

    It is immaterial that the seller has not yet delivered them or that the buyer has not yet paid the price. However, the seller may, and often does, stipulate that property shall not pass until the price is paid. If the seller insists on retaining the goods or documents relating to them, such as the registration book of a car which has been sold, until the price is paid it will readily be inferred that he intended (and the buyer agreed) that property would not pass on making the contract, but only on payment of the price.

    'Deliverable state' is defined in s62(4) as 'such a state that the buyer would under the contract be bound to take delivery.'

SALE OF GOODS

Case: Clarke v Reilly 1967 (I)
The plaintiff had been allowed by the defendant to continue to use his traded-in car pending the delivery of the new car he had bought. It (the old car) was damaged in an accident.

Held ownership in the old car had passed to the defendant as soon as the contract was made. As the plaintiff was merely the bailee of the car (he had a loan of it in this case) and since he had taken reasonable care of it, the defendant must bear the loss - Rule 1 applied.

55. <u>Rule 2</u>: If, under a contract for sale of specific goods, the seller is bound to do something to put the goods into a deliverable state, property does not pass until the seller has done what is required of him and the buyer has notice of it.

Case: Anderson v Ryan 1967
Motor car bought on the understanding that some panel-beating would be done to it.

Held: property did not pass until the work was done as only then would the vehicle be in a deliverable state.

A different aspect of the operation of Rule 2 is:

Case: Underwood v Burgh Castle Cement Syndicate 1922
Contract for the sale of an engine to be loaded on to a railway wagon. At the time of making the contract the engine was embedded in cement foundations at a factory and it was not in a deliverable state. In loading it into the railway wagon the sellers broke part of the machine. The buyers refused to accept it.

Held: Rule 2 and not Rule 1 applied. At the time of the damage the engine was still in the sellers' ownership and so at their risk. The buyers were entitled to reject it in its damaged state.

56. <u>Rule 3</u>: Where there is a contract for the sale of specific goods in a deliverable state but the seller is bound to weigh, measure or test them to fix the price, property only passes when he has done so and the buyer has notice of it.

The rule does not apply when it is the buyer who must take this action;

Case: Turley v Bates 1863
Contract for the sale of a heap of clay at £X per ton, the buyer to weigh the clay as he loaded it.

Held: Rule 1 not Rule 3 applied.

Note that the mere right of the buyer to weigh or test is immaterial and if the parties have agreed on a provisional estimate of the total price to be verified when the goods can be weighed etc an intention can be inferred that transfer of ownership will not be postponed until such weighting etc.

57. <u>Rule 4</u>: When goods are delivered to the buyer on approval, or 'on sale or return' or other similar terms, the property passes to the buyer:

(a) When he signifies his approval or acceptance to the seller or does any other act adopting the transaction; or,

(b) If he does not signify his approval or acceptance to the seller but retains the goods without giving notice of rejection, then, if a time has been fixed for the return of the goods, on the expiration of such time, and if no time has been fixed, on the expiration of a reasonable time.   What is a reasonable time is a question of fact.

The clear general rule is that the property in the goods does not pass until the buyer adopts the transaction but it is open to the parties to agree otherwise - trade customs may govern.

If goods are damaged while on approval the seller must bear the loss unless the damage was the fault of the buyer.

Unascertained goods

58. Where the contract is for unascertained goods (eg 100 tonnes of coal from a larger bulk or any 20 kegs of Guinness) or for future goods by description, section 16 provides that 'no property in the goods is transferred to the buyer unless and until the goods are ascertained.'

When the goods are in due course ascertained then the contract *may* provide for the transfer of the property (section 17) but if the intention of the parties cannot be established then Rule 5 will operate to determine the time when the property in the goods is transferred.

Rule 5: When there is a contract for the sale of unascertained or future goods by description, and goods of that description and in a deliverable state are unconditionally appropriated to the contract by the seller with the assent of the buyer, or by the buyer with the assent of the seller, the property then passes to the buyer.

Such assent may be express or implied and given before or after the appropriation is made. For example, if the buyer orders goods to be supplied from the seller's stock he gives implied assent to the seller to make an appropriation from his stock.

59. To bring rule 5 into operation, something more definite is required than merely selecting or setting aside goods for delivery to the buyer. The act must be irrevocable, for example where the seller sets aside goods and also informs the buyer that they are ready for collection.

Case: Pignataro v Gilroy 1919
Contract for sale of 140 bags of rice. The seller sent to the buyer a delivery order for 125 bags at a warehouse and asked him to collect 15 from the seller's premises. The buyer took no action for a month and meanwhile the 15 bags were stolen.

Held: the property and risk had passed to the buyer whose assent was inferred from his inactivity.

Case: Flynn v Mackin & Mahon 1974 (I)

Fr Mackin contracted to purchase from Mr Mahon, a garage proprietor, a new blue Vauxhall Viva motor car. Mahon did not have one in stock but undertook to obtain one from the main dealer in Athlone. He duly collected the car and while on the way home to Kinnegad, where he was to deliver the car to Fr Mackin, he was involved in an accident in which the plaintiff was seriously injured. A question that arose for consideration by the court was: who owned the car at the time of the accident?

Held by the Supreme Court, for reasons which do not concern us here, that the agreement was not an agreement for sale within the meaning of the 1893 Act but even if it had been it would have been an agreement for the sale of *future goods* and since at the time of the accident the car had not been unconditionally appropriated to the contract it was therefore still the property of Mr Mahon. The court accepted that Mahon had collected the car with the intention of delivering it to Fr Mackin in fulfilment of his contract but found there was nothing in the contract which would have prevented his selling the car in question to anyone else – his obligation under the contract was to deliver a new blue Vauxhall Viva to Fr Mackin and any new blue Vauxhall Viva would have satisfied his obligation.

60. Delivery of goods to the buyer, or to a carrier for transmission to the buyer, without reserving to the seller a right of disposal is an unconditional appropriation which brings rule 5 into operation.

61. Rule 5 only applies to appropriation of goods in a deliverable state.

Case: Philip Head & Sons v Showfronts 1970
Contract for supply and laying of carpet at the buyer's premises. A roll of carpet was delivered but it was stolen before it could be laid.

Held: the carpet was deliverable to the buyer when laid and not before. It was the seller's property when stolen – the risk of loss remained with him.

Summary of s 18 – passing of property

Rule	Goods	Contract	Property passes
1	Specific and deliverable	Unconditional	When contract made
2	Specific	Seller to put into deliverable state	When seller has done so, and buyer has notice
3	Specific and deliverable	Seller must measure to fix price	When seller has done so and buyer has notice
4	Specific or ascertained goods	Sale or return	When buyer signifies approval, or he retains them
5	Unascertained or future goods	By description	When goods, fitting description and deliverable, are unconditionally appropriated by either party, with assent.

Sections 21–26 of the 1893 Act deal with the title, or right to goods, which persons can obtain when they buy them from a party who has no property in them.

- **Sale by a non-owner – nemo dat quod non habet**

62. The general rule is that only the owner, or an agent acting with his authority, can transfer ownership (called 'title' in this part of the 1893 Act) of goods to a buyer. This is expressed in the Latin maxim *nemo dat quod non habet* – no one can give what he does not have.

63. To the general rule there are a number of *exceptions* to protect an honest buyer against loss. The exceptions fall under rules relating to:

    (a) agency;

    (b) estoppel;

    (c) market overt;

    (d) voidable title;

    (e) seller in possession;

    (f) buyer in possession;

    (g) special powers of sale.

These are now discussed in turn.

64. <u>Agency s21 1893 Act.</u> If an ordinary agent sells goods without actual or apparent authority, there is usually no transfer of title to the buyer. But a mercantile agent, that is an agent whose business is selling goods for others, may have possession of goods (or documents of title to them) with the owner's consent. He can then sell them, in the ordinary course of his business, to a buyer who buys in good faith and without notice that the agent had no authority to sell (or was exceeding his authority). The buyer acquires title to the goods: s21. See *Folkes v King 1923* in IBL Chapter 14 on law of agency.

65. <u>Estoppel</u>. If, by his conduct, the true owner leads the buyer to believe that the person who makes the sale owns the goods or has authority to sell them, the true owner is prevented (estopped) from denying the seller's authority to sell. Merely to put goods in the possession of another is not to represent that he is the owner.

Case: Central Newbury Car Auctions v Unity Finance 1957
A rogue was allowed by motor dealers to take a car (and its registration book) pending completion of arrangements to buy it from a finance company on hire purchase. He sold the car. The dealers sued the buyer.

Held: the dealers could deny that the rogue to whom they had given possession had authority to sell the car: transfer of possession is not a representation that the transferee is the owner.

Case: Stoneleigh Finance v Phillips 1965
Mr X wanted to raise cash on the security of his car. He agreed with a car dealer that the latter would represent to the HP company that X wished to take the car on hire-purchase and X signed a form which contained, *inter alia,* a statement that the car was the property of the dealer. The dealer then purported to sell the car to the HP company in the usual way. Mr X defaulted on the repayments and the HP company repossessed the car.

Held that since X was a party to this 'fiddle' he was estopped from denying the dealer's title to the car when he sold it to the HP company and therefore the HP company had acquired a good title to the car.

Case: Henderson v Williams 1895
The owners of a stock of sugar informed the warehouse at which it was stored that they should hold it to the order of F as purchaser from them. F re-sold the sugar to H who was told by the warehouse (in reply to his enquiry) that they held the sugar to the order of F. Later the owners repudiated their transaction with F (induced by F's fraud) and instructed the warehouse to refuse delivery to H.

Held: the owners were estopped from denying their previous statement that the sugar was now held to the order of F (as owner).

66. <u>Market overt (s 22 1893 Act).</u> If goods are sold in market overt according to the usage of the market, the buyer acquires good title if he buys in good faith and without notice of the seller's lack of title.

67. Market overt (open market) means a recognised public market established by statute, charter or long-standing custom. The goods must be of a type usually sold there, the sale must take place in the public part of the shop and must be a sale *by* the shopkeeper (not *to* him). Sale in any market overt must (to afford this protection) take place between sunrise and sunset. The principle which underlies these rules is that the buyer is protected if he buys openly in a market to which the public resort, and where the goods are on public display.

Case: Bishopsgate Motor Finance v Transport Brakes 1949
X, who had possession of a car obtained under a hire purchase agreement, offered it for sale by auction at Maidstone market. There were no bidders but later the same day X sold the car to Y at the same market by private treaty.

Held: this was market overt; sale by private treaty was in accordance with market usage and so the buyer obtained good title.

68. Sale under voidable title (s 23 1893 Act). A person may acquire goods under a contract which is voidable, say for misrepresentation. He then has title to the goods until the contract is avoided. If he re-sells before the sale to him is avoided, to a person who buys in good faith and without notice of his defective title, that buyer obtains a good title to the goods. Normally the first contract of sale is not avoided until the person entitled to avoid it communicates his decision to the other party but if that party has disappeared other evidence of intention to avoid the first sale, such as reporting the matter to the police, will suffice: *Car & Universal Finance Co v Caldwell 1965.* See also *Anderson v Ryan 1967 (I)* and *Lewis v Averay 1972.*

Where the goods were obtained by fraud they will not revest in the owner merely because of the conviction of the offender but if the goods were stolen they revest in the true owner on conviction of the thief notwithstanding any intermediate dealings s24.

69. Re-sale by seller in possession (s25 (1) 1893 Act). If a seller, or a mercantile agent acting for him, continues in possession of the goods (or documents of title to them), and he makes a sale of them to a person who receives them in good faith and without notice of the previous sale, the transaction takes effect as if the seller were authorised for that purpose.

Suppose that A sells specific goods to B and B, to whom the ownership of the goods passes, immediately leaves them in A's possession until B can collect them in his car. A by mistake then re-sells the goods and delivers them to C, who is unaware of the previous sale to B. C gets good title to the goods; B's only remedy is to sue A. But if A does not actually deliver the goods to C, B has the better right.

70. Re-sale by a buyer in possession (s25 (2) 1893 Act). The seller may permit the buyer to take possession of the goods before ownership has passed to the buyer, eg the seller makes delivery but retains title until the price is paid. If the buyer then makes a re-sale or other disposition with an actual delivery or transfer of the goods (or documents of title), to a person who takes them in good faith and without notice of the original seller's rights, title passes to that person as if the original buyer had acted as a mercantile agent. Note that he must have possession with the seller's consent.

Case: Newtons of Wembley v Williams 1965
X purchased a car and paid the price by cheque. The seller stipulated that title to the car should not pass until the cheque was cleared but allowed X to take possession of the car. The cheque was dishonoured and the sellers informed the police and thereby avoided the sale to X in the only way available to them. But X sold the car for cash in an established secondhand car market to Y who took delivery forthwith.

Held: Y acquired good title since X was a buyer in possession with the seller's consent (at the time of sale) and the re-sale in the Warren Street market was a disposition in the ordinary course of business of a mercantile agent - it was a commercial sale.

71. <u>Special powers of sale</u>. The court may order goods to be sold. Various persons, such as pawnbrokers, unpaid sellers and hotel keepers and bailees (eg dry-cleaners) in possession of abandoned goods for which charges are owing, have specific powers of sale: s21 (2)(b)

Performance of the contract

Part III of the 1893 Act specifies what will constitute performance of the contract. The relevant sections are 27-37 of which s34 &35 were rewritten by s20 of the 1980 Act.

● Delivery

72. It is the duty of the seller to deliver the goods and of the buyer to accept and pay for them, in accordance with the terms of the contract for sale: s27.

Unless otherwise agreed, delivery of the goods and payment of the price are concurrent conditions, that is the seller must be prepared to give possession of the goods in exchange for the price and vice versa: s28.

(a) <u>Method</u>: delivery is the voluntary transfer of possession from one person to another (s 62 1893 Act). It may be by physical transfer of possession, or of the means of control (eg the key of a warehouse) or by arranging that a third party who has the goods acknowledges ('attorns') to the buyer that he holds them on his behalf, or by delivery of a document of title to the goods.

(b) <u>Place</u>: delivery is to be made at the seller's place of business, or if he has none at his residence, unless the goods are specific and, to the knowledge of both parties when the contract is made, the goods are at some other place, then delivery is, in those circumstances, to be at that other place: s29(I).

(c) <u>Time</u>: if no time is agreed, delivery is to be made within a reasonable time and at a reasonable hour: s29(2) and (4) 1893 Act.

(d) <u>Expense</u>: the seller bears the expense of putting the goods into a deliverable state (eg by packing them up or bagging them): s29(5) 1893 Act.

---

73. Unless otherwise agreed the buyer is not obliged to accept delivery by instalments: s31 1893 Act. He may reject a delivery of part only of the goods.

Case: Norwell & Co v Black 1930 (I)
Held that a buyer was entitled to reject a delivery of carpets and other floor coverings because the whole order had not been delivered in one lot as the contract stipulated.

74. If the contract does provide for delivery by instalments with separate payment for each instalment, the contract is 'severable'. If one or more instalments under a severable contract are defective, this may amount to repudiation of the entire contract or merely give a right to claim compensation for the defective deliveries only. It depends on the ratio of defective to sound deliveries and the likelihood or otherwise that future instalments may also be defective.

75. If the seller delivers the wrong quantity the buyer may reject the whole quantity, but if he accepts what is delivered he must pay at the contract rate for the quantity accepted. When the seller delivers too much the buyer may also accept the correct quantity and reject the rest: s30 1893 Act.

76. If the seller delivers the contract goods mixed (ie accompanied by) with other goods the buyer may reject the whole or accept the contract goods and reject others: s 30 1893 Act.

77. Delivery through a carrier - sections 32 & 33 of the 1893 Act deal with the responsibilities of the parties for shipment, insurance and deterioration of the goods during transit:

    (a) delivery to a carrier for transmission to the buyer is deemed to be delivery to the buyer unless the contrary intention appears, eg when the seller consigns the goods to himself or his agent at their destination: s32 1893 Act;

    Case: Michel Freres S/A v Kilkenny Woolen Mills 1961 (I)
    Plaintiffs entered into a CIF contract to deliver goods to an Irish port. The goods were not unloaded in Dublin until after the contract delivery date.

    Held: that the French sellers had not delivered yarn until the carriers had landed the goods in Dublin and since this was after the contract delivery date the defendants were entitled to reject them.

    (b) the seller must make a reasonable arrangement with the carrier and (if the goods are sent by sea) give the buyer notice in time to permit the buyer to arrange insurance: s32 1893 Act;

    (c) the buyer must bear the risk of any deterioration necessarily incidental to the course of transit: s33 1893 Act.

● **Acceptance and rejection**

78. As already stated, acceptance of goods or part of them (unless the contract is severable), deprives the buyer of his right to treat the contract as discharged by breach of condition (for example as to the quality of the goods) on the part of the seller unless he is empowered to do so by an express or implied term of the contract: s11(3). But he may claim damages.

79. Buyer's right to examine goods

    Section 34 of the 1893 Act (as substituted by s20 of the 1980 Act) provides that where goods are delivered to the buyer, which he has not previously examined, he is not deemed to have accepted them unless and until he has had a reasonable opportunity of examining them for the purpose of ascertaining whether they are in conformity with the contract.

    Case: Marry v Merville Dairy 1954 (I)
    Held: it was reasonable for the defendants to defer acceptance of the plaintiff's milk until it had been tested.

    If the buyer either states expressly that he accepts or simply retains the goods beyond a reasonable time for examination, he has had his opportunity and he has accepted the goods. But re-sale (possibly with delivery direct from the seller to the sub-purchaser) may give the buyer no opportunity; for example the buyer may be unaware that the goods are defective until the sub-purchaser makes complaint to him. In these circumstances the buyer is permitted to reject the goods in spite of the re-sale.

Acceptance

80. The buyer is deemed to have accepted the goods (s35 of the 1893 Act (as substituted by s20 of 1980 Act)):

> (a) if he informs the seller that he accepts them; or,
>
> (b) subject to s34 when the goods have been delivered to him, if he does any act inconsistent with the seller's ownership such as re-selling the goods to a third party; or
>
> (c) if, after the lapse of a reasonable time, the buyer retains the goods without informing the seller that he has rejected them:
>
> *Case: Gill v Heiton 1943 (I)*
> *Held:* that the buyer lost his right to reject goods by allowing the unloading of a load of turf to continue after it had become quite clear that it did not conform with the quality contracted for.

81. Where the seller has breached a condition the buyer may treat the contract as repudiated and hence reject the goods. The buyer does not have to return the goods to the seller unless otherwise agreed - he merely has to inform the seller of his rejection: s36 1893 Act.

82. The buyer loses his right to reject goods if:

(a) he waives the breached condition;
(b) he elects to treat the breach of condition as a breach of warranty;
(c) he has accepted the goods (in a contract which is not severable); or
(d) he is unable to return the goods because, for example, he has sold them on to a buyer who keeps them.

Section 37 of the 1893 Act provides that where the buyer refuses to take delivery of goods within a reasonable time after the seller has requested him to do so, he is liable to the seller for any loss caused by his neglect or refusal to take delivery and also for a reasonable charge for the care and custody of the goods.

• Remedies in sale of goods contracts

83. As with any other contract, one for sale of goods may be breached. Aside from the usual common law remedies (damages, action for the price etc) the parties have rights peculiar to this type of contract. They are categorised as follows:

(a) seller's remedies against the goods;
(b) seller's remedies against the buyer;
(c) buyer's remedies against the seller.

The remedies which are against goods are described as 'real remedies'; all others are called 'personal'.

Seller's remedies against the goods (Sections refer to 1893 Act).

84. Ownership of goods often passes to the buyer before they are delivered to the buyer or the price paid. If the buyer then defaults, for example by failing to pay the price when due, the seller has rights against the goods in his possession or under his control although those goods are now owned by the buyer. It is usually more satisfactory to him to retain the goods as security for the price than merely to sue a buyer, who may well be insolvent, for breach of contract.

85. These rights are given only to an 'unpaid seller' (s 38). He is unpaid if either:

    (a) the whole of the price has not been paid or tendered to him; or

    (b) he has received a bill of exchange eg a cheque etc as conditional payment and the bill has been dishonoured.

86. An unpaid seller of goods which are now the property of the buyer has the following statutory rights in respect of the goods (s39):

    (a) a *lien* on the goods so long as they are in his possession; and
    (b) a right of *stoppage in transitu* if the buyer is insolvent and the goods are in the hands of a carrier;
    (c) a right of *re-sale* in certain circumstances.

87. The unpaid seller's <u>lien</u>, his right to retain the goods in his possession until the price is paid or tendered, exists (s 41):

    (a) where the goods are sold without any stipulation as to credit; or
    (b) where they have been sold on credit terms but the credit period has expired; or
    (c) where the buyer becomes insolvent.

    Even if part of the goods have been delivered to the buyer, the unpaid seller has a lien on the rest unless part delivery indicates his agreement to give up his lien altogether: s42.

88. The unpaid seller loses his lien (a) when he makes delivery of the goods to a carrier or warehouse-man etc for transmission to the buyer (unless the seller reserves a right of disposal), or (b) when the buyer or his agent lawfully obtains possession of the goods, or (c) when the seller waives his lien: s 43 or (d) when a third party has acquired title to the goods, *bona fide* and for value.

89. A lien merely gives a right to retain possession until the price is paid. It does not rescind the contract, deprive the buyer of his ownership nor entitle the seller to re-sell the goods. If ownership of the goods in the seller's possession has not yet passed to the buyer, the seller does not have lien (which is a right to retain the property of another person) but he does have a similar right to withhold delivery to the buyer (called a right of 'retention') in those circumstances where he would have lien or a right of stoppage in transitu if they were the buyer's goods.

90. The right of <u>stoppage in transitu</u> (ss 44-45) exists when the buyer becomes insolvent. He is insolvent if he has ceased to pay his debts in the ordinary course of business or cannot pay his debts as they fall due: it is not necessary to wait until he becomes bankrupt.

91. While goods are in transit, neither seller nor buyer has possession of the goods since they are in the possession of a carrier. The unpaid seller may stop the goods in transit by issuing an order to the carrier.

    The goods cease to be in transit and the seller's right of stoppage ends:

    (a) on delivery to the buyer or his agent (whether at the appointed destination or before); or

    (b) if the carrier acknowledges to the buyer or his agent that the goods (arrived at their original destination) are now held on behalf of the buyer; it is immaterial that the buyer may have indicated to the carrier that the goods are to be taken on to a further destination; or

    (c) if the carrier wrongfully refuses to make delivery to the buyer or his agent.

    But if the buyer refuses to accept the goods which remain in the possession of the carrier, they are still in transit.

92. When the unpaid seller exercises his right of stoppage in transitu he may either resume possession or give notice to the carrier of his claim pending re-delivery. But he must allow time for the carrier to transmit instructions within his organisation to give effect to the seller's notice etc to him: s46.

93. As between the unpaid seller and the buyer of the goods, the seller has a right of re-sale in the following circumstances only.

    > (a) If the goods are of a perishable nature, or
    >
    > (b) If the seller gives notice to the buyer of his intention to re-sell and the buyer fails within a reasonable time to pay or tender the price, or
    >
    > (c) The seller reserves a right of re-sale under the contract.

94. A re-sale by the seller rescinds the original contract but if the seller does not, by re-sale, recover the full amount of his loss he may sue the buyer for damages for breach of contract: s48. On a sale in these circumstances the second buyer gets good title to the goods.

95. If the unpaid seller, having exercised his right of lien, retention or stoppage in transitu re-sells the goods, the second buyer from him acquires good title if he takes in good faith and for value.

Retention of title

96. As mentioned above the seller can by agreement make the passing of property in the goods subject to conditions: s 19 of the 1893 Act. It is a common feature of commercial contracts that the passing of property is made conditional on the buyer paying the price. This type of clause is known as a 'retention of title' clause.

    A statement to the effect that no property in the goods, the subject matter of the contract, shall pass to the buyer until the purchase price for those goods has been paid, acts as a simple retention of title and the buyer only becomes owner when he pays for the goods.

More complex clauses are also possible and the so called 'all sums clause' can maintain property in goods in the seller until the buyer has not only paid the price owing for those goods but all sums that he may owe to the seller.

As a general rule the buyer under which a contract is free to sell or use the goods in the course of his business even though property has not yet passed to him and indeed such intention can readily be inferred into commercial contracts and the buyer can pass a good title under the exceptions to the *nemo dat* rule explained above. Because of this various attempts have been made to secure a right for the sellers over the proceeds of the sale of goods so retained. This has led to retention of title clauses of considerable complexity. Such extended conditions can be imposed as conditions in a sale but the practicalities are such, particularly when the buyer is a limited company, that they may be ineffective.

Case: Aluminium Industrie Vaassen BV v Romalpa Ltd 1976
Romalpa purchased aluminium foil on terms that the stock of foil (and any proceeds of sale) should be the property of the Dutch supplier until the company had paid to the supplier all that it owed. The receiver found that the company still held aluminium foil and proceeds of selling other stocks of foil and had not paid off its debt to the supplier. The receiver applied to the court to determine whether or not the foil and the cash were assets of the company under his control as receiver.

Held: the conditions of sale were valid – the relevant assets ie the foil and the proceeds, although in the possession of the company, did not belong to it. The receiver could not deal with these assets since his authority under the floating charge was restricted to assets of the company.

Case: Sugar Distributors Ltd v Monaghan Cash and Carry 1982 (I)
The defendant company, then in liquidation, had had a long series of dealings with the plaintiff who had supplied them with sugar. During that course of dealings the plaintiff had incorporated a retention of title clause into their standard conditions of business. The conditions, including the clause, were printed on the rear of their delivery notes and invoices and a note on the front of these referred to them.

Held: that the unsold sugar in the possession of the liquidator at the time he was appointed was the property of the plaintiff and not the company and that the liquidator had to account to the plaintiff for the proceeds of sale of sugar that he had sold.

97. Complications can arise with retention of title clauses when the buyer is a company. Such clauses can create charges which should be registered pursuant to s 99 of the Companies Act 1963.

Case: Carrol Group Distributors v G & J F Bourke Ltd 1990 (I)
Plainiff sold goods with retention of title clause. The buyer could resell the goods but was a trustee over the proceeds.

Held: that clause amounted to a charge on company assets and was invalid because it was not registered under s 99 of the Companies Act 1963.

Seller's remedies against the buyer

98. The seller has two possible remedies against the buyer personally plus rescission, but only where the buyer is in breach of a condition of contract.
 (a) Section 49 provides he may <u>bring an action for the price</u> if:
  (i) the ownership of the goods has passed to the buyer and he wrongfully neglects or refuses to pay the price according to the terms of the contract; or

(ii)　if the price is payable on a certain day (regardless of delivery) and the buyer wrongfully neglects or refuses to pay it, that day having passed.

In this latter case it is immaterial that property in the goods has not yet passed to the buyer or that goods have not been appropriated to the contract.

This is the usual action brought by the seller and the buyer will often plead that there was a breach of contract by the seller eg that the goods were defective or there was some misrepresentation.

(b)　The seller may <u>sue for damages for non-acceptance</u> if the buyer wrongfully refuses or neglects to accept and pay for the goods. In this case the claim may include any expense incurred by the seller, eg in storing the goods, caused by the buyer's failure to take delivery (after being requested to do so): s50.

99.　When the seller claims damages, the first head of the rule in *Hadley v Baxendale 1854* (see IBL Chapter 13 on remedies for breach of contract) applies. If there is an 'available market' for this type of goods, the measure of damages is usually the difference between the contract price and the market price on the day when the goods should have been accepted. For example, if the market price per unit of the goods is £10 below the contract price at the contractual delivery date that margin (plus any expenses) is the amount recoverable.

100.　The seller's claim is sometimes for loss of profit. If in fact he has been able to re-sell the goods to another buyer at a price equal to or above the contract price, he will usually be awarded only nominal damages. A claim that he has made only one sale instead of two is likely to fail; see the case of *Lazenby Garages v Wright 1976* in IBL Chapter 13 on remedies for breach of contract.

Buyer's remedies

101.　If the seller is in *breach of a condition* of the contract, the buyer may reject the goods unless he has lost his right to do so by accepting the goods or part of them. In addition he may also claim damages (see para 12 above with regard to position of 'consumers' under s21 of the 1980 Act).

102.　If there is *breach of warranty* by the seller, or if the buyer is obliged (or prefers) to treat a breach of condition as a breach of warranty (ie a claim for damages), the buyer may either reduce the amount paid to the seller by an allowance for the breach of warranty or sue for damages for breach of warranty. The amount of damages is determined on principles similar to those of the seller's claim against the buyer.

(a)　The first head of the rule in *Hadley v Baxendale* is applied - damages arising directly and naturally from the result of an ordinary course of events from the breach of warranty.

(b)　The difference between the value of the goods as delivered and the value which they would have had if they had complied with the warranty is the normal measure of the loss: s53 1893 Act.

103.　It is open to the buyer to base his claim on any circumstances within the general scope of these rules.

Case: Mason v Burningham 1949
The plaintiff had been sold a typewriter which turned out to be stolen property. She had to return it to the owner. In addition to the price paid she claimed damages for breach of implied warranty of quiet enjoyment including her expenditure in having the typewriter overhauled.

Held: damages should be awarded as claimed.

104. A buyer may also claim damages for non-delivery, calculated under the same principles as described earlier when a seller claims damages. This claim may be made if the seller either fails to deliver altogether or delivers goods which the buyer is entitled to, and does, reject.

105. The buyer's claim for damages for loss of profit or liability for damages arising on that contract is not affected by a resale by him, unless it can be shown that the parties to the original sale contemplated that there would be a re-sale.

Case: Williams v Agius 1914
Contract for sale of coal at 16s.3d per ton. The buyers resold at 19s.6d per ton. The market price at the date for delivery was 23s.6d. per ton. The sellers failed to deliver. The sellers contended that the buyer's actual loss was the difference between the contract price (16s.3d) and the re-sale price (19s.6d) per ton only.

Held: the buyers should be awarded damages of 7s.3d per ton - the full difference between the market price and the contract price; the re-sale contract should be ignored.

106. In an action for breach of contract to deliver specific or ascertained goods, the court may order specific performance or delivery of the goods. s52 1893 Act but only where damages would not be an adequate remedy.

Miscellaneous aspects of sale of goods

● **Auction sales (s 58 1893 Act).**

107. The legal authority of an auctioneer as agent is described in IBL Chapter 14 on the law of agency. The statutory rules on the conduct of an auction are:

(a) each 'lot' of goods put up for auction is the subject of a separate contract;

(b) a bidder may withdraw his bid at any time before the auctioneer announces that the sale is completed by dropping his hammer or other customary manner;

(c) unless the seller gives notice, it is not lawful for him (or for anyone on his behalf) to bid for his own property at the auction. Any sale contravening this code may be treated as fraudulent by the buyer.

● **Export sales**

108. When a contract for sale of goods requires that the goods shall be transported by sea the parties usually agree to 'fob' or 'cif' - terms which require brief explanation.

109. FOB ('free on board') requires the seller to place the goods at his expense aboard a ship nominated by the buyer who pays the cost of freight and insurance which it is the buyer's responsibility to arrange. Both property and risk usually pass as the goods are lifted over the ship's rail in the course of loading.

110. CIF ('cost insurance and freight') requires the seller to load the goods on to the ship and to arrange and pay the cost of insurance and freight (carriage by sea on the ship). The seller must then deliver the shipping and insurance documents to the buyer who must pay the price in

exchange for them. Unless otherwise agreed property does not pass until documents are delivered but risk passes when the goods go over the ship's rail. If they are later accidentally destroyed the seller may deliver the documents and may claim the price; the buyer must rely on his insurance to cover his loss.

- **Product liability**

111. The common law approach to the liability of suppliers of defective products is that they are liable in the tort of negligence for injuries or loss caused due to the defect in their product or workmanship, where the product is supplied in such a form as to show that the user is not likely to have an intermediate chance of examining the product: *Donoghue v Stevenson (1932)* and the supplier knew or ought to have known that an absence of reasonable care on their part was likely to result in injury or loss.

112. Since December 16, 1991 the law relating to defective goods has been extended by the Liability for Defective Products Act 1991, which is intended to bring Irish law into line with the requirements of the EC Directive on Product Liability. The scheme under the Act, which supplements rather than replaces the common law, is intended to be a *no fault regime*. This topic is discussed in IBL Chapter 17, Negligence in specific situations.

Consumer Information Act 1978

113. The Consumer Information Act 1978:

 (a) extends the definition of 'trade description' and 'false trade description' in Merchandise Marks Act 1887;

 (b) makes it an offence to give false or misleading statements as to services, prices and charges and advertisements. If goods or services are described as having been offered at a different price then they must have been openly offered for sale in that place and at that price for 28 consecutive days in the previous 3 months. An offer for sale at a particular price is deemed to be an offer to sell those goods at that price at every place where the seller does business within the State unless the advert says differently:

 (c) establishes the Office of Director of Consumer Affairs whose holder is known as Director of Consumer Affairs and Fair Trade who is empowered to keep under review practices in relation to advertising and to carry out examination of such practices and may initiate proceedings in the High Court to prevent malpractices.

Unsolicited goods

114. Section 47 of the 1980 Act sets out the circumstances where unsolicited goods can be deemed to be a gift to the recipient. This occurs where during a period of 6 months following receipt the vendor did not reposess the goods and the recipient did not unreasonably refuse to permit the vendor to do so *or* not less than 30 days before the expiration of that period the recipient gave notice to the vendor, and during the following 30 days the vendor did not take possession of the goods.

It is an offence to demand payment for unsolicited goods or to do any of the following with a view to obtaining payment:
- threatening legal proceedings;
- placing, or threatening to place, the name of the person on a list of defaulters or debtors; or,
- invoking, or threatening to invoke, any collection procedure.

Directory entries

115. Section 48 of the 1980 Act deals with directory entries. A person shall not be liable for any payment for a directory entry unless an order or note complying with s48 has been signed by him and, in the case of a note of agreement to the charge, a copy was supplied to him for retention before the note was signed.

The order for the directory entry must have been ordered on the firm's stationery or oder form and the firm must have agreed to pay the charge by signing a document which:

- contains the agreed charge directly above the signature;

- indicates the proposed date of publication of the directory and the name of the person producing it;

- indicates the prices and the number of directories which will be offered for sale and the number which will be available free of charge;

- gives reasonable particulars of the entry as it will appear in the directory.

Unless the section is complied with it is an offence to demand payment or to take proceedings and the firm is entitled to recover any payments made.

'Cooling-off' provision

116. Section 50 of the 1980 Act empowers the Minister to make Orders imposing a defined period during which consumers may cancel a contract in certain circumstances. The making of the European Communities (Cancellation of Contracts negotiated away from Business Premises) Regulations 1989 (SI 224 of 1989) gives effect to this section. This regulation applies to contracts under which a trader supplies goods and services to a consumer and which are concluded during an excursion organized by the trader away from his business premises or during a visit to the consumer's home or place of work where the visit does not take place at the express request of the consumer. Such a contract will not be enforceable unless the trader delivered to the consumer a 'cancellation notice' and a 'cancellation form.'

The cancellation notice stipulates the consumers's right to cancel within a specified period, which must be not less than 7 days. If the consumer decides to cancel the agreement within the specified period it renders the contract void.

A person who, not having reasonable cause to believe there is a right to payment, makes a demand for payment may be guilty of an offence.

Spare parts and servicing

117. Section 12 of the 1980 Act provides that in a contract for sale of goods there is an implied warranty that the seller will make available spare parts and aftersales service as are stated in any offer, description or advertisement by the seller on behalf of the manufacturer or on his own behalf for such period as is specified. If no period is mentioned they must be available for a reasonable period and the Minister is empowered to define what is a reasonable period in relation to any particular type of goods.

Any purported exclusion of these provisions is void.

Guarantees

118. The scope of sale of goods legislation has been extended by s15-19 of the 1980 Act to cover manufacturers' and suppliers' guarantees. A *guarantee* is defined by s15 as any document, notice or other written statement, however described, given by a manufacturer or other supplier (other than a retailer) in connection with the supply of any goods indicating that the manufacturer or other supplier will service, repair or otherwise deal with the goods after purchase.

There is no obligation on a manufacturer or other supplier to give a guarantee and the Act does not set out what must be covered in a guarantee so that a manufacturer or other supplier is free to decide the period of the guarantee and whether it covers the goods as a whole or only certain components and whether it includes labour or parts and such like. However, if a guarantee is given it must conform to certain rules set out in s16 and it is an offence to supply a guarantee which does not so conform. The rules provide that a guarantee:

- shall be clearly legible and refer only to specific goods or to one category of goods;

- shall state clearly the name and address of the person giving the guarantee and the procedure for making a claim under the guarantee, which procedure must not be more difficult than is usual in ordinary or normal commercial procedure;

- shall state clearly the period of the guarantee from the date of purchase but different periods may be stated for different components of the goods;

- shall state clearly what the manufacturer or other supplier undertakes to do in relation to the goods and what charges, if any, including the cost of carriage, the buyer must meet in relation to such undertakings.

A guarantee may not exclude or limit the rights of the buyer at common law or pursuant to statute and any provision in a guarantee which purports to impose obligations on a buyer additional to his obligations under the contract are void. Further, a provision in a guarantee which purports to make the guarantor, or anyone acting on his behalf, the sole authority to decide whether the goods are defective or whether the buyer has a claim is void: s18.

Section 17 provides that where a guarantee is supplied with the goods the retailer is responsible for seeing that the guarantee is honoured by the manufacturer or other supplier unless the retailer expressly makes it clear at the time of delivery that such is not the case. If the retailer provides his own *written* guarantee it will be presumed that he will not be responsible for seeing that the manufacturer's or other supplier's guarantee is honoured. Any guarantee given by the retailer must conform to the same rules as those which apply to a guarantee from a manufacturer or other supplier.

If a manufacturer or other supplier fails to observe any of the terms of the guarantee, s19 provides that the buyer is entitled to sue for breach of warranty and the court may order the manufacturer or other supplier to take such action as may be necessary to observe the terms of the guarantee or to pay damages to the buyer. It should be noted that s19 also provides that the guarantee applies not only to the original buyer but to anyone who becomes the owner of the goods during the period of guarantee so that someone who receives goods as a gift can claim directly under the guarantee. It should also be noted that where goods are imported the buyer may maintain an action against the importer.

6: SALE OF GOODS

● **Summary of the chapter**

119. The four most important things to bear in mind when studying sale of goods are as follows:

    (a) basic contract law is as of much importance as statutory rules;
    (b) implied terms of the statutes aim to give the buyer goods of a satisfactory quality which he needs;
    (c) time of passing of property is vital to determine who suffers loss;
    (d) there are exceptions to the rule *'nemo dat quod non habet'*.

120. The most important single topic in this complicated subject is the protection given to a buyer of goods by the conditions implied in his favour by ss12 – 15 of the Sale of Goods Act 1893 (as amended by the 1980 Act). All of these are designed to help him in obtaining goods which are satisfactory in quality and in accordance with his requirements. It is essential to develop a sound grasp of this subject.

121. There is often an overlap in examination questions between sale of goods and the law of contract (in respect of contract terms and clauses which attempt to limit or exclude liability). This results from the fact that sale of goods is a particular and common kind of contract. It has many special features but it also conforms to the basic principles of contract law.

122. The other very practical element in the law on sale of goods is the question of who bears the loss if goods are damaged or destroyed while the transaction is in progress. The rules on passing of 'property' in goods which are sold is therefore very important.

TEST YOUR KNOWLEDGE

Numbers in brackets refer to paragraphs of this chapter

1. What topics are covered by statutory conditions implied (as part of the contract) by the Sale of Goods Act 1893? (14)

2. What is the implied condition as to the seller's right to sell the goods? (20-23)

3. What is a sale of goods by description and what is implied in such a sale? (24-28)

4. When are defects of quality not a breach of the condition of merchantable quality? (31)

5. What is merchantable quality? (32-34)

6. In what circumstances is it an implied condition that the goods shall be fit for the purpose for which they are bought? (39-44)

7. What is implied in a sale of goods by sample? (45)

8. State (in outline) the statutory rules which determine when property in goods passes (53-61). Do these rules apply to every sale of goods? (53,58)

9. Give three exceptions to the rule *nemo dat quod non habet*. (63)

10. What is market overt? (66,67)

11. What is a severable contract? (74)

12. When is a buyer deemed to have accepted goods? (80)

13. What are the seller's remedies if he is not paid? (86, 98)

14. What is a 'retention of title' clause? (96)

15. What are the buyer's remedies for breach of contract? (101-106)

Now try illustrative questions 7-10 at the end of the study text.

Chapter 7

SUPPLY OF SERVICES

Points covered in this chapter are:

- Distinction between goods and services
- The Sale of Goods and Supply of Services Act 1980
- Contracts of hire
- Remedies

Purpose of chapter

Many contracts involving transfer of property also include elements of services supplied; some are only for services. This chapter looks at the importance of distinguishing the two, and at the terms implied by statute.

• Distinction between goods and services

1. The classification of a contract as being one for the sale of goods or one for the supply of services has a number of legal consequences. There is no clear-cut distinction, since very often when goods are sold, such as a washing-machine, a service, in this case installation, is also supplied. Likewise, an accountant providing his services for the preparation of a report in a prospectus is also in some sense 'selling' goods, being the document itself.

2. To test whether a contract is one or the other, its 'substance' should be looked at.

(a) If the substance is the *skill* and *labour* of the supplier, then it is a supply of services.

(b) If the substance is the *ultimate result* - the washing-machine - then it is a sale of goods.

---

3. What is the importance of such a distinction? Often there is none - similar terms are implied by statute into both. But there are matters for which the distinction needs to be made.

   (a) Time of passing of property - this may differ between a contract whereby, say, a carpet is *delivered* under a sale of goods, and one where it is to be *fitted* under a contract for supply of goods and services.

   (b) Advance payment - an advance payment for the supply of goods under an agreement which the purchaser then breaches is refundable, since there is complete failure of consideration.

However, where the agreement was for manufacture, the manufacturer/seller could retain the advance payment as remuneration for time spent manufacturing the goods (his service).

4.   This is not an exhaustive list, but serves to pinpoint some areas where the difference is significant.

● **The Sale of Goods and Supply of Services Act 1980**

5.   The Sale of Goods and Supply of Services Act 1980 Part IV Ss 39-42 of the Act deals with the supply of services.

6.   In a contract for the supply of a service where the supplier is acting in the course of a business the following terms are implied:

(a)   the supplier has the necessary skill to render the service;

(b)   that he will supply the service with due skill, care and diligence;

(c)   that, where materials are used, they will be sound and reasonably fit for the purpose for which they are required;

(d)   where goods are supplied under the contract they will be of merchantable quality within the meaning of the 1893 Act (as amended by the 1980 Act).

The implied terms set out above may be negatived or varied by an exemption clause or by the course of dealing between the parties (s40).

7.   However where the recipient of the services is dealing as a consumer for the purposes of the 1980 Act then it must be shown that the exemption clause is fair and reasonable and has been specifically brought to his attention (s40).

● **Hire**

8.   Where goods are let, otherwise than under hire purchase, to a person dealing as consumer s38 of the 1980 Act ensures that provisions relating to description, merchantable quality and fitness for purpose apply.

● **Remedies**

9.   As regards breach of contract where it contains transfer of goods, the same remedies are available as set out in Chapter 6 above on sale of goods.

10.   Where the contract includes or solely consists of a supply of services, the remedies consist of:

(a)   an action for the price;
(b)   damages;
(c)   rescission;
(d)   *quantum meruit.*

7: SUPPLY OF SERVICES

Action for the price

11. Where the price is agreed between the parties, or it is required to be 'reasonable', the unpaid supplier may bring an action for the price against the buyer.

Damages

12. As has been stated a supplier of services is now subject to certain implied terms which impose several duties on him. If it can be proved that a duty has not been fulfilled, then the person is in breach of a term of the contract for which damages are available as a remedy.

13. The rules relating to damages for breach of a contract for services are the same as for general contracts.

Rescission

14. Where a term in a contract for services is broken, the remedy of rescission is available. The terms as to skill and care, and time of performance, are implied by statute but are not stated to be either conditions or warranties. As such, they are 'innominate' terms, the consequences of breach of which can only be judged and remedied in the breach. If it is felt that the breach was such as to deprive the other party of 'substantially the whole benefit of the contract' then a condition is breached and the contract may be rescinded.

Quantum meruit

15. It is possible that the terms of a contract for services may not fix the remuneration - if not, a reasonable sum must be paid. The party who has performed his side of the bargain may claim reasonable recompense from the other, as detailed in IBL Chapter 13 on remedies.

TEST YOUR KNOWLEDGE

Numbers in brackets refer to paragraphs of this chapter

1. What is the test of substance used to determine whether a contract is for sale of goods or supply of services? (2)

2. What terms does the 1980 Act imply in to contracts for the supply of services? (6)

3. What remedies are available for breach of a term in a contract for the supply of services? (10)

Chapter 8

CONSUMER CREDIT

Points covered in this chapter are:

- Forms of consumer credit
- Hire purchase agreements
- Credit sale agreements
- Conditional sale agreements
- Credit cards
- Consumer Credit Act 1995

Purpose of chapter

As with sales of goods, the related topic of consumer credit is regulated by statute, chiefly in order to restore the balance in bargaining power and to protect the public.

Introduction

1. The present law on Consumer Credit is that as stated directly below. However this whole area of law has been somewhat altered by the new Consumer Credit Act 1995 which was enacted in the summer of 1995 but which is not yet in operation. It is expected to come into operation in 1996. This Act gives effect to a number of EU directives (Council Directive 87/102/EEC and Council Directive 90/88/EEC) which have the aim of providing a minimum level of consumer protection in the area of credit in all member states. However the Act goes beyond the simple implementation of these Directives. Effectively this Act repeals all existing consumer credit law and replaces it with a unified piece of legislation. The principal provisions of the new Act in relation to consumer credit are outlined in the latter part of the chapter after an explanation of the existing law in this area.

• Forms of consumer credit

2. Consumer credit takes a variety of forms. The following may be identified:

    (a) hire purchase agreements;
    (b) conditional sale agreements;
    (c) credit sale agreements;
    (d) consumer hire agreements.

3.   The simplest form is a loan to a customer which he may use to purchase whatever goods or services he requires. But the creditor often prefers to supply goods himself to the consumer on hire purchase terms so that the goods remain the creditor's property (and can be recovered if the debtor defaults) until the consumer has paid the price (including credit charges). It is a common business practice for a trader to sell his goods to a finance company so that the latter, in providing credit to a customer of the trader, can do so under a hire purchase or related transaction. There are also other special forms of credit transaction such as a bank credit card (Visa, Access Card etc), shop 'budget accounts', loans by pawnbrokers on the security of chattels deposited with them etc.

● **Hire purchase agreements**

4.   There are two elements in a hire purchase transaction:

> (a)   goods are bailed or delivered to the possession of the hirer, for his use; and
>
> (b)   the hirer has an option to purchase the goods when he has completed payment of a number of instalments which represent the cash price plus a charge for credit: s1 Hire Purchase Act, 1946.

5.   The legal effect of a hire purchase agreement is that the hirer is *not* a buyer in possession of goods, the property in which has not yet passed to him. He has an option to buy the goods but he is not bound to exercise that option - he has not 'agreed to buy'. He does not yet own the goods nor can he pass ownership to another person by an unauthorised sale as a buyer in possession (which he is not). The significance of this point appears in Chapter 6 on Sale of goods. It protects the owner of the goods from losing title to them: the hirer is not legally competent to deprive him of it (with an exception limited to motor vehicles).

6.   The law on hire purchase is to be found in the Hire Purchase Act 1946, Hire Purchase (Amendment) Act 1960, and Part III of the Sale of Goods and Supply of Services Act 1980.

7.   Section 3 of the 1946 Act sets out a number of requirements for a Hire Purchase agreement to be enforceable. They are:

(a)   before the agreement is entered into the owner will state in writing otherwise than in the note or memorandum of the agreement the cash price of the goods. This requirement will be satisfied if:

> (i)   the hirer has inspected the goods and at the time there were tickets or labels attached to the goods showing the price;
> (ii)   the hirer selected the goods from a catalogue price list or advertisement which stated the cash price;

(b)   a note or memorandum of the agreement is made and signed by the hirer and by or on behalf of all other parties to the agreement;

(c)   the note or memorandum contains:

> (i)   the HP price;
> (ii)   the cash price;
> (iii)   details of instalment;
> (iv)   list to identify goods;

(v)   a notice which is at least as prominent as the rest of the contents of the note or memorandum in the terms set out in the Schedule of the 1946 Act (this deals with the right of the hirer to terminate agreement and a restriction on owner's right to re-posesss goods);

(vi) in the case of motor vehicles the Schedule in the 1946 Act was amended by the 1960 Act to give increased rights to re-possession in the case of motor vehicles; and

a copy of the note or memorandum is delivered or sent to the hirer within 14 days of the making of the agreement.

8.   The court may dispense with the need to comply with all or any of the requirements set out at para 7 above where it would not prejudice the hirer and where it would be just and equitable to do so.

Right of hirer to determine the HP agreement

9.   The hirer may put an end to the HP agreement by giving notice in writing. The hirer must pay any arrears and must in total pay one half of the hire purchase price. Where there has been a charge for installation then the amount is added to the HP price and half this amount must be paid.

Owners right to re-possession

10. Prior to the passing of the 1946 Act the owner had almost an unlimited right to re-possess goods where a default had been made in payment. This included entry onto the hirer's premises to re-possess. This situation has been modified by the 1946 Act and the 1960 Act.

11. Under s6 of the 1946 Act a provision of a HP agreement entitling the owner to enter upon any premises to re-possess the goods is void.

12. Section 12 of the 1946 Act provides that the owner may not enforce any right to re-possess the goods where one third of the HP price has been paid other than by Court action.

If an owner acts in contravention of this provision the HP agreement will determine and the hirer will be entitled to recover all sums paid under the HP agreement.

13. There are special provisions in relation to the re-possession of motor vehicles. Section 16 of the 1960 Act provides:

(a)   in the case of a motor vehicle a provision in a HP agreement enabling the owner to enter premises (other than a dwelling house) to re-possess a motor vehicle will not be invalid.

(b)   where the owner of a motor vehicle has commenced an action to recover it and one third of the HP price has been paid before the commencement of the action *and* the vehicle has been abandoned or left in circumstances which may result in its damage then the owner may be entitled to enforce a right to recover it.

(c)   where an owner recovers a vehicle as aforesaid he must make an application to the court within 14 days of doing so. If the court finds that he was not entitled to recover the vehicle damages may be awarded to the hirer.

Part III of the Sale of Goods and Supply of Services Act 1980

14. Part III of the 1980 Act gives to persons who buy goods on hire purchase similar protections as are given to persons who buy goods. These protections may be summarised as follows:

   (a)   an implied condition that the owner will have a right to sell the goods at the time when property is to pass;

   (b)   an implied warranty that the goods will be free from undisclosed charges or encumbrances;

   (c)   where goods are let by description an implied condition that the goods will correspond with the description;

   (d)   an implied condition that the goods will be of merchantable quality and fit for the purpose for which they were supplied;

   (e)   an implied condition that where goods are let by reference to sample the bulk of the goods will correspond to the sample.

15.   Where the hirer deals as a consumer these implied conditions and warranties cannot be exempted. (See Chapter 6 on Sale of goods where similar provisions apply).

16.   Where goods are let under an HP agreement to a person dealing as consumer and for example, a finance house was involved in the negotiations, then that finance house will be deemed to be a party to the agreement and thus liable for any breach and any misrepresentation (see section 14 of 1980 Act).

17.   In the case of motor vehicles s13 applies (see chapter on Sale of Goods) to such a hire purchase agreement.

● **Credit sale agreements**

18.   A credit sale agreement is an agreement for the sale of goods where the purchase price is payable by instalments. Where the agreement provides that the purchase price is to be payable by five or more instalments then the credit sale agreement to be enforceable must comply with the provisions of s4 of the Hire Purchase Act 1946. The requirements set out in s4 are similar to those required for a hire purchase agreement (see paras 7 and 8 above).

19.   As a credit sale is a sale of goods the provisions of the Sale of Goods Act 1893 and the Sale of Goods and Supply of Services Act 1980 apply.

● **Conditional sale agreements**

20.   The conditional sale agreement was developed as a means of avoiding the controls applied to hire purchase agreements. The essential features of a conditional sale agreement are:

   (a)   the buyer agrees to buy goods (or land) and to pay the price by instalments;

   (b)   he obtains immediate possession but the transfer of ownership is postponed until he has paid all the instalments;

   (c)   he is not a buyer or person who has agreed to buy goods for the purposes of Sale of Goods Act 1893 and so he cannot transfer the ownership (which he has not yet obtained) to another person.

It is an agreement for the sale of goods to which the Sale of Goods Act 1893 and the Sale of Goods and Supply of Services Act 1980 apply.

8: CONSUMER CREDIT

Personal loans

21. The personal loan is a form of credit which is frequently offered by financial institutions to customers for the financing of contracts of sale. Essentially the finance provided by these financial institutions would constitute a separate agreement distinct from any contract for the sale of goods itself. Thus an agreement to provide a personal loan will be governed by general contract principles. In practice the financial institution will only lend money to a customer if he has a reasonably good credit standing with the institution or alternatively can provide some form of security to the company. Security provided may be in the form of rights over the property of the borrower, real or personal, or alternatively the lending institution may insist that the borrower provide a third party called a surety who would agree with the financial institution to repay the loan in the event of default by the borrower himself. In this situation the finance company would have a personal right of action not only against the borrower but also against the third party. Typically the personal loan agreement would take the following form.

The customer would obtain a loan from the financial institution and then in a separate transaction would purchase the goods required on an ordinary sale of goods contract. The loan would then be repayable by instalments. Generally speaking the agreement would provide that the whole debt would become immediately repayable if the borrower defaults in making repayments. The clear advantage from the finance company's point of view is that it distances itself from the sale of goods contract and thus will not incur any liability in relation to faulty or defective goods which might typically arise in an HP agreement situation. It should be noted, however, that if the money borrowed is paid directly to the seller by the lending institution and the borrower of the goods deals as a consumer within the meaning of the Sale of Goods Act then the finance company and the seller of the goods will be jointly and severally liable under the contract for the sale of goods - see para 14 Sale of Goods and Supply of Services Act, 1980.

• Credit cards

22. The use of credit cards (as opposed to charge cards) is now quite extensive, some people using them because of their convenience instead of cash or cheques and settling the whole of their credit card account on a monthly basis so as to avoid the payment of the company's interest charges. The two leading bank credit cards in Ireland are Access and Visa.

23. The use of a credit card involves three parties and three transactions between them.

    (a) on producing his card to a supplier for goods and/or services, the card-holder can obtain what he requires without paying for it immediately;

    (b) the supplier recovers from the credit card company the price of the goods or services less a discount which is the credit card company's profit margin;

    (c) at monthly intervals the credit card company sends to the credit card-holder a monthly statement. The card-holder may either settle interest free within a specified time or he may pay interest on the balance owing after the specified time. He is however required to pay a minimum sum.

24. The exact nature of a transaction completed by charge card is that there are three contracts - one between cardholder and supplier, one between supplier and card company and the other between cardholder and card company. Payment by credit card is *not* a conditional payment, unlike payment by cheque where the drawer of the cheque is not discharged from his debt until the cheque has been honoured. Hence as soon as a buyer completes and signs a valid credit card voucher which is accepted by the supplier, the former's obligations are complete.

Case: Re Charge Card Services Ltd 1987

Charge Card Services Ltd operated a chargecard scheme for garages. A buyer signed a voucher filled out by the supplier, who then claimed payment from CC. Since CC usually paid the supplier before being paid by the cardholder, it financed its operations by factoring debts. It went into liquidation, and the garages who were creditors sought a declaration that they could claim payment from the cardholders since their debts had not been discharged at the point of sale.

Held: the garages had no claim against the cardholder in the card company's insolvency – the former's obligations to the garages had been discharged.

• Consumer Credit Act 1995

25. The Consumer Credit Act 1995 became law on the 31 July 1995. It is expected to come into operation on 1 May 1996. The Act covers the areas of credit agreements, credit sale agreements,hire purchase agreements and moneylending agreements to which a consumer is a party. In addition, it confers powers on the Director of Consumer Affairs, who is to have responsibility for the functioning and enforcement of the legislation.

Credit Agreements

26. A credit agreement is defined by s2 CCA 1995 'as an agreement whereby a creditor grants or promises to grant to a consumer a credit in the form of a deferred payment, a cash loan or other similar financial accommodation'. A consumer is defined by the same section as a 'natural person acting outside of his trade, business or profession'.

27. Part III of the 1995 Act (ss29–31) sets down requirements in relation to the form and contents which a credit agreement must take. The principal requirements are as follows:

    (a) it must be in writing and signed by the parties: s30;
    (b) the consumer is to be given a copy of the agreement within 10 days of signing: s30;
    (c) the consumer may withdraw from the agreement within 10 days of receipt of copy of the agreement (referred to in the Act as the 'cooling off period': s30;
    (d) specifically the agreement must contain:
         (i)   the annual percentage rate of charge (APR), ie the total cost of the credit;
         (ii)   description of goods or services covered;
         (iii) cash price and credit price;
         (iv)   amount and number of repayments;
         (v)   amount of interest to be paid;
         (vi)   the total amount repayable;
         (vii) the intervals at which interest is calculated: s31;
         (viii) in the case of a credit card, the credit limit and the terms of repayment

Enforcement

28. Failure to comply with the requirements at 27 (a)and (b) above will make the agreement completely unenforceable.

    If the other requirements are not complied with, the Court has a discretion whether to enforce the agreement or not. If the Court is satisfied that the creditor's failure to comply with the requirements of the Act was not deliberate and it has not prejudiced the consumer and that it would be just and equitable to dispense with the requirement, the Court may, subject to any conditions that it sees fit to impose, decide that the agreement shall be enforceable: s38.

Currency of agreement

29. Part IV of the Act (ss 40-50) deals with matters that may arise in the currency of the agreement and obliges a creditor to supply documents and information on request to the consumer, written communications from creditor to consumer must be in sealed envelopes, prohibits telephone calls and visits to the creditor, family, or employer.

30. In addition the Director of Consumer Affairs may, where he believes the total cost of the credit is excessive, apply to the Circuit Court and the Court may alter the cost: s47-48.

31. In respect to the cooling off period (see 27(c) above) a consumer has the right to withdraw from the agreement within 10 days of receiving a copy of it, by giving notice to the creditor or owner. A consumer may forgo this right to a cooling off period by signing a statement to this effect separately from any other term of the agreement. Any such statement by which the consumer waives this right must carry a warning to that effect in a prominent position.

Termination

32. Para V of the 1995 Act (ss 51-55) deals with the termination of credit agreements.

    The consumer may at any time discharge his obligations under a credit agreement (except hire purchase agreements) before the time fixed, by giving notice in writing to the creditor. Where he does so, he will be entitled to a reduction in the total cost of the credit in accordance with a specified formula.

33. In accordance with a set procedure, the creditor has the right to enforce an agreement or any provision thereof or to recover possession of goods by reason of a breach of the agreement by the consumer. S 54 limits the creditors' rights in the enforcement of an agreement and sets down the steps which must be taken by him.

    The procedure involves the serving of a notice at least 10 days before the creditor proposes to take action giving particulars of the agreement in question, the nature of any alleged breach, a statement to the effect that he intends to enforce the agreement and giving the consumer 21 days to remedy the default or pay compensation for the breach. If the consumer complies, the breach shall be treated as if it had not occurred.

Hire Purchase Agreements

34. The Consumer Credit Act 1995 (Part vi) replaces all the existing legislation in elation to hire purchase (The Hire Purchase Act 1946, Hire Purchase Act 1960 and Part III of the Sale of Goods and Supply of Services Act 1980). By and large however, the old law is simply restated in the new Act with a few new provisions. The principal sections of Part VI are as follows:
    (a) Section 56 defines an HP agreement in much the same terms as the old s1 of the 1946 Act (see para 4 above);
    (b) Section 57 restates in effect the contents of s3 of the 1946 Act (see para 7 above);
    (c) Section 58 deals with the contents of an HP agreement and restates the existing requirements as set out at para 7(c) above. However in addition there are some new requirements. They are as follows:
        (i) that a copy of the agreement must be given or sent to the hirer within 10 days (in place of the present 14 days) of making the agreement;
        (ii) the HP agreements must also state any costs or penalties to be paid by hirer if he breaches the agreement;
        (iii) a statement that the hirer may withdraw from the agreement without penalty by giving written notice to the owner within 10 days of receipt of a copy of the agreement (the cooling-off period).

Enforceability

35. Section 59 deals with the enforceability of the agreement and essentially reiterates the statements set out at para 8 above except that the agreement will be completely unenforceable where it is not in writing and/or signed by the parties and if the owner fails to give a copy of the agreement to the hirer within the aforesaid 10 days of the making of it.

Right of hirer to determine the HP agreement

36. Section 63 restates the contents in para 9 above.

Owners right to re-possession

37. Section 63 restates the contents of para 11 above while section 64 restates the position in paras 11, 12 and 13 above.

Implied terms in HP agreements

38. Section 74 restates the position as that set out in para 14(a) and (b); section 75 restates para 14(c); section 76 restates para 14(d); section 77 restates para 14(e).

39. Section 79 deals with the exclusion of these implied terms and conditions:
    (a) the exclusion of the provisions of s74 (title) shall be void;
    (b) the exclusion of the provisions of ss75, 76 and 77 shall also be void and unenforceable unless it is shown that it is fair and reasonable. Sections 80 and 82 essentially restate the contents of paras 16 and 17 above.

40. In additions to the hire purchase agreement outlined above, the CC Act 1995 also introduces a new type of HP agreement, namely, a consumer hire agreement. This is defined in s2 of the Act as an agreement of more than three months duration for the bailment of goods to the hirer under which the property remains with the owner. Part VII (ss84 to 91) of the 1995 Act regulates this agreement. Essentially the same provisions as to its contents, enforceability, etc apply to it as to an HP agreement.

Termination

41. Note however that unlike an hire purchase agreement the hirer under a consumer hire agreement may at any time determine it by giving notice to the owner. The agreement shall then determine after 3 months of receipt of the notice: s91.

Credit sale agreements

42. The 1995 Act also regulates this type of agreement:
    (a) section 2 defines a credit sale agreement as a credit agreement for the sale of goods under which the purchase price or part of it is payable in instalments and the property in the goods passes to the buyer immediately upon the making of the agreement;
    (b) section 32 of the 1995 Act sets out the requirements of a credit sale agreement which are broadly similar to those of an hire purchase agreement (see para 7 above).

Credit cards

43. This is essentially a credit agreement operated by means of a credit card and therefore it is subject to regulation by the 1995 Act (see paras 26 to 33 above). Specifically s31(2) states that such an agreement shall contain a statement of:

(a) the amount of the credit limit;
(b) the rate of interest charged and the annual percentage rate (APR) of charge;
(c) the terms of use and repayments; and
(d) the means and the cost of termination of the agreement.

Advertisements offering credit

44. The 1995 Act also regulates advertising of credit facilities in respect of goods and services (including hire purchase and consumer hire agreements). Essentially advertisements must state the cash price, the number, amount and frequency of repayments, details of any payments to be made prior to acquisition, including deposit, of any, and the total cost of the credit to the consumer: s22. In addition where any advertisement of credit refers to a rate of interest, then it shall be in the form of a clear and prominent statement of the annual percentage rate (APR): s21.

45. The Act also prohibits the display or publication of false, misleading or non-compliant advertising: s26.

Director of Consumer Affairs

46. Under the Consumer Credit Act 1995, the Director of Consumer Affairs is given certain functions and powers for the purposes of the operation and enforcement of this Act. Specifically he is given the function to investigate breaches of the Act and may institute legal proceedings to enforce its provisions and to publish Codes of Practice. In addition he is obliged to make an annual report to the Minister of Enterprise and Employment in relation to the performance of his functions under the Act.

TEST YOUR KNOWLEDGE

Numbers in brackets refer to paragraphs of this chapter

1. What are the various forms of consumer credit? (2)

2. What are the requirements to make a Hire Purchase agreement enforceable? (7,8)

3. What special provisions apply to the re-possession of motor vehicles let under a Hire Purchase agreement? (13)

4. What is a 'credit sale' agreement? (18)

5. When a credit card is used what parties are involved in the transaction? (23)

Now try illustrative question 11 at the end of the study text.

PART E
NEGOTIABLE INSTRUMENTS AND CHEQUES

Chapter 9

NEGOTIABLE INSTRUMENTS

Points covered in this chapter are:

- Assignment
- Negotiable instruments
- Bills of exchange
- Cheques
- Promissory notes

Purpose of chapter

Negotiable instruments are defined and various terms relating to them are set out as an introduction to the subject.

Introduction

1. Property which is an actual physical possession is described as a 'chose in possession' and includes all tangible moveable property. If however the property does not exist in any tangible form but is a *right* which can be enforced in a court then it is called a 'chose in action'. Examples of choses in action are debts, shares in a company, rights under an insurance policy, patents, copyrights and, of particular relevance to the area of law being discussed, claims to money.

   Such a claim or right may be evidenced by a document and the document itself as representative of the right or claim is also referred to as a chose in action. The commonest types of such documents in commercial use are *'documents (or instruments) of title'* which evidence the right of some person to money or goods not in his actual possession - examples are bills of lading (claim to goods) and bills of exchange and cheques (claims to money).

   At its simplest such documents will name the party who is liable to deliver the money or goods and also the party with the right to claim them and is evidence that the party who is to pay the money or deliver the goods is contractually bound to do so.

- **Assignment**

2. It is generally possible for the owner of a chose in action to assign the benefit of it to another person but there are difficulties with this procedure:

   (1) on each assignment (or transfer as it is often called) notice has to be given to the party

liable on the instrument;

(2)   the new owner of the instrument (called the assignee or transferee) takes the instrument subject to any equities affecting the title of the previous owner (called the assignor or transferor).

For example, a policyholder may assign the benefit of his life insurance policy (a chose in action) but, notice of the assignment must be given to the insurance company and the title of the new owner is subject to any equitable interests that affected the assignor - so, for example, the assignor's wife may have some interest and/or the insurance company may have a right of set-off in respect of money loaned to the assignor.

The situation is therefore that an assignee has no better rights than the assignor had. The debtor may dispute his liability to the original creditor or claim set-off against him. The assignor, especially if he is not the original creditor but himself an assignee under a previous assignment, may have an imperfect or completely defective title to the ownership of the debt. To avoid uncertainty as to his own rights the assignee may have to investigate the past history of the debt.

3.   The business world however requires <u>simplicity</u> and <u>certainty</u>. This need arises particularly in providing short-term finance for trading transactions. An example will demonstrate this point.

A may consign goods to B, an overseas customer, on the basis that payment is due 6 months after shipment. But A wishes to transfer the debt at once to C, his bank, in return for immediate cash (to replenish A's working capital), less a discount on the amount of debt representing 6 months interest until C receives payment. It can be done but assignment (including obtaining evidence that notice has been given to B) and the possibility that B, on receiving the goods, may claim a deduction for shortages or defects, is inconvenient and risky.

For a bank which handles many such transactions for many customers assignment becomes unworkable.

●   **Negotiable instruments**

4.   In order to obviate the inconveniences associated with assignment of a chose in action as outlined above, the custom arose among merchants of simply ignoring those requirements in the case of some choses in action.   This had the effect that it became possible to transfer by simple delivery (ie by handing over) of the document of title so that the transferee obtained a complete legal title to the subject matter of the document without notice of transfer being to the party liable on the instrument and, further, provided the transferee took the instrument in good faith and gave value or consideration to the transferor, he became the full and legal owner of the instrument and all it represented even though the title of the previous owner was defective or subject to any equity such as a right of set-off.

Such an instrument is called a *negotiable instrument* and the following features of such instrument should be noted:

(a)   simplicity of transfer:
        - no memorandum or 'transfer form' evidencing the transfer;
        - no notice to the party liable on the instrument;

(b)   mere delivery of the document by the owner (plus in some cases his signature or indorsement on the document) to the transferee is sufficient to give the latter a full legal title to the instrument;

(c)   provided the transferee gave value and acted in good faith ie in ignorance of any equity affecting the title (such transferee is called a holder in due course) he obtains an *unqualified right to payment of the full amount*. He may therefore have better rights than his transferor had and need not concern himself with the past history of the transaction. In technical terms he takes it 'free of equities' - it is not subject to rights of other persons.

If any of these features of negotiability is absent the instrument is *not* negotiable.

5.   The principal negotiable instruments are:

(a)   bills of exchange (which include cheques and promissory notes); and
(b)   some other more specialised documents such as bearer bonds, certificates of deposit, share warrants and dividend warrants, provided they are in what is described as a 'deliverable state' (discussed below).

It should be noted that some documents of title such as postal orders, share certificates, insurance policies, debentures and documents of title to goods (such as bills of lading) are not negotiable.

(i)   A share certificiate is not negotiable because it is not transferable by mere delivery (plus possibly an indorsement) - a form of transfer is required and notice of the transfer must be given to the company by sending the form of transfer for registration of the name of the new owner of the shares.

(ii)   A bill of lading is freely transferable by delivery (plus possibly an endorsement) but it is not negotiable because mercantile practice has decided that title to the goods cannot usually pass free from equities which affect the title of a previous owner - so that a person who acquires a bill of lading from a thief obtains no title to the goods and can be compelled to restore them to the true owner.

Two points should be noted:

(1)   The terms *transferable* and *assignable* are not synonymous. They both can arise in the context on a change of ownership of an instrument of title transfer, but, *transferable* is the appropriate word to use to describe an instrument whose ownership can be changed by mere delivery (plus possibly an indorsement) - so that a bill of lading is transferable; *assignable* is the appropriate word where the change of ownership is effected by the execution of a separate document evidencing the change of ownership and which operates to give notice to the party liable on the instrument - so that a share certificate is assignable because of the necessity to complete a *share transfer form* (the title is confusing!) and send it to the company for registration. Other assignable instruments are life insurance policies and debentures.

(2)   The words *negotiable* and *transferable* are not synonymous. A cheque is a negotiable instrument but if it has been marked not negotiable it loses its character of negotiability as defined above, however it is still freely transferable by delivery (and possibly indorsement) but the new owner takes it subject to equities and any defect in title of any previous owner.

> Negotiable instruments are simply those commercial documents which are transferable (or negotiable) on the basis described above. This and the chapters which follow deal only with bills of exchange and cheques, which are commercial documents concerned with the payment of money.

To be negotiable, an instrument must embody a promise or ground of action in itself. It must purport to be transferable by delivery or by endorsement and delivery; it must, either by statute or by the custom of the mercantile community, be recognised as so transferable and as conferring, upon a person who takes it honestly and for value, independent and indefeasible property in, and right of action on, it: *Crouch v Credit Foncier of England 1873.*

The rights of an owner of a negotiable instrument do not automatically accrue to him unless certain conditions are fulfilled:

(a)   the transfer must be for value;

(b)   the transferee must act *bona fide*;

(c)   the instrument itself must be complete and regular on the face of it;

(d)   the instrument must be in a deliverable state.

If these conditions, which are discussed in the following chapters, are not met, the transferee may find that some or all of the rights usually accruing to the holder of a negotiable instrument are lost and his title may be affected by equities or non-existent.

●   **Bills of exchange**

6.   Bills of exchange are a particular class of negotiable instrument which includes cheques and promissory notes.

The Bills of Exchange Act 1882 is the basic legal code. References in later chapters to numbered sections are to sections of the 1882 Act unless otherwise stated. It is unnecessary to memorise these numbers which are given for reference. Certain aspects of the law relating to cheques is to be found in the Cheques Act 1959 and there is a considerable amount of case law which illustrates how the rules work.

Except where stated otherwise, the provisions of the Bills of Exchange Act, 1882 apply equally to promissory notes.

The bill of exchange was one of the first choses in action to be accepted as negotiable in mercantile practice and its early use was for the settlement of debts between merchants located some considerable distance apart to avoid the physical movement of coin or gold. For example, if John in London owed £1,000 to Claude in Paris and Louis in Paris owed £1,000 to the same John, a single payment of £1,000 by Louis to Claude would discharge both these obligations without the necessity to ship cash back and forth between London and Paris with all the attendant risks en route. John would arrange the transaction by sending, through Claude, an instruction to Louis to pay Claude £1,000. Such an instruction was the forerunner of the bill of exchange.

Sometimes the instructions would be that Louis should pay Claude immediately (or as we say *on demand*) or they could provide for the payment to be made at some future date. In the latter case, Claude (to whom John owed the money) on receipt of the instructions would take it to Louis and get the latter's confirmation that he (Louis) would pay Claude as instructed on the due date – ie Louis would *accept* liability to pay Claude and he would indicate his acceptance of liability by signing the instructions or as we would call it today the *bill*. On the due date Claude would again present the bill to Louis for payment and Louis would honour his acceptance by paying the bill.

Thus there are 3 parties to a bill of exchange:

(i)   the party who sent the instructions or drew the bill, called the *drawer* ie John in the above example;

(ii) the party who is to receive payment, called the *payee* ie Claude;

(iii) the party instructed to pay or the party on whom the bill is drawn, called the *drawee*, and if he accepts the bill is called the *acceptor* ie Louis.

The same triangular relationship applies to a transaction involving a cheque:

(a)   John is now a person with money in a bank account;

(b)   Louis is the bank with which John keeps his account and which *owes* money to John;

(c)   Claude is John's creditor whom John wishes to pay.

The sequence of events is that John draws a bill of exchange on his bank (ie he writes a cheque) instructing the bank to pay the creditor and he sends the cheque to the creditor who presents it to the bank for payment. Thus John is the drawer, the bank is the drawee and the creditor is the payee - as will be seen later there is no acceptor since the cheques are not *accepted*.

● **Cheques**

7.   It must be emphasised - since it is sometimes not fully understood - that cheques, although they are subject to a number of special rules, are a form of bill of exchange which in turn is one type of negotiable instrument. Cheques are negotiable instruments subject to variations reflecting modern banking practice. Section 73 states that 'a cheque is a bill of exchange drawn on a banker payable on demand'.

● **Promissory notes**

8.   As mentioned in paragraph 4 above, promissory notes are one form of negotiable instrument.

9.   A promissory note is:

> an unconditional promise in writing made by one person to another signed by the maker, engaging to pay on demand or at a fixed or determinable future time a sum certain in money to or to the order of a specified person or to bearer: s83.

10. Much of the wording is the same as that of the definition of a bill of exchange and has the same effect (see Chapter 10).

11. A promissory note differs from a bill in being a *promise by the maker to pay* instead of *an order to pay issued by the drawer to the drawee*. A bank note is a bearer promissory note issued by the Central Bank. An IOU, which is a mere acknowledgement of a debt, is not a promissory note.

12. The rules on negotiation are essentially similar to those for bills of exchange, but a promissory note cannot be 'accepted' since there is no drawee.

TEST YOUR KNOWLEDGE

Numbers in brackets refer to paragraphs of this chapter

1. What are the advantages of a negotiable instrument as compared with a document giving rights which are merely transferable? (4)

2. Is a cheque a negotiable instrument? If so, why? (7)

3. Define a promissory note. (8,9)

Chapter 10

BILLS OF EXCHANGE

Points covered in this chapter are:

- Definition
- Unconditional order in writing
- Parties to the bill
- Time for payment
- Sum certain in money
- Other matters affecting bills
- Dealings with bills of exchange

Purpose of chapter

The 1882 Act defines a bill of exchange using certain terms which require further definition. This chapter explains how these terms serve to distinguish a bill from other forms of negotiable instrument.

- **Definition**

1. A bill of exchange is defined as

'an unconditional order in writing, addressed by one person to another, signed by the person giving it, requiring the person to whom it is addressed to pay on demand, or at a fixed or determinable future time, a sum certain in money to or to the order of a specified person, or to bearer': s3(1).

---

2. The core of the definition is that a bill of exchange (sometimes abbreviated 'B/E') is *an order to pay money*. The purpose of the other points of the definition is to make a bill of exchange as simple and precise as possible to facilitate dealings with it. An order which satisfies the requirements of the definition may be *negotiated*, in which case it:

    (a) is transferable by delivery (plus indorsement if relevant);
    (b) gives unqualified right to payment of the full amount to the transferee; and
    (c) can, in certain circumstances, give transferee a better title than the transferor had.

3. Section 3(2) provides that unless the instrument fulfills all the requirements of s.3(1) it cannot be a valid bill of exchange but it may still be a chose in action on which there will be a party liable and a person giving value for it will probably be an assignee and so be entitled to sue the party liable on the instrument - but since it has lost its feature of negotiability the ordinary rules of assignment apply to determine the rights of the transferee - he has no better rights than his transferor had.

4. A typical bill of exchange looks like this:

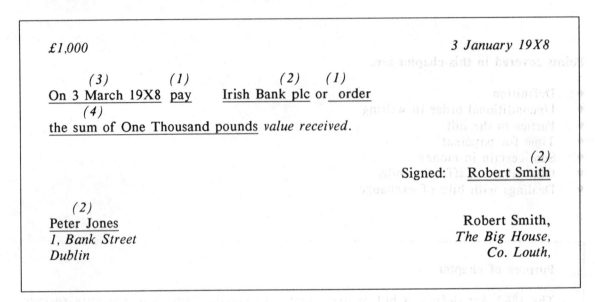

This bill includes the obligatory particulars required by the definition (underlined) plus some particulars which are only customary (in italics).

5. By *convention* (it is not legally necessary) it may be:

   (a) dated (3 January 19X8);
   (b) express the amount in both words and figures (£1,000);
   (c) state that consideration (value received) has been given; and
   (d) give the addresses of the person by whom it is issued and to whom it is addressed.

There is no objection to these additional particulars provided they do not infringe the definition. The meaning and importance of the obligatory particulars required by the definition (underlined in the above example of a bill) are discussed in paras 6 to 19 below.

● An unconditional order in writing (1)

6. It must be an order to pay though words of politeness ('Please pay') are permitted. The word 'pay' itself need not, however, be used, so long as the order is imperative.

Because a bill is an *order* to pay it does not operate as an assignment of funds, so there is no disposition until the monies are paid by the drawee.

7. It may be written on any material though paper alone is convenient. The banks issue pre-printed numbered forms for use as cheques, but this is merely a convenient arrangement between banker and customer. A bill may be written in pencil but this obviously facilitates fraud.

8. It must be <u>unconditional</u>. If the order is conditional upon a certain event or upon satisfying a certain condition then it is not a bill of exchange: *Creative Press v Harman 1973(1)*. Thus an order 'Pay out of the proceeds of sale of my goods when received' is not a bill of exchange since payment is made conditional on (1) receipt of the goods (2) sale of the goods (3) sufficient proceeds of sale to meet the payment. Any of these conditions might not be realised. But it is permissible to give instructions such as 'Pay and debit my No 1 account' or to refer to the transaction to which the payment relates ('Pay £1,500 being the purchase price of my car'). Neither is usual.

9. If the signature of the payee (Irish Bank plc in the above) is required this must be expressed as an instruction to him ('the receipt at the foot must be signed') and not as a pre-condition for payment.

    Case: Bavins & Sims v London & SW Bank 1900
    Order to pay 'provided that the receipt form at the foot hereof is duly signed'.

    Held: this made it a conditional order ('provided that') and so not a bill of exchange.

10. In modern practice when a receipt is required a large and prominent letter 'R' is printed in heavy type. This is simply an instruction which is well understood in the banking world.

● **Parties to a bill of exchange (2)**

11. The definition refers to and requires that there shall be three parties to a bill of exchange:

    (a) the *drawer;*

    (b) the *drawee;*

    (c) the *payee.*

    (a) Drawer

    The drawer is the person who issues the order and whose signature is an essential part of a bill of exhange (Robert Smith in the above example).

    If the bill is not signed by the drawer or by someone with his authority it is not a valid bill. If it is signed without authority or if the drawer's signature is forged, it cannot be a bill of exchange but a person in possession of it may acquire rights by operation of s 54(2), see below.

    (b) Drawee

    The drawee is the person on whom the bill of exchange is drawn, meaning that the order to pay is addressed to him (Peter Jones); the definition does not require that he should add his signature, but he may do so later and is then described as 'the acceptor'.

    The drawee must be named or indicated with reasonable certainty - joint drawees are allowed but alternate drawees are not: s6.

    The definition requires the order to be addressed by one *person* to *another* so that:

    (i) if the drawer and drawee are the same person as eg where a bank draws a cheque on itself (this is called a banker's draft) the instrument is not strictly a bill of exchange as it it not addressed to another but s 5(2) provides that the holder has the option of treating it as a bill or as a promissory note made by the drawer;

(ii) if the instrument is addressed to no one it cannot be a bill of exchange but if a person purports to accept it he may make himself liable on it as the maker of a promissory note.

It may also be noted that if the drawee is fictitious or without capacity to contract, s 5(2) provides that the holder may treat it as a bill or a promissory note made by the drawer.

(c) Payee

The payee is the person to whom payment is ordered to be made (Irish Bank plc). If no payee is specified the bill of exchange may be expressed to be payable to 'bearer', and so it is payable to any person in possession of it. The definition does not require that the payee shall sign, but if he wishes to negotiate and transfer the bill to someone else he must sign on the back of the bill to *indorse* it.

Except where the bill is payable to bearer, the payee must be named 'or otherwise indicated *with reasonable certainty*': s 7. A bill may be drawn payable to the holder of an office ('The City Manager') or to a person by the name under which he trades ('George Hotel' denotes the proprietor). But an impersonal payee - 'pay cash', 'pay wages' - is neither an order to pay a specified person nor one to pay bearer. It is very doubtful whether such an instrument is negotiable. Since however this practice is confined to cheques, bankers are in the same position, whether collecting or paying them, as if they were valid cheques by virtue of s 1(2) of the Cheques Act 1959 and the courts have also held banks entitled to treat such instruments as a mandate to pay the bearer: *Orbit Mining and Trading Co v Westminster Bank 1963.*

Joint or alternate payees are allowed, but if there are joint payees each of them must be indicated with reasonable certainty - so that a cheque expressed to be payable to 'P Murphy and Another' is not a valid bill of exchange.

Non-existing and fictitious payees

12. Section 7(3) provides that where the payee is a fictitious or non-existing person the bill may be treated as payable to bearer. The Act does not state what is meant by 'fictitious' or 'non-existing' but the courts have decided that a fictitious person is not the same as a non-existing person and that it is necessary to establish what was the drawer's intention when he drew the bill in order to determine whether the payee is:

(a) existing;

(b) non-existing;

(c) fictitious.

If the drawer knew of the existence of the payee when he drew the bill and intended the payee to receive payment - then the payee is existing.

13. A *non-existing payee* is a payee of whose existence the drawer had no knowledge when he drew the bill notwithstanding that there may have been an actual living person of that name:

Case: Clutton v Attenborough, 1879
A dishonest employee of C induced him to sign cheques payable to 'Brett', saying that C had trade debts owing to Brett. In fact there were no such debts and while C intended payment to be made to Brett, he had never heard of him. The employee then 'forged' the non-existing Brett's signature and negotiated the cheques to A for cash. When the fraud was discovered C

sued A to recover his money.

Held:
(i)   that the payee was non-existing and hence the cheques were to be treated as payable to bearer;

(ii) since the cheques were to be treated as payable to bearer, indorsements whether forged or genuine could be ignored and thus A was a *bona fide* transferee for value of bearer cheques ie he was what is called a holder in due course and was entitled to retain the moneys received (see discussion on s 29 in Chapter 11 below).

It should be observed that if Brett had been an existing payee then even though A was a *bona fide* transferee for value the forgery of an essential indorsement (ie Brett's) would have defeated A's claim to the cheques and he would have been compelled to make refund to C (see discussion on s 24 in Chapter 11 below).

14.   A *fictitious* payee is a payee known to the drawer but to whom he does not intend to make payment:

Case: Bank of England v Vagliano, 1891
Vagliano's clerk produced to his employer bills apparently drawn by V's customers and expressed to be payable to persons known to V. V accepted the bills and the clerk then forged the payees' indorsements on the bills and negotiated them to the Bank of England for cash.

Held: that the real drawer of the bills was the clerk and since he knew of the existence of the payees but did not intend them to receive payments, the payees were deemed fictitious and hence the bills were to be treated as payable to bearer - with the same effect as in *Clutton v Attenborough*.

The *ficititious* payee rule has no bearing on the law of cheques as distinct from other bills. This is because the drawer of a cheque is deemed always to intend that the payee shall receive payment. A cheque transaction is very much a direct means of payment and intention to make that payment by that means must always be presumed:

Case: Vinden v Hughes, 1905
A clerk falsely told his employer that moneys were due to certain customers well-known to his employer. The employer drew the cheques and it seems some cheques were signed before the payees' name was inserted. The clerk forged the payees' indorsements and negotiated them to the defendant.

Held: the drawer had intended the payees, whoever they might be, to receive payment and therefore they were not ficitious. Since the defendant held order bills, the forged indorsements meant that he had no title to them.

15.   Although the definition requires three parties, it does not stipulate that they shall be different persons. The same person may appear in two roles, for instance:

(a)   when a cheque is drawn payable to 'self' (or to the drawer by name), drawer and payee are the same person;

(b)   a bank may draw a cheque on itself called (a 'bankers' draft'); drawer and drawee are then the same person.

- **Time for payment (3)**

16. A bill is payable on demand if it is so expressed or if nothing is written on it to fix a time for payment: s 10. The effect of this is that a holder can demand payment immediately - the most common type of bill of exchange payable on demand is the *cheque*, defined by s 73 as 'a bill of exchange drawn on a banker and payable on demand.'

    It is not usual and by virtue of s 10(1) not necessary for the words 'on demand' to appear on a cheque.

17. A bill of exchange may also be made payable at a future time which is either specified (3 March 19X8 above) or determinable. In these cases, either:
    (a) payment is due after a fixed period from the date of the bill or from the date of presentation for acceptance (the latter is called a period 'after sight' of the bill); or

    (b) payment is due on a future event or after a period after that event (eg '7 days after my death') provided that the event is of a kind which must happen at some time; '7 days after my marriage' will not do (he may never marry).

    Similarly, a bill expressed to be payable X days after acceptance is not a valid bill because the drawer's acceptance is not certain.

    The English courts *(Williamson v Ryder, 1963)* have held that the words 'on or before' a certain date import an element of contingency so that the instrument is not a valid bill. The Irish courts have taken the opposite view: in *Creative Press v Harman, 1973, Williamson v Ryder* was not followed and the court approved the Canadian case of *John Burrowes v Subsurface Surveys, 1968* which had also refused to follow that case.

    If a date for payment is not a business day, such as a Sunday, the bill is due for payment and 'matures' on the next following business day.

- **Sum certain in money (4)**

18. If the order requires that anything be done except pay a sum of money it is not a bill of exchange. A bill of exchange may, however, provide for a fixed sum payable with interest or a sum payable in a different currency ('£1,000 in US dollars') provided that the rate of interest or of exchange is indicated. It may also provide for payment of the sum by stated instalments, the crucial thing is that the amount shall be capable of exact calculation, so that a bill expressed to be payable 'with interest' where the rate is not stated is invalid: s 9.

19. If the bill expresses the sum in both words and figures (it need not do so) and there is a discrepancy between them, the words prevail: s9 of the 1882 Act.

    Students should note the emphasis on *certainty* in relation to bills - they are intended to circulate freely and therefore any uncertainty on the face of the bill would hamper this intention. Thus there must be certainty as to:

    A   the identity of the drawer;
    B   the identity of the drawee;
    C   the identity of the payee;
    D   the time of payment; and,
    E   the sum payable.

• Other matters affecting bills of exchange

20. So far we have looked at the nature of a bill, its definition and compulsory elements. We shall now briefly look at other matters which affect bills of exchange.

Value

21. In the law on bills of exchange, 'value' is used instead of 'consideration'. The definition does not require that value shall be given for a bill; but in the absence or subsequent failure of consideration the instrument is invalid between the parties and cannot be enforced against the drawer by the original payee. It is, however, valid in the hands of a holder for value even with notice of the absence of consideration.

    Section 27(1) provides that 'Valuable consideration for a bill may be constituted by -
    (a) any consideration sufficient to support a simple contract;
    (b) an antecedent debt or liability. Such a debt or liability is deemed valuable consideration whether the bill is payable on demand or at a future time.'

22. Most bills of exchange are issued in commercial transactions for value. Any consideration which will support a contract and also any past consideration, such as an existing debt, constitutes value for this purpose.

Signatures

23. A person is only liable on a bill of exchange if it has been signed by him (as drawer, acceptor or indorser), or by his agent duly authorised. For example, the holder of a cheque which the drawee bank refuses to pay has no claim against the bank (which has not signed it), though he usually has against the drawer since he has signed it: s 23.

    A bill of exchange may be signed in the name of a firm; it is normal practice for partnership cheques to be signed in this way. This form of signature is equivalent to the signatures of all the individual partners: s 23.

    A person may sign a bill of exchange under the business name which he uses or even under an assumed name. If he does so he is liable as if he had signed in his personal or real name: s 23.

Forged and unauthorised signatures

24. Section 24 provides that where a signature on a bill is forged or placed thereon without the authority of the person whose signature it purports to be the forged or unauthorised signature is wholly inoperative ie it is no signature at all and the space it occupies can be treated as a blank piece of paper and no one can acquire through such signature any right to:

    (a) - retain the bill;
    (b) - discharge it; or,
    (c) - enforce payment of it.

    The act does not distinguish between a *forged* signature and an *unauthorised* signature one except that it allows for the ratification of an unauthorised signature which is not itself a forgery.

    The relevance of this discussion will only be appreciated later when the liabilities of the various parties to a bill are discussed in Chapter 11 below.

25. If the *drawer's* signature is forged or unauthorised then the document is not a bill at all and consequently there can be no holder and no title to it and insofar as it purports to be a bill it is worthless. For example, if Black's cheque is stolen by White who forges Black's signature and gets Green to cash it for him, Green cannot sue Black on the cheque and if Green had presented the cheque to Black's bank and obtained payment, the bank would not be entitled to debit Black's account for the bank's only authority to do so is Black's genuine signature.

Where there has been a forgery of an *essential indorsement* eg of the payee's signature on an order bill or that of the person to whom the bill has been negotiated by special indorsement, such forged indorsement is inoperative for the passing of title and the bill, in effect, remains as it was before the forgery so that a person in possession of such a bill is a person in possession of an unindorsed bill payable to another that is to say, no title can be obtained through the forgery of an essential indorsement and no one can be a *holder* where there is such prior forgery.

An *acceptor's* signature is not essential and the effect of a forged acceptance is that the bill is simply unaccepted.

It is worth reiterating that a *bearer bill is* transferable by mere delivery and therefore any indorsements, genuine or forged, can be ignored as far as the title of the holder is concerned. Where an *order bill* has been indorsed in blank no further indorsement is necessary while it remains payable to the bearer. If the bill is indorsed and the indorsement has been forged, the title of the holder will not be affected. In both cases the person is in possession of a bill payable to bearer and is therefore the holder of it.

26. There are exceptions to the general rule that one cannot retain, discharge or enforce payment of a bill where an essential signature has been forged:

    (i)   sections 54 & 55 may allow a person in possession to have the rights which he would otherwise enjoy protected, but he would never get a good title;

    (ii) sections 60 & 80 operate to protect bankers dealing with cheques with forged indorsements;

    (iii) section 4 of the Cheques Act 1959 protects bankers collecting cheques with forged indorsements.

    These exceptions and protections are discussed in Chapters 11 & 12 below.

Agent's liability

27. An agent who signs a bill of exchange should add words to indicate that he signs for or on behalf of his principal, for example:

> J Smith Director
> *for and on behalf of*
> Smith Enterprises Ltd

He is not then personally liable on the bill. But if he merely specifies his position:

> J Smith, Director
> Smith Enterprises Ltd

he is treated as signing in a personal capacity and is liable accordingly: s 26 (but not where he is sued by a party who is in fact aware of his true position).

28. Some doubt on this point now arises from a recent decision *(Bondina Ltd v Rollaway Shower Blinds Ltd 1986)* where a director signed a company cheque below the printed name of the company. The Court of Appeal held that in doing so the director had done enough to indicate that he signed in a 'representative capacity' and so was not personally liable because he had adopted all the words printed on the cheques, including the company's name.

29. An agent who makes a 'procuration' signature (eg 'H Brown per pro') discloses that he may have only limited authority, since he is signing 'on behalf of'. If he is exceeding his actual authority the principal is not bound: s26.

Case: Morison v Kemp 1912
A clerk was authorised to sign business cheques drawn on his employer's account and he signed 'per pro'. Using this style he drew a cheque to pay a personal debt to a bookmaker.

Held: the employer could recover the money since the payment was in excess of the clerk's authority and the existence of a limit on it had been disclosed.

30. The principle above is subject to any overriding apparent authority given by the principal. In modern practice a bank insists that a customer shall supply a mandate to the bank authorising it to pay cheques signed by the customer's authorised cheque signatories. In giving the mandate the customer represents that any cheque (even if signed 'per pro') signed by an authorised signatory has his authority. He is estopped against the bank from denying it (but he would not be estopped against a third party unaware of the mandate as in *Morison's case* above).

Capacity

31. The rules on capacity to assume liability on a bill of exchange are the same as the rules on capacity to make contracts: s22. As regards minors:

   (a) a minor can never be liable on a bill which he has signed. For example, if a minor draws a cheque to pay for necessaries and the cheque is dishonoured by the bank, no one can sue the minor as drawer of the cheque though he remains liable to pay for the necessaries;

   (b) if a minor draws a cheque and the bank pays it, the bank may debit his account and the payee may retain the money;

   (c) if a minor indorses a cheque to negotiate it, he has no liability on it as indorser but the indorsement is effective to transfer ownership to the indorsee.

   Other persons with defined powers, such as companies, are subject to the same rules. The position of a person under a disability is determined by contractual rules on capacity.

Banker's drafts

32. A banker's draft is a bill drawn on a bank by itself. It is not a cheque and it is equivalent to a promissory note since it is essentially a document by which the bank guarantees payment to the payee. It is the practice of solicitors to obtain a banker's draft to deliver in a property transaction as payment of the price. The vendor would not hand over his title deeds in exchange for a solicitor's cheque, but a banker's draft is acceptable since the drawee/drawer bank would not dishonour it.

33. A bank which has issued a draft at the request of a customer will not accept instructions to stop payment (in any normal circumstances).

● Dealings with bills of exchange

34. Having defined a bill of exchange and discussed the elements which must be present to make it valid, we shall now look at how dealing on a day-to-day basis with bills of exchange is effected.

Order bills and bearer bills

35. Every bill of exchange must state to whom the money is to be paid otherwise it is not a bill as defined by s 3 of the Act. The payee may be indicated as follows:

    (a) Pay 'Black' or 'Pay Black or Order';

    (b) Pay 'Bearer';

    (c) Pay 'Black or Bearer'.

    In (a) we have an *order bill*, that is one expressed to be payable to a particular person or to him 'or order' (the words 'or order' are implied if not expressed). This means that Black is entitled to payment but he may, if he wishes, order (by indorsement) that payment shall be made to someone else.

    Until Black transfers the bill to someone else (which he can do since it is a negotiable instrument) it is payable to Black only. If Black wants to negotiate it to White he will write on the back (ie indorse it) 'pay White or order' plus his signature 'Black'- the bill then becomes payable only to White until such time as he transfers it to someone else. This type of indorsement is called a *special indorsement*, since in this example Black indorses the bill specially to White.

    But Black is not obliged to write the words 'pay White or order' in the above example. The simple signature 'Black' is sufficient to put the bill in a deliverable state for transfer to another. The effect of the simple indorsement 'Black' (called an *indorsement in blank*) is to render the bill payable to anyone in possession of it ie it would be then payable to bearer.

36. It should be observed that a bill may, however, prevent the possibility of transfer, eg 'Pay X only' or 'Pay X' with 'Not transferable' written anywhere on the bill. X may still claim payment but he cannot transfer his rights to anyone else. *A bill which is not transferable is not a negotiable instrument.*

37. The effect of (b) and (c) of para 35 above is to order payment to whomever is in *possession* of the bill. In (c) the name 'Black' can be ignored and the bill is payable just as in (b). Such a bill is called a *bearer bill* and a person in possession of such a bill is called the *bearer*. Note that the word 'bearer' is only used in the sense of a person in possession of a bearer bill - a person in possession of any other type of bill is not a bearer within the meaning of the Bills of Exchange Act, 1882.

    Note that an order bill which has been indorsed in blank is also a bearer bill - but it can be reconverted into an order bill by a subsequent special indorsement.

Thus a bearer bill is one of the following:

(a)   a bill drawn payable to bearer originally; or

(b)   an order bill bearing a single or last indorsement in blank; or

(c)   a bill drawn payable to a non-existent or fictitious payee - it appears to be an order bill but in reality it is not: s 7. See paragraphs 12 to 14 above.

Such bills are transferable by mere delivery whereas an order bill can only be negotiated by indorsement by the *holder* and by delivery - delivery without indorsement merely transfers possession not ownership: s 31.

It should be noted that a bearer bill originally drawn as such is always payable to bearer no matter how many times it is transferred and any purported special indorsement is without effect and can be ignored.

Bearer, holder and true owner

38.   It is worth repeating that the word 'bearer' means a person in possession of a bill which is payable to bearer - a person in possession of any other type of bill is not a 'bearer' within the meaning of the Act.

The word 'holder', which occurs frequently in the context of this area of law, is declared by s 2 to mean 'the payee or indorsee of a bill who is in possession of it, or the bearer thereof'. That is to say a *holder* means a person in possession of a bill of exchange which is payable to him as the payee or indorsee or which is payable to the bearer. Referring back to the meaning of 'bearer' it follows that the person in possession of a bearer bill is also always the holder of it.

A person who steals a bearer bill is the holder of it because he is in possession of a bill payable to bearer but he is not the true owner because the bill belongs to the person from whom it was stolen. Thus there can be at the same time one person who is the holder another who is the true owner. If the thief negotiates the bill to a party who takes it *bona fide*, ie not knowing it was stolen, and for value that party becomes both the holder and the true owner and can defeat any claim against him by the original true owner - it is a bit like money which has been stolen and used to buy goods, the person from whom the money was stolen would generally have no claim against the shopkeeper.

Where there has been no theft or fraud or anything which would make the holder's title defective, the bearer (of a bearer bill) or the payee or indorsee of an order bill will be both the holder and the true owner. If however eg the drawer's signature is forged or if an indorsement on an order bill has been forged, the person the person in possession of such a bill cannot be the holder of it. This topic is dealt with in s 24 and 29 and will be considered later.

Delivery

39.   Delivery, or voluntary transfer of possession, is necessary for the negotiation of any bill. A person who signs or indorses a cheque but retains it does not confer any new rights on anyone else. It remains his property in spite of his presumed intention at some later stage to issue or transfer it by delivery. But:

(a)   there can be constructive delivery (if A sends to B a letter of authority to collect a bill drawn by A held by C);

(b) if a bill is no longer in the possession of a party who has signed it, unconditional delivery by him is presumed until the contrary is proved;

(c) in favour of a holder in due course, it is conclusively presumed that every party prior to him made due delivery: s21.

> As an example of (b) and (c), suppose that X steals a bearer bill drawn by Y and negotiates it to Z in circumstances which make Z a holder in due course. While the bill is in the hands of X it will be presumed that Y delivered it to him until it is shown that X stole it. But against Z, Y cannot escape liability nor deny Z's title by showing that he did not 'deliver' the bill to X. It is conclusively presumed that he did.

Note: For meaning of the term 'holder in due course' see Chapter 11 below.

Inchoate instruments

40. An inchoate bill of exchange is one lacking some essential particular eg no sum stated, payee's name omitted etc. A person in possession of such a bill has *prima facie* authority to complete the bill as he wishes but in order to bind prior parties it must be completed within a reasonable time and in accordance with the authority given: s 20.

It should be observed that the section only operates when delivery for the purpose of completion has in fact been made. If for example the drawer can prove he did not deliver the bill he will not be liable even though the bill is in possession of a holder in due course. Thus there is no delivery if a thief steals a signed incomplete cheque.

Indorsement

41. There are two main types of indorsement: s 34.

(a) <u>Indorsement in blank</u> - a simple signature of the holder on the reverse of the bill

> (signed) 'J Smith'

This converts an order bill to a bearer bill, since it authorises payment to anyone to whom the bill is delivered.

(b) <u>Special indorsement</u> - the holder's signature plus instructions to pay a particular person (the indorsee)

> 'Pay H Brown
>
> (signed) J Smith'

The bill remains an order bill. If the bill is delivered to H Brown, he becomes the holder and may in turn negotiate the bill to another person by indorsement (special or in blank) plus delivery. If the bill comes into possession of anyone other than H Brown, he is not the holder since the bill is not payable to the mere possessor (nor is it payable to bearer).

42. Other types of indorsement include:

   (a) *conditional indorsement* eg 'Pay X if he delivers the goods on order'. The payer then has a choice. He may refuse payment until the condition is satisfied or pay in disregard of the condition: s 33;

   (b) *restrictive indorsement* which prohibits further negotiation, eg 'Pay X only', or which merely gives directions without transferring ownership to the indorsee, eg 'Pay X for the account of Y'. The bill is no longer a negotiable instrument but the indorsee can demand payment.

43. The indorsement must equate with the order to pay the indorser (as payee or indorsee) which precedes it.

If, for example, a cheque payable to 'F Smyth' is delivered to the payee who actually spells his name 'Smythe' with a final 'e' and he wishes to indorse, he should do so as 'F Smyth' though he may add if he wishes his correct signature (F Smythe) as well: s32.

If there is any discrepancy between the order to pay and the indorsement, then the indorsement is 'irregular' and no subsequent holder of the bill can be a holder in due course (unless he is a banker handling a cheque to whom special rules apply - see Chapter 13 below on protection of banks). However, an irregular indorsement is effective to transfer ownership, though not with the benefits of negotiability.

44. A valid indorsement is an essential link in the chain of ownership of an order bill of exchange. If it is a forgery, ownership remains with the party whose indorsement is forged and he can recover the bill from the person who has possession; the latter is not the holder (since it is not payable to him). A bearer bill need not be indorsed in order to negotiate it (but it may be indorsed by way of guarantee as described in Chapter 11 below).

Acceptance

45. If a bill is payable on demand, the holder should present it for payment within a reasonable time (a few days at most). If, however, the bill is payable at a future time, its purpose is usually to effect a transfer by which the original holder sells it for cash and the transferee buys it (at a discount on its value at maturity) as a short-term investment. The transferee will be readier to enter into the transaction if he knows that the drawee accepts liability to pay the bill when it falls due. The drawee however is not liable unless he adds his signature to the bill, and signs as 'acceptor'.

General acceptance

46. It is general practice to present 'time' bills (a bill due for payment at a future time) for acceptance as soon as they are issued, since acceptance increases their commercial value. If the drawee is willing to accept that he will pay when it falls due, he writes his signature on the

front of the bill. It is usual, but not legally necessary, to add 'Accepted' and possibly the date (essential if the bill is payable at a period after sight), as follows:

```
Accepted
D Black - 31.10.8X
```

If he proposes to make payment at his bank he may add words such as 'Payable at Irish Bank plc, Dublin'.

If the drawee accepts without qualification to the order as drawn, he is said to give a *general acceptance*.

Qualified acceptance

47. An acceptance may be qualified in any of the following ways.

(a) *Conditional acceptance* – 'Accepted provided goods received by 31 March'.
(b) *Partial acceptance* in respect of part only of the amount of the bill.
(c) *Local acceptance* – an undertaking to pay *only* at a particular place: eg 'accepted, payable at Bank of Ireland, College Green Branch only' – but if the word 'only' is omitted it is a general acceptance.
(d) *Acceptance qualified as to time* – agreement to pay at a different date from that specified in the bill.
(e) *Acceptance by some but not all drawees* when the bill is drawn on two or more persons jointly: s19.

Presentation for acceptance

48. In general there is no obligation to present a bill for acceptance. But it is necessary to do so:

(a) if the date for payment is defined as a specified time 'after sight'. It must then be presented within a reasonable time after issue;

(b) if the bill expressly requires that it be presented for acceptance; or

(c) if the bill is drawn at some place which is neither the place of residence nor the place of business of the drawee: s39.

49. A bill payable on demand can never be presented for acceptance (agreement to pay at a later date), since by its nature a demand bill is due for payment as soon as presented for the first time to the drawee. Cheques therefore are never accepted (in the technical sense) by the drawee bank.

Effect of non-acceptance or qualified acceptance on liability of parties

50. The drawee has usually agreed with the drawer that he (the drawee) will accept his bill when presented. It may therefore be breach of contract on his part to refuse acceptance. But he has no liability to the holder to pay the bill unless and until he accepts. If he does accept, he undertakes that he will pay the bill 'according to the tenor of his acceptance' in accordance with the terms of the bill unless he has made a qualified acceptance only: s 54. The holder of

a bill may refuse to take a qualified acceptance and if he does not obtain an unqualified acceptance ie a general acceptance, he is entitled to treat the bill as dishonoured by non-acceptance: s 44(1).

51. Where a qualified acceptance is taken the drawer and indorsers are discharged form liability unless they have expressly or impliedly authorised the holder to take a qualified acceptance or have not indicated their dissent within a reasonable time of their having received notice from the holder of a qualified acceptance: s 44 (2) & (3).

A partial acceptance does not discharge the drawer and indorsers. The acceptor is liable for the part amount and the holder can treat the bill as dishonoured by non-acceptance as to the balance and provided he notifies the other prior parties to the bill ie the drawer and indorsers, they are liable in full whether they consent or not.

52. The acceptor has usually received value for his acceptance. But if he has received none he is still liable under his acceptance if value for the bill by some other party.

For example, A may agree to give financial support to B by accepting without receiving value a bill drawn on him (A) by B in favour of C to whom B is indebted. The existing debt is value from C to B and C therefore can claim payment of the bill at maturity from A although A has received nothing.

This is an accommodation bill. It is also possible to assume gratuitous liability on a bill by signing as drawer or as indorser. An acceptor, drawer or as indorser who does not receive value is called an *accommodation party*: s28.

Once the acceptor has accepted the bill, he becomes primarily liable on it and may be sued by a holder. He also warrants the drawer's existence, signature and authority.

Presentment for payment

53. Section 45 provides that a bill of exchange must be duly presented for payment and that failure to comply with the rules governing presentment discharges the liability of the drawer and indorsers. The rules require that a bill which is not payable on demand must be presented for payment to the drawee/acceptor on the day it falls due at the proper place for payment and at a reasonable time on a business day. If the bill is expressed to be payable on demand then it should be presented within a reasonable time after its issue to make the drawer liable and within a reasonable time after its indorsements to make the indorser liable. In determining what is a reasonable time regard is to be had to the nature of the bill, usage of the trade with regard to similar bills and the facts of the particular case.

The practical importance of presenting a bill of payment in accordance with the rules is that if the acceptor, who is primarily liable on the bill, refuses to pay, the holder loses his right to recover from the drawer and indorsers if the bill is eg presented after the due date or not within a reasonable time in the case of a bill payable on demand.

It should be noted that the rules for presentment of cheques are modified by s 74 and are discussed in Chapter 12 below.

Dishonour

54. A bill is dishonoured in the following two circumstances.

   (a) If the drawee fails to accept a bill when presented for acceptance the bill is dishonoured for non-acceptance: s 42.

   (b) If a bill (whether accepted or not) is presented for payment at the proper place and is not paid, it is then dishonoured for non-payment. This is also the position in cases where presentment for payment is excused, eg the drawee cannot be found or is fictitious, and the bill is overdue and unpaid.

55. In case of dishonour by non-acceptance or non-payment, the holder should give notice of the dishonour to the drawer and to any indorsers within a reasonable time (normally within 24 hours). If he does not do so the other parties are discharged from their liability on the bill (except that if the holder at the time of dishonour later negotiates the bill to a holder in due course, the latter may still sue all previous parties).

56. If notice of dishonour is given to an indorser he should, to protect his rights, give notice to the drawer or any intermediate indorser before himself.

57. Delay in giving notice of dishonour is excused when the delay is caused by circumstances beyond the control of the person who eventually gives the notice. In a number of specified circumstances the duty to give notice is dispensed with altogether (s50):

   (a) when, after exercise of reasonable diligence, the notice cannot be given;
   (b) if the person entitled to it has waived it;
   (c) where the drawer has countermanded payment of the bill;
   (d) where the drawee is a fictitious person; or
   (e) where the drawee lacks capacity to contract.

58. The notice may be given orally or in writing. With dishonoured cheques it is normal practice to return the cheque to the drawer by way of notice. The notice is sufficient if it is accurate when received.

Case: Eaglehill v J Needham Builders 1973
The bill was due for payment on 31 December 1970 but the acceptor went into solvent liquidation before that date. The holder posted on 30 December 1970 a notice of dishonour dated 1 January 1971. It reached the acceptor on 31 December 1970.

Held: the notice took effect when received and so on these facts it was valid. Notice given and received before dishonour (even if dishonour followed) would be invalid.

59. Failure to give notice of dishonour to the acceptor does not discharge him from liability which continues over the normal six year period of limitation.

60. When a 'foreign bill' is dishonoured (and in certain other cases), it is necessary to follow the procedure of 'noting or protesting' the bill to obtain formal evidence of dishonour. A foreign bill is one which is either drawn or payable outside the British Isles or drawn within the British Isles on a person not resident therein. The procedure is:

   (a) *noting*: a public notary re-presents the bill and, if it is again dishonoured, he notes the relevant facts on the bill;

   (b) *protesting* is a formal declaration by the notary of what he has done: s51.

61. Dishonour of a bill can be damaging to the reputation of the drawer and any indorsers. To avoid this situation, either may insert on the bill the name of a *referee in case of need* - a person (usually the drawer's bank in the place where the drawee resides) to whom the holder may apply (after formal protesting) for payment. In this way the bill is paid without further commercial repercussions.

Documentary bills

62. In foreign trade, a seller who has shipped his goods to the buyer in another country may send off (i) the bill of lading which entitles the buyer to obtain delivery of the goods from the ship and (ii) a bill drawn on him for payment of the price. The shipping documents are released to the buyer by the seller's local agent, usually his bank, when the drawee accepts (or sometimes when he pays) the bill drawn on him. This procedure is not common.

Discharge of a bill of exchange

63. A bill is discharged when no one has any outstanding claims arising from it.

Section 59(1) provides that if the drawee or acceptor pays the bill to the *holder* in good faith and without notice of any defect in his title, that is payment in due course which discharges the bill.

64. If the drawee or acceptor dishonours the bill by non-payment the holder can enforce payment against any prior party eg an indorser or drawer, but such payment would not discharge the bill because an indorser compelled to pay the bill is entitled to recover from any prior indorser or from the drawer and if the drawer is compelled to pay he can sue the drawee/acceptor for dishonour; that is to say payment of the bill which still leaves a party liable on it does not discharge the bill.

It should be observed that discharge requires payment in due course to the holder. If an essential signature has been forged or placed on the bill without authority, the person in possession of it cannot be a holder so that if the drawee/acceptor pays such a person the bill has not been paid in due course and therefore it has not been discharged and hence the drawee/acceptor can be compelled to pay again to the true owner. However s 60 relieves a paying banker in such a situation from liability to the true owner in respect of an *order cheque* where an essential indorsement has been forged or made without authority - this is discussed in Chapter 13 below.

65. A bill is also discharged if:

    (a) the acceptor becomes the holder of it; or

    (b) the holder renounces in writing his rights against the acceptor or delivers the bill to him; or

    (c) the holder (or his agent) intentionally makes a cancellation of the bill which is 'apparent'. Any particular party is discharged from liability if the holder intentionally cancels that party's signature.

    (d) the bill is subject to material alteration without the assent of the parties liable; it is discharged except against the person making the alteration and subsequent indorsers (see paragraph 68).

66. Unintentional, mistaken or unauthorised cancellation is inoperative. But the party who alleges that it was unintentional must prove that it was so.

Alterations and additions

67. Section 64(1) provides that a material alteration to a bill or acceptance unless made with the assent of all the parties liable on it, avoids the bill except against:

    (a) a party who made, authorised or assented to the alteration; and

    (b) any person who indorses it after the alteration has been made.

    An alteration of the date, the sum payable, the time or place of payment and, where a bill has been accepted generally, the addition of a place of payment without the acceptor's consent are material alterations: s64(2). Case law has established that alterations to the name of the drawee or payee, the changing of the word 'order' to 'bearer' and any deletion of a crossing are material alterations.

68. If, however, the alteration is not 'apparent' or obvious, and the bill comes into the hands of a holder in due course, he can enforce the bill in its original form as if it had not been altered.

    Consider the following example:

    (i)   A draws a bill for £500 on
    (ii)   B, who accepts it, and delivers it to
    (iii) C as payee, who alters the amount to £5,000 and indorses it for value to
    (iv) D, who indorses it to
    (v)   E for value.

    (a) If the alteration is *apparent*, E is not the holder in due course but C, who made the alteration and D who indorsed the bill after it was made, are liable to E for £5,000. E has no rights against A or B. E is in the same position as a person in possession of a bill where an essential indorsement has been forged – he cannot recover from the parties who signed prior to the forgery but he is entitled to recover from any party who signed subsequent to it – see s 55 discussed in Chapter 11 below.

    (b) If the alteration is not apparent and E is a holder in due course, E has the same rights against C and D and can also claim £500 from B (acceptor) or from A (drawer) if B defaults. E cannot, of course, recover more than £5,000 in total.

The House of Lords has held that the acceptor of a bill owes no duty of care to a holder to guard against alterations to the bill after acceptance but different rules apply to cheques and are discussed in Chapter 12 below.

69. An addition is often a material alteration to which the above rules apply. But additions may be made without avoiding the bill in the following cases.

    (a) A drawer may issue a signed bill (an 'inchoate instrument') with authority to the holder to complete it by inserting the amount, the payee's name etc. If it is then completed within a reasonable time and strictly in accordance with the authority given, it becomes enforceable in its completed form. If it comes to a holder in due course he can enforce it as it stands whether or not the additions were authorised.

(b)   A bill may be undated or accepted without the addition of the date of acceptance. If the missing date is necessary to fix the time for payment, a holder may insert the correct date. If the holder by mistake but in good faith inserts an incorrect date and the bill comes into the hands of a holder in due course, he may claim payment in accordance with the date written on the bill as if it were correct.

(c)   A holder of a bill which has been indorsed in blank by the previous holder may add words to convert it to a special indorsement for payment to himself or some other person: s34.

(d)   Any holder of a cheque may cross it or add to the crossing: s77. But only the drawer may cancel a pre-printed crossing.

TEST YOUR KNOWLEDGE

Numbers in brackets refer to paragraphs of this chapter

1.   Define a bill of exchange. (1)

2.   What items on the face of a bill of exchange are only customary? (5)

3.   Who are the three parties to a bill of exchange? (11)

4.   What is a 'holder'? (38)

5.   What is the legal effect of a forged signature on a bill of exchange? (24-25)

6.   What is the effect of a procuration signature on a bill of exchange? (29)

7.   What is the distinction between a bearer bill and an order bill? (35-37)

8.   What is the difference between a non-existent and a fictitious payee? (12-14)

9.   What are the two main types of indorsement? (41)

10.   In what ways may acceptance of a bill be qualified? (47)

11.   In what ways may a bill be (i) dishonoured (54) and (ii) discharged? (63-66)

12.   How does an alteration or addition affect a bill? (67-69)

Now try illustrative questions 12 and 13 at the end of the study text.

Chapter 11

BILLS OF EXCHANGE - RIGHTS AND LIABILITIES

Points covered in this chapter are:

- The concept of value
- Holder for value
- Holder in due course
- Liabilities of the parties

Purpose of chapter

Having examined how a bill of exchange works in practice, this chapter sets out what each party to the instrument undertakes.

---

1. A person who puts his signature to a bill of exchange as the drawer, acceptor or indorser thereby assumes certain liabilities to the holder and to other parties through whose hands the bill passes. The holder who transfers a bearer bill without indorsement (as none is necessary) is also liable as transferor by delivery to his immediate transferee. On the other side the rights of the holder of the bill vary according to his status - he may merely be the holder, or the holder for value or the holder in due course (which is the best position of all).

    It is necessary first to consider how value may be given for a bill.

- **Value**

2. Value for a bill of exchange is essentially the same as consideration for an ordinary contract except that 'an antecedent debt or liability' or past consideration is sufficient for a bill: s27. Most cheques and other bills are in fact issued to discharge existing debts. A cheque or a bill given in respect of a pre-existing debt operates as a conditional payment thereof, and on the condition being performed by actual payment, the payment relates back to the time when the cheque or bill was given. Should, however, the cheque or bill be one drawn by the creditor on the creditor's own account and indorsed back by the debtor and delivered to the creditor the instrument operates as an unconditional discharge of the debt at the time of delivery, because the creditor could hardly question the value of his own cheque or bill.

3. The value given for a bill need not be equal to the full amount of the bill. The essence of 'discounting' a bill is that it is sold before maturity for less immediate cash than it will later produce. The 'discount' is a form of interest charge paid to the transferee who must wait until the bill matures before receiving the full sum. There may also be an allowance for the risk element. If, in the commercial negotiation of a bill, the discount greatly exceeded a due allowance for interest and risk, value would have been given but doubt might arise as to the transferee's motives (good faith is a necessary condition of being a holder in due course).

4. The value given is usually money or other property. But it may take some other form.

    Case: Pollway v Abdullah 1974
    P, an auctioneer, sold property to D and accepted D's cheque in payment of a 10 per cent deposit. D later stopped the cheque and the owners of the property, for whom P was acting as agents, treated the contract as discharged by breach. P sued D (as drawer) on the cheque and D argued that no value had been given for it.

    Held: in selling as agent for the owners P warranted that he had authority to sell. This was sufficient 'value' by the normal rules applicable to consideration. (NB. P as agent would have to account to his principals for the proceeds of the cheque, but the owners could not have recovered direct from D since the owners gave no consideration as they had rescinded the contract).

5. As will be explained later, value need not be given by the holder. But where the value given is an antecedent (existing) debt it must be a debt owing by the person who issues the bill.

    Case: Oliver v Davis 1949
    D owed £400 to O which he could not pay. D persuaded W to draw a cheque for this amount payable to O. The cheque was delivered to O. W later changed her mind and stopped the cheque. O sued W on the cheque.

    Held: no value had been given for the cheque since W owed O nothing and antecedent debt is limited to a debt of the person who issues the bill. If there had been a bargain with W (in fact there was none) by which O accepted W's cheque in return for forbearing to press his claim against D, his forbearance would probably (an *obiter dictum*) have been sufficient value for the cheque.

6. Oliver's case above was decided on the basis that no value had been given to W. But where value is received it need not be provided by the holder.

    Case: Diamond v Graham 1968
    H, in obtaining a loan from D, issued a cheque to G in exchange for G's cheque payable to D. H's cheque was dishonoured and G stopped payment of his cheque to D. D sued G who argued that no value had been given by D for G's cheque.

    Held: H's cheque, although it did not come from D, was value for G's cheque payable to D. (D himself had provided value by making his loan to H).

● **Holder for value**

7. As explained in Chapter 10 above, a bill for which no value has ever been given is a valid order to pay - the drawee is entitled to pay it and the holder to retain the money. But if the drawee refuses to pay, the holder has no rights on the bill against anyone. The donor of a gift cheque may stop payment and the donee has no claim.

8.   *A holder for value is the holder of a bill for which value has at some time been given* - but not usually by him. For example, A issues a cheque to B in payment of A's debt to B; B gives and A receives value. B then indorses the cheque to C and delivers it to C as a present:

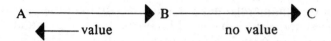

C, who has given no value himself, is nonetheless a holder for value of the cheque.

But note that whether or not he has given value the party in possession of the bill must be a holder - no one can be a holder if there has been a forgery of a prior essential indorsement.

The rights of a holder for value are discussed in paragraph 17 below.

● **Holder in due course**

9.   A *holder in due course* is defined by s 29 as a person who:

(i)   is a *holder*;

(ii)   who has taken a bill *complete and regular* on the face of it;

and where the following conditions are satisfied:

(a)   that he became the holder of if:
(1)   *before it was overdue*; and,
(2)   *without notice of any previous dishonour* (if such was the case);

(b)   that he took the bill:
(1)   *in good faith*; and,
(2)   *for value*; and,
(3)   *without notice of any defect in the title of the person who negotiated it to him.*

The words emphasised in the defintion are important and must be analysed.

10.   The conditions of s 29 must be satisfied at the time when the bill is negotiated or transferred to him. Hence the original payee cannot be a holder in due course since there is no negotiation to him.

Case: Jones v Waring & Gillow 1926
B owed £5,000 to WG. By fraud B persuaded J to draw a cheque for £5,000 payable to WG which G delivered to WG. J later sued to recover the money from WG on the ground that the cheque had been obtained by fraud. WG claimed that they satisfied the conditions of s29 and were a holder in due course entitled to the proceeds of the cheque.

Held: the wording of s29 precludes the payee from asserting that he is a holder in due course. The money had been paid under a mistake of fact and must be returned.

11.   If there has been the forgery of an essential signature no one taking the bill after that forgery can be a holder - see discussion of s 24 in Chapter 10 at paras 24 and 25 above. An indorser's signature is an essential signature on an order bill but note that an acceptor's signature is not essential.

12. Two of the conditions of s 29 relate to the condition of the bill when negotiated:

> (a) it must not then be overdue for payment; and
> (b) it must be complete and regular on the face of it.

A person taking a bill after the date on which it became due for payment cannot be a holder in due course but he may be a holder for value. A cheque is deemed to be overdue when it has been in circulation for an unreasonable length of time - what is an unreasonable time depends on the facts of the case: s 36(3).

13. The requirement that a bill be complete and regular on the face of it includes essential indorsements on the back of the bill:

Case: Arab Bank v Ross 1952
R issued two promissory notes (subject to the same rules on this point as bills of exchange) to 'FFN and Company'. The payee indorsed the notes to AB (the plaintiffs) by signing on the reverse 'FFN' without 'and Company'). AB claimed to be holder in due course.

Held: an indorsement which does not correspond exactly with the payee as named is irregular. It is an effective indorsement to transfer ownership but the bill is no longer 'regular', so that a subsequent holder cannot be a holder in due course.

An inchoate bill (see Chapter 10 para 40 above) is not complete and regular so that a person taking it, even though he may have authority to complete it, cannot be a holder in due course.

A bill marked 'not negotiable' or 'not transferable', although quite valid, is not regular and thus a person in possession of it cannot be a holder in due course.

Note that acceptance is not necessary to make a bill complete.

14. The other requirements of s 29 relate to the circumstances in which the holder acquires the bill. He must do so:

> (a) in good faith;
> (b) for value;
> (c) without notice of:
>   (i) previous dishonour, or
>   (ii) defect in the title of the person who negotiates it to him.

To comply with the good faith requirement the holder must be able to show that he acted honestly and had no knowledge of any defect in the transferor's title or any suspicion about it - this does not mean that he will be considered to have acted not in good faith because eg he was not smart enough to suspect something was wrong or was just careless.

The giving of value is discussed at paragraph 2 above and in Chapter 10 at paragraphs 21 & 22.

Requirement (c) only arises if there is in fact previous dishonour or a defect in the title of a previous party. The holder has then to show that when he took the bill he had no notice (knowledge or strong grounds for suspicion) of the facts in question. It is presumed that a holder is a holder in due course unless and until some irregularity is established in the history of the bill. Only then must the holder show positive proof that he gave value and took the bill in good faith (and without notice): s 30.

It has already been pointed out that an acceptor's signature is not essential but if a bill was presented for acceptance before the due date and acceptance was refused by the drawee this would be dishonour by non-acceptance and although the bill might not be overdue, anyone taking it with knowledge of its non-acceptance would not be a holder in due course. Likewise dishonour of a cheque by the drawee bank (eg by marking the cheque with the words 'refer to drawer' or 'words and figures differ') is clear notice of dishonour and anyone taking it cannot be a holder in due course.

A person taking a bill in the knowledge that the transferor's title is defective or subject to an equity cannot be a holder in due course. It is not necessary that the holder should have knowledge of some particular fact which renders the bill defective, it is enough if the holder has knowledge of some illegality or fraud surrounding the bill, even if he is unaware of the precise details or if he neglected to investigate the circumstances surrounding the bill when he clearly ought to have made such investigation.

Rights of a holder in due course

15. The holder of a bill who complies with all the requirements of s 29 is a holder in due course and as such has a complete and unassailable title to the bill: he is the true owner and has all the rights that accrue to the holder of a negotiable instrument, in particular, the right to be free from all prior defects in title and equities affecting prior holders (such as rights of set-off which one may have against another) and he may enforce payment against all parties liable on the bill ie the drawer, acceptor and prior indorsers: s 38(2).

    A person need not necessarily meet all the requirements of s 29 to get a good title to the bill - where there has been no prior irregularity, defect in title or equity then the holder will be the true owner. It is only where there is some defect in title or equities exist that s 29 is of importance because only by complying with its requirements can a holder be free from defects in title and equities and be in fact the true owner of it.

16. A holder of any kind who derives his title through a holder in due course has the same rights against parties before the holder in due course as the latter had, unless the subsequent holder is a party to some fraud or illegality affecting it: s 29. If, for example, a holder in due course gives the bill to his wife, she is a mere holder for value but with the same rights as he has against all previous parties. If the holder in due course had acquired the bill from a person who obtained it by fraud that would still be the position. But if, to vary the facts, the holder in due course negotiated the bill back to the crook from whom he originally acquired it, the latter (as a party to the fraud) would not be protected by this rule.

17. The rights of a holder for value are limited and differ from those of a holder in due course in two respects.

    (a) A holder for value's rights are against the latest party to the bill who received value and all parties previous to that latest party whether or not they received value:

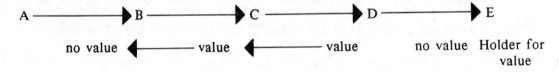

A issues a cheque to B as a gift; B and then C negotiate it for value; D gives the cheque to E as a gift. If the cheque is not paid E can sue A, B or C but not D. B and C received value; A did not but he is liable because value was given after he issued his cheque. E has no rights against D who received no value from E; C is the latest party in the sequence to receive value.

(b) A holders for value's rights are no better than those of his immediate transferor. If, for example, a thief steals a bearer bill, for which value has been given, the thief is not the holder (since there has been no delivery to him). If he gives it to his wife she, as holder for value, has no better title than the thief - she therefore has none at all.

18. Apart from the general protection of a holder in due course, he has a number of presumptions in his favour.

Duties of a holder

19. A holder's rights are subject to his due observance and performance of his duties. He should present the bill for payment at the due date and loses his rights against all parties except the acceptor (if any) if he fails to do so. He must observe the rules on presentment for acceptance, and notice of dishonour. Again if he fails to do so he may lose his rights. The 1882 Act contains elaborate procedural rules on all these matters.

• Liabilities of the parties

20. The liabilities of the parties to a bill are provided for by ss 54 & 55 which should be studied together in conjunction with s 24, which deals with forged and unauthorised signatures, discussed in Chapter 10 above.

21. By signing a bill as drawer, acceptor or indorser, the signatory becomes a party to whom special liabilities and restrictions apply.

There is a chain of responsibility. Each signatory is liable to subsequent parties (other than the acceptor who is always the primary debtor) and each party has rights against any previous signatory.

The liabilities of the drawer

22. By drawing and issuing the bill the drawer accepts the following liabilities: s 55(1).

(a) He undertakes that on due presentment it shall be accepted and paid at the due date, and that if it is dishonoured he will compensate the holder or any indorser who is compelled to pay, provided that the proper action is taken when it is dishonoured. That is to say before the bill is accepted the drawer is primarily liable for payment; after the bill is accepted the drawer is liable should the acceptor dishonour it by non-payment. In the simple case of a cheque the drawer guarantees that he will pay it if his bank does not. But like any other party he is only liable if value has been given.
(b) He may not deny to a holder in due course the existence of the payee and his capacity to negotiate the bill to the holder directly or through intermediate holders.

Liabilities of the acceptor

23. A drawee incurs no liability until he accepts a bill - if he does accept it s 54 (1) provides that he will pay it according to the terms of his acceptance.

Section 54(2)(a) further provides that the acceptor cannot deny payment to a holder in due course on the grounds that:

(a) the drawer did not exist; or,
(b) the drawer's signature is not genuine; or,
(c) the drawer had not the capacity or authority to draw the bill.

Referring back to the discussion of s 24, it will be remembered that the forgery of an essential signature (drawer's or indorser's) means that the person in possession of the bill has no title to it and cannot therefore be a holder in due course. But s 54(2)(a) confers the rights of a holder in due course against the acceptor on a person who but for the forgery etc of the drawer's signature would be a holder in due course so that he becomes entitled to enforce payment by the acceptor.

Note however that the acceptor is not responsible for the genuineness of indorsements so that if an essential indorsement is forged the possessor of the bill has no title to it and cannot enforce payment by the acceptor.

Liability of the indorser

24. By indorsing a bill the indorser: (s 55(2)):

(a) gives the same undertaking regarding payment etc as the drawer, but his liability is limited to the holder or any indorser *after* himself; that is to say he is liable to pay the bill should the drawee or acceptor refuse to do so;

(b) may not deny to a holder in due course the genuineness and regularity of the drawer's signature and any indorsements *before* his own so that if eg the drawer's signature is forged or unauthorised the possessor of the bill has the rights of a holder in due course against all indorsers (and by virtue of s 54 against the acceptor as well); and if an indorsement is forged the possessor of the bill has the rights of a holder in due course against all parties who indorsed the bill subsequent to the forgery (but he has no claim against the acceptor - see s 54(2));

(c) may not deny to his immediate or a subsequent indorsee that at the time of his own indorsement the bill was valid and he had good title to it.

25. The general effect of indorsement is thus to guarantee to subsequent parties that:

(a) all previous signatures are genuine;
(b) the bill is valid and will be paid; and
(c) the indorser will pay if parties previous to himself default.

It is this which protects the transferee who finds that he is not even a holder (and so not a holder in due course) because some indorsement is (unknown to him at the time) a forgery. He cannot recover from the acceptor (who is only liable to the holder) but he can recover damages for his loss from any indorser who signed after the forgery. For example:

A ——▶ B ——▶ C   forged   D ——▶ E ——▶ F
                        indorsement

(Acceptor)   (Drawer)   (Payee)

C remains the owner of the bill and can compel F to hand it back to him. But F can claim compensation from either D or E (because they guaranteed that C's apparent indorsement was genuine) provided that he gives them due notice of dishonour. In practice F would recover from E and E from D. The loss (arising from forged indorsement) always falls on the first indorser (D) after the forgery. D of course will have a claim against the forger but it is likely to be valueless.

26. Indorsement of an order bill thus serves a double purpose:

   (a) combined with delivery it transfers ownership; and
   (b) it serves as a guarantee.

27. It is possible to indorse a bill, for example a bearer bill or an order bill to which the indorser is not a party, merely to provide a guarantee to a holder in due course.

   Case: Rolfe Lubell v Keith 1979
   A company accepted a bill drawn on itself. A director and the secretary also signed their names on the back 'for and on behalf of the company'. The company defaulted.

   Held: these signatures (although expressed in agency terms) must be treated as personal indorsements (they served no other purpose) and so the indorsers were liable as guarantors.

28. It is also possible to indorse for the purposes of transfer but without normal personal liability as indorser by adding to the indorsement *'sans recours'* - without right of recourse against the indorser: s16. But even in this case the indorser has the restricted liabilities of a transferor by delivery (see below).

Liability of a transferor by delivery

29. If the holder of a bearer bill negotiates it by delivery without indorsement he is called a 'transferor by delivery' and he does not become a party and has no liability on the bill itself: s58. But he warrants or guarantees to his immediate transferee (but not to any subsequent holder) that if the transferee is a holder for value:

   (a) the bill is what it purports to be;
   (b) he has the right to transfer it; and
   (c) at the time of transfer he is unaware of any fact which renders it valueless.

> If, for example, a bearer bill passes without indorsement through the hands of several holders and is then dishonoured, the ultimate holder can claim against his immediate transferor (but only on the grounds of invalidity in (a) (b) or (c) above) and he in turn against his transferor and so on. But the ultimate holder has no direct right of action against previous transferors further back along the sequence such as indorsement of an order bill would give.

30. Even a transferor by delivery may only indorse a bearer bill by way of guarantee. He is then liable down the chain to any subsequent holder.

Transfer of an order bill without indorsement

31. If the holder of an order bill delivers it for value without adding the necessary indorsement the transferee:

    (a) has all such rights on the bill as his transferor had; and
    (b) has a right against the transferor to require him to add his indorsement: s31.

    In effect absence of a necessary indorsement can be remedied after the bill has been negotiated without it.

TEST YOUR KNOWLEDGE

Numbers in brackets refer to paragraphs of this chapter

1. Explain the meaning of 'value' in the context of bills of exchange. (2,3)

2. Define a 'holder for value'. (7,8)

3. Define a 'holder in due course'. (9)

4. What are the differences between a holder for value and a holder in due course? (17)

5. What are the specific liabilities of a drawer of a bill of exchange (22), an acceptor (23) and an indorser (24)?

6. What does the holder of a bearer bill warrant when he transfers it? (29)

Now try illustrative questions 14 and 15 at the end of the study text.

Chapter 12

CHEQUES

Points covered in this chapter are:

- Nature of a cheque
- Crossing a cheque
- Relations between bank and customer
  - bank's duty
  - customer's duty

Purpose of chapter

As a special type of bill of exchange, cheques have a number of unique features. This chapter sets out how a cheque is distinguished, and how the parties involved have special duties.

- **Nature of a cheque**

1. Cheques are dealt with specifically in Part III (ss 73 to 82) of the Bills of Exchange Act, 1882 and by the Cheques Act 1959. A cheque is defined by s 73 as

    > 'a bill of exchange drawn on a banker payable on demand'

    and the section further provides that 'except as otherwise provided in this Part the provisions of this Act applicable to a bill of exchange payable on demand apply to a cheque.'

2. The two definitions of bill and cheque may be combined to describe a cheque as

    ---

    an unconditional order in writing addressed by a person <u>to a bank</u>, signed by the person giving it requiring <u>the bank</u> to pay <u>on demand</u> a sum certain in money to or to the order of a specified person or to bearer.

    ---

3. A cheque form completed with 'Pay Cash' or any other impersonal 'payee' is not a cheque though it is subject to some rules which protect bankers. A post-dated cheque is a cheque due for payment at the date it bears.

4. Cheques differ from other bills of exchange in a number of respects.

    (a) A cheque cannot require payment at a future time (it must be payable on demand) and so it is never 'accepted' by the bank on which it is drawn and the bank is never liable to the holder of a cheque.

(b) Although a cheque is a negotiable instrument, cheques are not often negotiated. About 97 per cent of cheques are paid to the original payee.

(c) As a cheque must be drawn on a bank, it is subject to terms implied by banking practice as part of the contract between bank and customer.

(d) Cheques (and a few other negotiable instruments such as dividend warrants) may be *crossed* (explained later in this chapter). An ordinary bill of exchange is never crossed.

(e) Certain principles of negotiable instruments, notably the rules on indorsement, are modified to give protection to banks in respect of cheques.

(f) The effect of delay in presenting a cheque for payment is different from other bills of exchange.

Presentment of cheque for payment

5. With an ordinary bill of exchange (not a cheque) the drawer and any indorser guarantee payment by the drawee at the due date only. If payment is not demanded at that date their liability is discharged but the acceptor continues to be liable until the 6 year limitation period expires. Delay in presenting a cheque discharges any indorser from liability but not usually the drawer (the bank as drawee is not liable in any case) who is liable on his signature for the usual limitation period of 6 years.

6. If, however, the drawer has money at the bank available to meet the cheque when due and the bank becomes insolvent, the drawer is discharged from his liability to the holder in respect of the drawer's loss resulting from the holder's delay in presenting the cheque for payment: s 74. For example, D draws a cheque for £1,000 payable to P who fails to present it for payment within a reasonable time and who would have been paid by the drawee bank had he done so. If the bank became insolvent before the cheque was presented then the drawer would only be liable to the holder for that part of the £1,000 which the drawer recovers in the liquidation and he is discharged as to the amount he fails to recover.

7. A cheque (or any other bill of exchange) payable on demand is due for payment within a reasonable time. Section 36(3) declares that a cheque is deemed to be overdue when it appears on the face of it to have been in circulation for an unreasonable length of time. What is a reasonable time depends on the circumstances but it is not more than 10–14 days (in special and urgent circumstances 3 days delay was held to be too long - *Wheeler v Young 1897*). The holder of an overdue cheque cannot be a holder in due course, the consequences of which are discussed in Chapter 11 above, but it is for the party seeking to avoid liability on the cheque to prove it is overdue.

8. An overdue cheque should be distinguished from a 'stale cheque'. A cheque becomes 'stale' if it is not presented until 6 months or more after issue. The bank upon which it is drawn then considers that its authority from the drawer to pay the stale cheque has expired and it refuses to pay it unless he confirms it (he is usually asked to issue a new one). But subject to that, a bank will usually pay a cheque which is overdue but not yet stale.

12: CHEQUES

● Crossings

9. Crossings are placed on cheques as instructions to the banks who may deal with them and they also serve to give some security against forgery and theft and also afford protection to banks handling them provided the instructions are observed. These aspects of crossings are discussed in Chapter 13.

    There are four types of crossing: general, special, with or without the words 'not negotiable': s 76. In addition there are certain crossings and alterations of crossings that are not recognised by the Act eg 'account payee' or 'account payee only'.

10. A <u>general</u> crossing is two transverse lines across the cheque (usually pre-printed on the cheques when issued by the bank to customers). The words 'and company' or an abbreviation ('&/Co') may be written between the lines but it is no longer usual to do so. <u>A general crossing instructs the paying bank to make payment only to another bank</u>. It is a considerable safeguard to the paying bank against liability if payment is obtained by a person not entitled to it.

11. A <u>special</u> crossing is the name of the collecting bank (and often its branch address) written across the cheque. It is usual (though not strictly necessary) to have two transverse lines and to write the name of the bank between them:

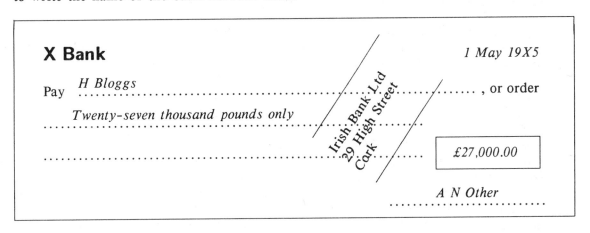

This is an instruction to X Bank to make payment only to the branch of the Irish Bank (the collecting bank) designated by the special crossing. The words of the special crossing are often added by the collecting bank (for identification) before the cheque is put through the clearing between banks in which very large numbers of cheques are handled. It is a precaution against loss in the clearing. Payment contrary to any crossing is negligence on the part of a banker, and if loss ensues, the banker cannot charge the customer.

12. The words '<u>not negotiable</u>' may be written (between the lines of the crossing) by the drawer or any subsequent holder. The effect is that any person into whose hands the cheque may come does not have (and cannot give to his transferee) any better title than that which the transferor to him had: s 81. It is primarily a protection against theft of bearer cheques which are transferable merely by delivery.

> For example, A delivers a cheque payable to B in payment of A's debt to B, who indorses the cheque in blank, converting it to a bearer cheque.
>
> C steals the cheque from B and negotiates it to D who takes it in good faith, for value and qualifies in all other respects as a holder in due course. D has then acquired good title to the cheque though C as the thief had none. But if A or B had crossed the cheque 'not negotiable' D could have no better title than C, who had none.

13. The 'not negotiable' crossing is less significant on an order cheque. To vary the facts of the above example, C steals B's cheque when it is unindorsed, forges the indorsement of B, and negotiates it to D. The forged indorsement has no legal effect: the cheque remains the property of B. D's remedy is a claim (probably worthless) against C. If an order cheque is obtained by fraud, indorsed by the payee and negotiated for value to an honest indorsee, the 'not negotiable' crossing would deny to the latter any better rights than the payee had.

14. The not negotiable crossing on a cheque does not prevent its transfer. It merely ensures the transferee has no better rights than his transferor had. On an ordinary bill of exchange however, the words 'not negotiable' prevent it from being transferable at all.

    If the words 'not negotiable' are written on an uncrossed cheque, or not within the lines of the crossing as part of it, they probably have no effect at all. (The alternative view is that the cheque ceases to be transferable.)

15. The 'account payee' or 'account payee only' crossing is not recognised by statute and is not in any sense an addition to the crossing but its effect is clear. It is an mere direction to the receiving bank as to how the money is to be dealt with after the receipt: *Akrokerri (Atlantic) Mines Ltd v Economic Bank 1904*. It is an instruction to the collecting bank to collect payment only for the original payee. A collecting bank would be negligent if it ignored that instruction and would thereby forfeit its statutory protection (which is described in the following chapter on protection of banks). In law an 'account payee' crossing in no way prohibits the transfer of a cheque nor alters the rights of the transferee: *National Bank v Silke 1891*. But in practice such a crossing makes it almost impossible to negotiate the cheque since no bank would collect payment for the transferee. Many public utilities request payment by cheque crossed in this way since it reduces the risk of theft of the very large number of cheques which they receive. They do not need transferable cheques but pay them into their own bank accounts.

Crossing a cheque

16. Section 77 provides that a cheque may be crossed generally or specially by the drawer or by the holder ie a holder of an uncrossed cheque can cross it generally or specially and can convert a general crossing into a special one and may add the words 'not negotiable'. Where a cheque is crossed specially the banker to whom it is crossed may cross it again specially to another banker for collection and where a cheque (uncrossed or crossed generally) is sent to a banker for collection he may cross it specially to himself.

    The effect of the above is to allow successive holders of a cheque to add crossings or to make them more restrictive but they may not reverse the effect of a crossing so that eg while a holder can convert an 'open' (ie uncrossed) cheque into a crossed cheque he may not do the reverse.

12: CHEQUES

Opening a crossed cheque

17. The drawer (but no one else) may alter a cheque which bears a pre-printed general crossing by writing between the lines 'Pay Cash' and adding his signature or initials: see *Smith v Union Bank of London 1875*. If a subsequent holder did this he would be altering the drawer's instructions for payment and this would be a material alteration: s 78.

18. Banks will usually pay a crossed cheque at the counter to the drawer or any other person well known to them since there is no risk. But in law the bank is at fault in disregarding the crossing.

• The nature of the relationship between bank and customer

19. There is a contract under which the bank holds the customer's money (or if he has an overdraft facility, agrees to lend him money) with the obligation on the part of the bank:

> (a) to make payments (within the limits of funds available to the customer) in accordance with the customer's instructions (usually in the form of a cheque); and
>
> (b) not to make payments on behalf of the customer without his authority; if the bank does so it may not usually (but there are exceptions) debit the payment to the customer's account; and
>
> (c) to maintain secrecy over his affairs, and not to divulge details without authorisation.

20. The customer on his side owes the bank certain duties of care and disclosure. If he fails in those duties the bank may be entitled to debit cheques paid without his authority to his account.

21. These rights and obligations and the bank's duty of secrecy are implied by law as part of the customary relationship between a bank and its customers.

22. Banks may also undertake to provide other services such as safe-keeping of documents, advice on financial matters etc.

• Bank's duty - to honour cheques

23. The bank owes to its customer (but not to the holder) a duty to honour the customer's cheques up to the amount of his credit balance in its books (and any agreed overdraft). If the bank wrongly refuses to pay a cheque it is liable for damages for breach of contract and it may incidentally be liable to pay damages for the tort of defamation.

24. If the customer claims damages for breach of contract he will recover only nominal damages unless he can prove that he has suffered actual damage. General damages may not be given for 'distress' caused by non-payment: *Rae v Yorkshire Bank plc 1987*. Usually damage will be much easier for a trader to prove (his credit may be damaged or he might lose a particular contract) than for a private individual. Note that the smaller the amount of the cheque which is dishonoured, the greater the potential damage to a person's credit.

Case: Gibbons v Westminster Bank Ltd 1939
G delivered to the bank a cheque payable to her for credit of the proceeds to her account. By mistake the proceeds were credited to another account. G's own cheque drawn on her account in payment of rent due to her landlord was presented by him for payment and dishonoured as there were insufficient funds in G's account. The landlord insisted that in future G must pay her rent to him in cash but she did not claim special damage on that account. The bank offered G one guinea in settlement of her claim but she rejected it and sued for substantial damages.

Held: in the absence of proof of actual damage a claim by a non-trader for substantial damages must fail. G was awarded nominal damages of £2.

25. When the bank refuses to pay a cheque it usually returns the cheque marked 'Refer to drawer' (or 'Not Sufficient'). It has been held in *Jayson v Midland Bank 1968* that the words 'Refer to Drawer' may be defamatory by innuendo and that their use is not protected by qualified privilege – the bank has no duty to communicate to the holder its reasons for refusing payment. As a result the bank may be liable to damages for injuring the customer's reputation; if there is no actual damage caused then only nominal damages will be awarded: *National Westminster Bank Ltd v Oceancrest Ltd 1985*.

26. The bank's duty and authority to pay the customer's cheque is terminated by any of the following:

> (a)   notice to the bank of the death or insanity of the customer;
>
> (b)   notice of a petition or order for bankruptcy against him;
>
> (c)   notice of a petition for compulsory winding up of a company customer or of a resolution for voluntary winding up;
>
> (d)   service on the bank of a garnishee order *nisi* – a court order in favour of a judgment creditor whereby the customer's bank balance is 'frozen';
>
> (e)   countermand of payment;
>
> (f)   becoming aware of breach of trust or fraud.

27. Since a bank is at risk in refusing payment of a customer's cheque, any countermand of payment by him is effective only when correct and complete details come to the actual notice of the branch of the bank on which the cheque is drawn.

Case: Curtice v London City and Midland Bank 1908
C drew a cheque for £63 in payment for goods. As the goods were not delivered on time, C sent a telegram to the bank to countermand payment of the cheque. The telegram was put through the bank's letterbox at 6.15 p.m. after it had closed. On the following day the telegram remained unnoticed and the cheque was presented and paid. On the day after that, C's letter of confirmation was received and the telegram found in the letterbox. In his action against the bank C claimed return of £63 paid without his authority.

Held: at the time when the cheque was paid there had been no effective countermand. The claim must fail. (C might have claimed for negligence but he would have recovered no damages for it since the cheque served to pay the price of the goods for which he was presumably still liable).

See also *London Provincial and South Western Bank Ltd v Buszard 1918*:
The drawer of a cheque stopped payment of it by giving notice, in the usual way, to the branch

of the bank on which it was drawn. The payee endorsed the cheque and took it to another branch of the same bank, which advanced money on it in good faith and without notice that the cheque had been stopped.

Held: the bank was entitled to succeed as holder for value against the drawer.

• Bank's duty - payment without authority

28. The bank has no authority to pay (and if it does so may not debit the customer's account):

    (a) if there has been effectual countermand or other termination of its authority;
    (b) if the apparent signature of the drawer is forged: it makes no difference that the forgery is difficult to detect, as it is the bank's duty to distinguish a genuine from a forged signature of the customer;
    (c) if the cheque is void for material alteration.

    But the bank may be protected by fault on the part of the customer, such as negligence or non-disclosure, by subrogation or by recovery from the payee. All these points are considered further in the following paragraphs.

29. If an unauthorised payment by the bank discharges a debt owed by the customer, the bank is subrogated to the creditor's claims against the customer which have been discharged with the bank's money - the bank may recover a similar amount from the customer.

30. A bank which has made an unauthorised payment may usually recover its money from the payee as a payment under mistake of fact. If the cheque was presented for payment by another bank (as must be the case when it is crossed) the paying bank simply claims from the collecting bank which is likely therefore to bear the loss (if the payee is insolvent or has disappeared).

31. Difficult questions may arise over a joint account (eg in the names of two executors or trustees), when one forges the signature of the other on a cheque and adds his own. Obviously the forger cannot hold the bank accountable. The current view is that the bank owes a duty to each customer separately only to pay cheques which he (among others) has signed. Hence the innocent account-holder can deny the bank's right to pay a cheque which he has not signed (*Jackson and White v Midland Bank 1967*).

• Bank's duty - secrecy

32. In *Tournier's Case* (below) the Court of Appeal held that a bank owes a general duty to the customer to keep information about his affairs confidential. But to that rule there are four exceptions.

(a) Where the bank is compelled by law to divulge information.

(b) Where disclosure is required in the public interest.

(c) Where disclosure is required to protect the interests of the bank, such as when it sues a customer to recover sums advanced to him.

(d) Where the customer consents, say by naming his bank to a third party who wishes to have a 'banker's reference'.

Case: Tournier v National Provincial and Union Bank of England 1924
T defaulted in agreed instalments of repayment of his overdraft. The bank telephoned his employers to obtain T's home address. In that conversation the bank disclosed that T had suffered betting losses (paid by cheque). When T's contract of employment expired soon afterwards it was not renewed. T sued the bank.

Held: the bank owed its customer a duty of secrecy and was in breach of the duty since none of the above exceptions applied.

● **Customer's duty to bank**

33. In connection with cheques, the customer owes a *duty of care* to the bank and also a *duty to notify* the bank if he discovers that his signature has been forged.

34. The duty of care is to take those precautions in drawing a cheque which are usual, such as writing a cheque in ink and not in pencil. But it is not a duty to take every possible precaution.

    Case: London Joint Stock Bank v Macmillan & Arthur 1918
    A dishonest clerk presented to his employer for signature a bearer cheque on which £2 had been inserted as a figure (but so that space was left for another digit before it) and no amount at all in words. After the cheque had been signed the clerk altered '£2' to '£120' and inserted that amount in words and obtained payment. The employers denied the bank's right to debit £120 (as distinct from £2) to their account.

    Held: the employer owed a duty to take usual precautions against alteration and had failed in that duty. The bank might debit the full £120 to the account.

    Case: Slingsby v District Bank 1932
    A space was left between the payee's name and the printed words 'or order' on the cheque. Into this space a solicitor wrote 'per' and the name of his firm and obtained payment.

    Held: there was no negligence. It is not usual (and there is no duty) to draw a horizontal line across any remaining blank space to prevent additions. (NB. practice changes and a modern court might consider that this was now a usual precaution.)

35. If the customer becomes aware that his signature has been forged on a cheque, he should notify the bank as soon as possible to enable the bank to protect itself if it can. If the customer fails to do this and the bank suffers prejudice thereby, the customer may be estopped from denying to the bank that his forged signature is genuine.

    Case: Greenwood v Martins Bank 1933
    A husband discovered that his wife had been drawing on his account by forging his signature on cheques. He did not tell the bank. The wife later committed suicide. The husband claimed from the bank £410 which was the amount of the forged cheques.

    Held: by his non-disclosure the husband had represented to the bank that the forged cheques were genuine and he was estopped from denying that they were signed by him. The bank has suffered loss because under the law at that time its undoubted right to claim the money from the wife was terminated by her death. In any future case a bank would probably have to show, as in this case, that its position had been prejudiced by the customer's non-disclosure.

36. The customer has no duty to check his bank statements - in fact, the following recent case (decided in a Hong Kong case by the Privy Council) shows that the customer's duties are few.

Case: Tai Hing Cotton Mill Ltd v Liu Chong Hing Bank Ltd and others 1986
The plaintiff ran accounts with three different banks, all of whom had mandates to honour cheques bearing particular signatures. The company had a long-serving employee whom it trusted, maintaining no supervision or financial control over him. Over six years the employee forged over 300 cheques worth $5.5 million. All the banks in question had written terms stating that monthly statements should be deemed correct unless Tai Hing informed the bank of an error within a short space of time. The terms required Tai Hing to examine the statement and sign a confirmation slip that all was in order, silence being deemed to be assent.

Held: in the Privy Council, that:

(a) even by express terms, bank statements are not conclusive evidence;

(b) the customer was not estopped by its own negligence from asserting that the bank acted without authority;

(c) the customer has no duty to inspect statements;

(d) the customer has no duty to supervise employees so as to prevent forgeries; and

(e) the customer only owes a duty to draw cheques with care and to inform the bank of known forgeries.

TEST YOUR KNOWLEDGE

Numbers in brackets refer to paragraphs of this chapter

1. Define a cheque. (1,2)

2. How do cheques differ from other bills of exchange? (4)

3. Distinguish between an overdue cheque and a stale cheque. (7,8)

4. What is the effect of a 'not negotiable' crossing? (12)

5. What is the effect of an 'account payee' crossing on a cheque? (15)

6. What obligations has a bank to its customer? (19)

7. What is the legal position of a private customer whose cheque is wrongly dishonoured by his bank? (24)

8. In what ways may a bank's duty to honour a customer's cheques terminate? (26)

9. When has a bank no authority to pay a cheque? (28)

10. When may a bank divulge information about its customers? (32)

11. What duties does a customer owe his bank? (33-36)

Chapter 13

PROTECTION OF BANKS

Points covered in this chapter are:

- The need for protection
- The paying bank's protection
- The drawer's protection
- The collecting bank's protection
- Cheque guarantee cards

Purpose of chapter

The volume of cheques which is processed by banks means that each one cannot be given the careful scrutiny we have seen would be necessary. Hence bankers are given protection against liability in law.

- **The need for protection**

1. The banks are the main mechanism for the transfer of money between customers, commercial or private. Huge amounts in aggregate are transferred by cheques every working day. The banks have standard procedures for dealing with cheques which afford some safeguards. But they cannot give to each individual cheque a detailed scrutiny in the light of their knowledge of customers' affairs. They are therefore given *statutory protection against liability* subject to certain conditions.

2. In most cheque transactions two banks are involved.

For example, Adam gives a cheque to Beatrice to settle a debt. Adam's bank, the X Bank, is the drawee but in banking terminology it is the *paying bank*. Beatrice has an account at Y Bank. Since Adam has generally crossed his cheque (his cheque-book has preprinted crossings), X Bank can only pay to another bank. Y Bank then is called the *collecting bank*.

---

3. The cheque is drawn on one bank (the '*paying bank*') which has a duty to the customer to honour his cheques and to make only such payments as he has authorised. The paying bank could, however, pay a person not entitled to the money. It may then be liable:

   (a) to its customer - if it was an unauthorised payment it cannot debit his account; or

      (b) to the payee or other 'true owner' of the cheque for conversion of his property. ('Conversion' is dealing with someone else's property so as to prejudice his rights of ownership).

4.   If the cheque is presented to the paying bank for payment by another bank *('the collecting bank')* - as it must be if it is a crossed cheque - and payment is thereby obtained for a person not entitled, the collecting bank may be liable in conversion to the true owner of the cheque.

A collecting bank may be negligent where it delays in presenting a cheque for collection. Presentation by one bank to another by post is sufficient. In such case it would seem that the paying bank receives as agent for presentation to itself and so can hold the cheque until the day after receipt. Presentation is made on receipt of the item but as a result of an agreement between banks or commercial usage the presentation is deemed not to be made to the paying bank until after the expiration of 24 hours. There is no liability then on a collecting bank where there is a delay by the drawee bank in presenting an item to itself for collection.

The duties of the collecting bank are such that it is bound to use reasonable skill, care and diligence in presenting and securing payments of the drafts entrusted to it for collection and in placing the proceeds to its customer's account or in taking such other steps as may be proper to serve its customer's interests.

Case: Royal Bank of Ireland v O'Rourke 1962 (I)

Held: a collecting bank or bank presenting as holder might incur a responsibility if it failed to use diligence in requiring the paying bank to deal with the bill presented or failed to treat a bill as dishonoured if there was undue delay on the ground that payment could not be obtained.

5.   Obviously the collecting bank is better able to discover whether the person who puts in a cheque for collection is the true owner, since it holds the account which is to receive the funds. So the bias of the protection system is to shift the burden of care on to the collecting bank and to relieve the paying bank of liability insofar as (in good faith and without negligence) it makes payment to the collecting bank. But it is also necessary to make rules for payment of cheques across the counter.

- **The paying bank's protection**

6.   When a cheque is presented, the paying bank must first satisfy itself that it has the customer's authority to pay (and funds available). The protection rules have no effect if the cheque is forged or altered so that it is not a genuine authority from the customer to pay at all.

7.   The bank must next consider the possibility of a claim by the true owner (if he is not the person claiming payment). If the cheque is crossed, the paying banker has a duty to pay according to the crossing, general or special, and make payment to a collecting bank. Unless it does so it is liable to the true owner if the latter suffers loss: s 79 1882 Act.

8.   A *paying banker* who pays a crossed cheque:

      (a) in accordance with the crossing; and
        (b) in good faith; and
        (c) without negligence;

      is in the same position as if he had made payment to the true owner (even if in fact he has not) s80 1882 Act.

13: PROTECTION OF BANKS

- **The drawer's protection**

9. A paying bank which acts in bad faith or ignores a crossing (unless there is no risk, eg when the drawer presents his own cheque to obtain cash at the counter) is deservedly not protected by s 80 1882 Act from claims by the true owner. But the real area of risk for the paying banker left by s 80 is:

    (a) if he fails to detect some defect of indorsement this might be negligence which deprives him of the protection of s80; or

    (b) when the holder of an open and uncrossed cheque (other than the drawer) presents it for payment in cash at the counter. An open cheque is outside the scope of protection under s80 which is limited to crossed cheques.

10. The paying bank usually has no means of knowing whether an indorsement is genuine (or authorised if made by an agent). Accordingly, it is relieved of liability if it is not: s60. This protection is limited, however, as the paying bank must still be concerned with irregularity and discrepancy, and with the fact that an indorsement which should be there - say, because the holder is not the original payee - is absent. These problems are now covered by the Cheques Act 1959 s 1. Section 60 does not protect the banker if the drawers signature is forged, except where the customer is estopped from denying the forgery: *Carpenters Co v British Mutual Banking Co Ltd 1938.*

11. The combined effect of s 60 (of the 1882 Act) and s 1 (of the Cheques Act 1959) is that

> a paying banker is deemed to have made payment of a cheque 'in due course' (to the person entitled) in spite of any forged, unauthorised, or irregular indorsement or the absence of any indorsement if it pays:
>
>   (a) in good faith; and
>   (b) in the ordinary course of business.

Note that requirement (b) is satisfied if the normal banking procedure is followed even though there was negligence in doing so.

12. The banks themselves decided that in paying open cheques at the counter it should be a normal precaution (in the ordinary course of business referred to by the above rules), to require the person who presents the cheque to sign it on the back. Such a signature is more of a receipt and identification than a true indorsement. Some banks do not insist on it if the person presenting the cheque is well known to them, such as the cashier of a company customer making his weekly call for money for wages, or the customer himself drawing cash.

13. Moreover when payment is made (as described above) of a cheque which the drawer has delivered into the hands of the payee, the drawer also is in the same position as if payment had been made to the true owner.

If, for example, A draws a crossed cheque and delivers it to B in payment of a debt and C steals it and obtains payment, B bears the loss and cannot demand payment a second time from A. But if the cheque were stolen from A by C before it came into the hands of B, then B's claim as creditor of A is unaffected and he may demand payment from A by other means: s80.

13: PROTECTION OF BANKS

- **The collecting bank's protection**

14. The main statutory protection of a collecting bank is now found in s4 Cheques Act 1959. The collecting bank is protected if it:
    (a) receives payment for a customer;
    (b) in good faith; and
    (c) without negligence.

    In these circumstances the bank is not liable to the true owner (if payment is obtained by someone else through the bank). This protection applies not only to cheques but also to written orders for payment such as a cheque form completed 'Pay Cash'. The bank is further protected where it receives payment of the cheque for itself, having paid over the amount of the cheque: *Midland Bank Ltd v Charles Simpson Motors Ltd 1960*.

Negligence by collecting bank

15. The considerable body of case-law is concerned with the standard of care to be observed by the collecting bank if it is to avoid negligence and so retain the statutory protection. In some earlier cases (for example *Savory's Case* described later in the chapter) the mere observance of standard banking procedures has been treated as insufficient evidence of due care. In other (notably *Marfani's Case*, also described later) the court has accepted the argument that in modern conditions a bank, dealing with many customers and thousands of transactions, avoids negligence if (without much attention to an individual transaction) it follows its standard routine. In *Lloyds Bank Ltd v Chartered Bank of India 1929*, it was stated that the bank must excercise the same care and forethought in the interest of the true owner, with regard to cheques paid in by the customer, as a reasonable business person would excercise in their own business. Each case has to be considered on its own particular facts.

16. Where there is negligence by a collecting bank it usually arises in one of the following circumstances.

(a)	Obtaining payment for a customer of a cheque drawn by his employer in favour of a third party, or drawn by a third party in favour of the employer, and in either case indorsed over to the customer. The same principle is applied to the company and partnership cheques if the customer is a director or a partner as the case may be.
(b)	Obtaining payment for a customer of a cheque for an abnormally large amount in relation to his circumstances.
(c)	Opening an account for a previously unknown customer without proper enquiry.

    In cases (a) or (b) – as with (c) – it is a defence that the bank made proper enquiries (which requires that credible and reliable information should be obtained). It is not required to concern itself with irregularity etc of indorsement.

    Case: Towey v Ulster Bank Limited 1987
    The defendant bank were in possession of a considerable body of evidence, built up over a lengthy period, which cast doubt on the reliability of A. They co-operated with the plaintiff to the extent that he built up large overdrafts etc to facilitate his dealings with A.

    Held: in failing to advise the plaintiff in a careful manner when consulted about his business dealings with A and in failing in its capacity as collecting banker to take the steps necessary to protect the interests of its customer, the bank was in breach of its duty owed to the plaintiff.

13: PROTECTION OF BANKS

(a) Employers' cheques

17. The best opportunity for stealing a cheque is usually at the thief's place of work. A bank is expected to obtain particulars of a customer's employer (company, firm etc) in opening his account. If the customer presents a cheque drawn by the employer in favour of a third party (or to bearer), or a cheque drawn by a third party in favour of the employer, and the bank is aware of the connection, it should make enquiries to satisfy itself that the customer is the owner of the cheque.

Case: Savory & Co v Lloyds Bank 1933
S (a stockbroker) drew bearer cheques to settle with other firms. Two employees of S stole cheques which were paid in to accounts in the names of the employee in one case and his wife (in the other). These accounts were at suburban branches. The cheques were paid in at City branches for credit to the accounts elsewhere. Hence the branches to which the money was credited never saw the cheques (as the accepting branch cleared the cheques straight to the paying bank). S sued the collecting bank which argued that it followed normal practice in accepting cheques at City branches without enquiry and was not negligent.

Held: through its branches the bank as a whole was in possession (or should have been) of sufficient information to detect that these were cheques drawn by the employers. With that information available within the bank it had been negligent and so was liable.

18. A bank may also be put on notice and should make enquiries (and obtain credible answers) when the customer:

> (a)   pays in a cheque drawn in favour of a company of which he is known to be a director and indorsed by him as director to himself *(A L Underwood Ltd v Bank of Liverpool & Martins 1924)*. But the bank is not negligent if it does not know him to be a director and collects without enquiry *(Orbit Mining & Trading Co v Westminster Bank 1963)*;
>
> (b)   pays in to his personal account a cheque payable to him in a representative capacity, for example as agent *(Bute v Barclays Bank 1955)*, or a cheque drawn by him as agent on his principal's account in favour of himself.

(b) Cheques for abnormal amounts

19. This is obvious. As an example:

Case: Nu-stilo Footwear v Lloyds Bank 1956
A customer told his bank that he was setting up on his own account as a freelance agent. He paid in stolen cheques to a total of £4,855. The bank obtained payment for him without enquiry.

Held: the bank had been negligent in failing to enquire about cheques of a total amount which was inconsistent with the customer's description of his modest business.

(c) Opening an account for a customer

20. If a stranger appears with a cheque for collection, the bank would not present it for payment on his behalf unless he first opens an account. He then becomes a 'customer' with respect even to the very first cheque paid in for collection. Duration of the relationship is not of the essence: *Taxation Commissioners v English, Scottish and Australian Bank Ltd 1920*. It is not necessary before the person becomes a customer that they should have drawn any money or even

that they should be in a postion to draw money: *Ladbooke & Co v Todd 1914*. But in thus acting for a new customer, the bank would be negligent if it failed to make proper enquiries about him. These enquiries should include obtaining at least one satisfactory reference about the new customer: *Harding v London Joint Stock Bank Ltd 1914*.

21. A common method of dealing with a stolen cheque is as follows.

> A thief opens an account in the name of the payee (whose identity he assumes) at a bank where both thief and the payee are unknown. In this way the thief avoids having to indorse the cheque to himself; indorsement of a cheque is uncommon and so invites inquiries. As a matter of routine the bank, in agreeing to open the account, asks the thief where he is employed and whether he has previously had a bank account elsewhere. It also asks him for personal references. The thief may name as a reference a respectable person to whom the genuine payee is known - in the hope that the referee will respond without making enquiries of the genuine payee. Alternatively the thief may give himself, under his true name, as a reference and thus keep the matter in his own hands. It is difficult, though not impossible for a bank to probe the veracity of a well-constructed but fraudulent story.

22. Let the cases illustrate the point.

Case: Marfani & Co v Midland Bank 1968
K, an employee of MC, assumed the identity of E (with whom MC did business) and in that name developed an acquaintance with A, a business customer of the bank. After this preparation, K stole a cheque for £3,000 drawn by MC in favour of E and opened an account at the bank in the name of E. K told the bank that he had only recently arrived from Pakistan to do business in UK; he had had no bank account in UK before and had no previous employment etc in UK. The bank did not ask to see his passport. He was asked to give referees and named A and another person who did not reply to the bank's enquiries. A replied verbally that he had known E (K under his assumed name) 'for some time' but gave no other details. K paid in to his new account a cheque for £80 (not stolen) and then the stolen cheque for £3,000. When the proceeds were credited to his account (as E), K withdrew most of the money and absconded. MC sued the bank for conversion. The issue was whether the bank had acted negligently. The bank contended that only by quite exceptional enquiries could it have uncovered K's fraud and there was nothing to arouse its suspicions.

Held: the bank had done as much as could be expected in accordance with normal practice. It was not guilty of negligence and so was protected by s 4.

Case: Lumsden & Co v London Trustee Savings Bank 1971
L (stockbrokers) settled periodically with other stockbrokers by issuing cheques made payable to the payees in an abbreviated form, eg 'Pay Brown' instead of the payee firm's full name Brown, Smith & Co etc. Blake, an employee of L, opened an account in the name of Brown, explaining to the bank that he had recently arrived from Australia; he gave himself as one referee and an non-existent person as the other. The bank did not ask to see his passport or make any other enquiries as to his identity and present business address. Blake stole his employer's cheque payable to 'Brown' and obtained the proceeds through his bank account in that name. L sued the bank.

Held: the bank had been negligent, especially in failing to obtain the passport to check that the new customer was an Australian named Brown newly arrived in UK. But L had been guilty of contributory negligence (assessed at 10 per cent of their loss) in failing to insert the payee's full name on the cheques.

23. It can be seen that the case-law is not entirely consistent. It would probably be true to say that a bank should:

   (a) ask to see a person's passport if they claim to be newly arrived; and
   (b) make enquiries as to the status of a referee.

Other safeguards of the collecting bank

24. When a customer delivers a cheque to his bank for collection and credit of the proceeds to his account, the normal result is that the bank deals with the cheque as agent for the customer. Although it has no interest in the cheque, the bank may be liable for conversion unless it is protected by s4 and to rely on that defence the bank must not have been negligent.

25. However, if the bank itself becomes the holder for value of the cheque (by giving value for it) that status will improve its position in two respects.

   (a) If the drawer of the cheque stops payment the bank as holder for value may recover payment from him (or from an indorser).

   (b) The bank may by negligence have forfeited the protection of s4 against a claim by the true owner. But if the bank is a holder in due course it can resist a claim for damages by the true owner since the bank has superior title. Negligence in acquiring a bill does not prevent the holder from being a holder in due course. It is only necessary that he should have acquired it in good faith, that is honestly.

   Case: Lloyds Bank Ltd v Hornby 1933
   A new account was opened and the customer paid in a cheque for £250 against which he was allowed to draw before clearance and before any reference had been obtained. The drawer stopped payment of the cheque and resisted a claim by the bank as holder in due course on the ground that it had been negligent in opening the account.

   Held: on the facts of the case there had been no negligence but even if there had been it would not have disentitled the bank from claiming as a holder in due course.

26. A number of factors may, however, operate to prevent the bank from becoming a holder with those improved rights.

   (a) If the customer delivers an order cheque for collection which bears a *forged indorsement* he is not the holder. The bank as transferee cannot be in any better position so it cannot become the holder.

   (b) In the ordinary course, negotiation of an order cheque requires that it be *indorsed* by the holder (the customer) to the transferee (the bank): s31. Otherwise the transferee merely has possession and is not the holder. The effect of Cheques Act 1959 s1 is that a customer does not ordinarily indorse cheques on delivering them to the bank for collection (but there are exceptions). However the need for indorsement to constitute the bank a holder, *if* it also gives value, is removed by s2 of the 1959 Act (see paragraph 27).

   (c) If the cheque is crossed 'not negotiable' the bank, if it is the holder at all, has no better rights than the customer had as the previous holder.

27. Section 2 of the Cheques Act 1959 was enacted as a consequence of the removal (by s1) of the need to indorse cheques handed to the bank for collection. The section reads:

> 'A banker who gives *value* for, or has a lien on, a cheque payable to order which the *holder* delivers to him for collection without indorsing it, has such (if any) rights as he would have had if, upon delivery, the holder had indorsed it in blank': s2.

- ● Cheque guarantee cards

28. The drawee bank is never liable *on the cheque* to the holder. Liability on any bill is restricted to those who have signed it: s 23 1882 Act. The bank cannot sign (as acceptor) a bill payable on demand. The purpose of a cheque guarantee card is to create a collateral contract by which the bank (through the customer as its agent) undertakes to pay the holder of the cheque the lesser of either its value or a fixed amount (now usually set at £100).

29. As a means of limiting fraudulent use of stolen cheque cards the following conditions apply.
    (a) Only one cheque may be used in one transaction. This is to block the device used successfully in *Metropolitan Commissioners of Police v Charles 1976* where a large number of cheques (each for an amount within the limit) were issued to make up a large aggregate amount.

    (b) The cheque card bears a specimen signature and the signature on the cheque must be written in the presence of the payee and must correspond – the payee should compare the two before accepting the cheque.

    (c) The cheque card bears a serial number which the payee must write on the back of the cheque as evidence that is has been produced to him.

30. The other risk is that the customer, while in possession of the card, will use it to obtain acceptance of cheques (which the bank must pay) for larger sums than his credit balance (and any agreed overdraft facility) at the bank. This can be a criminal offence.

TEST YOUR KNOWLEDGE

Numbers in brackets refer to paragraphs of this chapter

1. Define (i) paying and (ii) collecting bank. (2)

2. How does s80 protect a paying bank? (8)

3. When is a bank deemed to have made payment of a cheque 'in due course' in spite of a forged indorsement? (12)

4. In what circumstances is a bank entitled to the protection of Cheques Act 1959 s4? (14)

5. When should a bank be put on notice with regard to (i) employer's cheques and (ii) fiduciary relationships? (17,18)

6. How does the fact that a collecting bank is holder for value of a cheque protect it? (25,26)

7. What should a bank do when considering opening a new customer account? (20-23)

8. What conditions are imposed on the use of cheque guarantee cards? (29)

Now try illustrative question 16 at the end of the study text.

PART F

INTELLECTUAL AND INTANGIBLE PROPERTY

Chapter 14

INTELLECTUAL AND INTANGIBLE PROPERTY

Points covered in this paper

- Breach of confidence
- Trade secrets
- Patents
- Copyright
- Design registration
- Trade marks
- Service marks
- Passing off
- The tort of injurious falsehood

Purpose of chapter

Just as the ownership of goods, land or shares in a company are valuable property rights, so also are those rights that arise from a person's creative effort, their trading activity or the effort that they have made to have their business or goods identified as being theirs. Such rights in intellectual property are assets that can be dealt with, protected or assigned to others and a knowledge of the relevant law is important.

Introduction

1. Within the limits of the law as discussed below a person is entitled to exercise property rights, or similar rights, over the fruits of their own intellectual or creative efforts. Thus if a person reveals information to another in confidence they will be able to restrain that other from making that information generally known or using it for their own business purposes in *breach of confidence*. They may also be able to protect to an extent their *trade secrets*

A person who reveals the secrets of an invention to the world by applying for and being awarded a *patent* is afforded an exclusive right to make use of the method or process in the patent for a period. Similarly the registration of a distinguishing form of words or a distinguishing design or logo gives the owner the exclusive right to use that as a *trade mark* in connection with the class or classes of goods in respect of which the mark is registered and to prevent others using the mark or a deceivingly similar mark in respect of those classes of goods or services.

Copyright, which under Irish Law comes into existence without the need for any formal registration, gives the creator of a copyright work, such as writers, artists, composers, film-makers, or persons who record works, the exclusive right to publish the work, adapt it, convert it to another form, broadcast it, etc.

Apart from trade mark protection the commercial goodwill which the owner of the business has in the enterprise can be protected by an action to prevent Passing Off which will restrain others from trading in such a way as would be likely to associate their goods or services with those of the owner of the goodwill.

A person can also be restrained from making statements about another's goods, business or rights of ownership which are false by an action for the tort of injurious falsehood.

- **Breach of Confidence**

2. While information imparted in circumstances where there is a duty of confidentiality cannot be regarded as property in the sense that patents, trade marks or copyright are, the person who has an interest in keeping the information confidential has a right of action to restrain others from breaching the confidence.

3. The obligation to keep information confidential will most often arise in a commercial context, as where an employee is under a general or a specific duty of confidentaility arising out of his contract of employment or information has been made available in the context of some business or professional dealing.

4. In order for an action for breach of confidence to lie there are three requirements which must be met. These were set out in the case of *Coco v A N Clarke (Engineers) Ltd 1969*:

   (a) the information must be such that it will be protected by the law and have the 'necessary quality of confidence about it' i.e. it must be something which is not in the knowledge of the public;

   (b) the information must be imparted in circumstances that give rise to a duty of confidence;

   (c) there must be an actual or imminent use or disclosure of the information in breach of a duty or in bad faith.

The quality of the information

5. The information must be something which the informant knows which others in general do not, such as a scientific discovery or a unique business idea. However, it could also be the fruits of collating known data, of research or of a proposal to manufacture a commonplace item.

The circumstances

6. A duty to keep the information confidential must exist. This can arise either by agreement or can be inferred from the circumstances eg if the relationship is normally one where a duty is owed, as in the relationship between a professional advisor and client.

Employees owe a general duty of fidelity to their employers so that they cannot reveal to others what they learn in the course of employment. It should be borne in mind that what an employee learns in the course of a particular employment can be separated into knowledge of facts or information which the employer is entitled to have kept confidential and general professional or vocational skill and competence which is inseparable from the employee. The revelation of the former can be restrained while the employee is entitled to use the latter for his own economic purposes subject to such reasonable contractual restraint as the law will permit.

In general a person coming upon information by chance, such as an innocent eavesdropper, owes no duty to keep what was learned confidential. But a person who learns something which another has endeavoured to keep secret by actively spying or by reading a found confidential document would probably be restrained from using or disclosing the information so acquired.

Disclosure or use

7. A person who seeks to use information imparted to him in circumstances where he is under a duty to keep it secret will be prevented from imparting the information to others and indeed others will be restrained from further publishing the information so acquired.

    It is not necessary that there be bad faith: an innocent breach of confidence will give rise to the right of action *(Segar v Copydex Ltd, 1967)*.

Exception

8. Courts will not restrain the disclosure of confidential information where they form the view that it is in the public interest that there be disclosure. What constitutes the public interest will depend on the circumstances of the case but it would be difficult to get the courts to restrain or punish a disclosure of information concerning a crime or civil wrong.

    Circumstances can also exist where there is a duty to inform, so crimes should be reported to the police and misconduct to the appropriate professional body.

9. The possible remedies for breach of confidence are:

    a. an injunction;
    b. damages;
    c. an account of profits; and
    d. the delivery up and/or destruction of goods.

● Trade Secrets

10. An important area of the law relating to breach of confidence involves the protection of trade secrets. Considerable commercial advantage can be gained by keeping a manufacturing process, a business method or a recipe a closely guarded secret.

    Case: Facenda Chicken Ltd v Fowler and Others 1986
    F had been FC's sales manager; he had established a van sales operation offering fresh chickens to retailers and caterers from refrigerated vehicles. He left and set up a rival company and eight other former employees of FC joined him. It was alleged they had wrongly used information relating to the names and addresses of customers; the most convenient delivery routes; the usual requirements of customers as to quantity and quality and days and times of delivery; and the varied prices charged to different customers.

    Held: neither this sales information looked at as a whole nor the prices alone (alleged to be the most significant information), constituted confidential information which could be protected under the *implied* term of confidence.

11. If the secrecy is lost without there being bad faith on the part of another there will be no relief. Another person can through his own efforts come to a knowledge of the secret and no action will lie against him. The recent appearance of own brand Colas which compete with a famous brand is an example of this.

- **Patents**

12. A patent gives the holder monopoly rights in respect of the subject matter of the patent for 20 years from the date of filing. However, all elements of secrecy are lost as the application process requires a full revelation, and subsequent publication, of the details of the invention. The underlying rationale of the patenting system is that in return for the disclosure which advances human knowledge the patent holder is granted a monopoly right for 20 years to exploit the invention.

13. The law on patents in Ireland is regulated by the Patents Act, 1992 and the Patent Rules, 1992. The Act regulates the Irish patents, European patents in Irish law (Part XII) and Short Term patents (Part III).

14. In order that an invention be patentable (Section 9 of the Patents Act, 1992) it must:

    (a) be new;
    (b) involve an inventive step; and
    (c) be susceptible to industrial application.

15. Various things are excluded from being patented (s9):

    - a discovery, a scientific theory or a mathematical method;
    - an aesthetic creation;
    - a scheme, rule or method for performing a mental act, playing a game or doing business;
    - a program for a computer;
    - a presentation of information.

    Methods of treatment and diagnosis for humans or animals are excluded from being regarded as being inventions susceptible of industrial application (s9).

    Further, patents will not be granted in respect of inventions whose publication or exploitation would be contrary to public order or morality (s. 10). Nor will patents be granted in respect of plant or animal varieties or essentially biological processes for the production of plants or animals (s.10) but microbiological processes or their products are not excluded.

16. In order to get a patent you must make an application to the Patent Office. Since the 1992 Act it is also possible to apply to apply for a European Patent in the European Patent Office and when Ireland is designated in that patent it is equivalent to an Irish patent (s119).

Novelty

17. Novelty is a central requirement for patentability. To be new the invention must not form part of the state of the art at the time filing the application. The state of the art comprises of whatever knowledge is available to the public, through publication or use, anywhere in the world before that time (s11).

18. If knowledge became available to the public in the six months prior to the filing as a result of a breach of confidence or of agreement then this does not prevent the invention qualifying as being new.

19. In the Irish case of *Wavin Pipes Ltd v Hepworth Iron Company Ltd (1991)* the High Court decided that a patent could be revoked if there had been any prior use or publication of the subject matter. The test of novelty applied is that laid down in *General Tire and Rubber Company v*

Firestone Tire and Rubber Company (1975). 'A signpost, however clear, upon the road to the patentee's invention will not suffice. The prior inventor must be clearly shown to have planted his flag at the precise destination before the patentee.'

Inventive step

20. 'An invention shall be considered as involving an inventive step if, having regard to the state of the art, it is not obvious to a person skilled in the art.' (s13).

21. Difficulty can be encountered when the invention is a combination or collage of known products or processes. The test is whether creation of the new thing involves genuine inventive ingenuity. To merely combine two existing machines or devices to make a device that serves the functions of both may not be patentable, but an innovative use of existing technology which involves an inventive step can lead to a patentable invention. Examples are the Black and Decker 'Workmate' and the 'Ball Barrow', both of which were patented.

Application for a patent

22. It is the inventor or his successor in title who has the right to apply for a patent. An applicant must identify the inventor or inventors and if the applicant is not the inventor he must show how his right to apply derives from the inventor(s).

   The application must be in the form prescribed and contain:

   (a) a request for the grant of a patent;

   (b) a specification containing a description of the invention, the clear and concise claims being made for it and any drawings referred to in the description or claims;

   (c) an abstract of technical information.

Priority date

23. The date of filing establishes the *priority date* for the patent. The priority date secures the inventor against his rivals making applications for patents of similar inventions.

   The date of filing is the earliest date on which the applicant paid the filing fee and filed documents which contain an indication that a patent was being sought, information identifying the applicant and a description of the invention.

After the application

24. Once the Controller has satisfied himself of the applicant's entitlement to the patent applied for he requests the applicant to pay the prescribed fee. If the fee is paid within the prescribed time the patent is granted.

Grant

25. The Controller publishes a notice of the grant and at the same time publishes a specification of the patent containing the description and claims, any drawings that were submitted and any other matter or information that appears to him to be useful or important.

Duration of a patent

26. A patent is granted for a period of 20 years subject to the payment of renewal fees. These fees become payable annually starting two years after the patent is granted. If the fees are not paid the patent lapses. An application can be made to the Controller to renew a lapsed patent within two years of it having lapsed.

The effect of a patent

27. The holder of a valid patent has a virtual monopoly on the commercial exploitation of the subject matter of the patent. He can do this himself or he can grant licences to others to do so. Full commercial exploitation of patents is encouraged by a system of voluntary and compulsory licensing under Part IV of the Act.

Licences as of right. The proprietor of the patent can apply to the Controller to have an entry made in the register that licences under the patent are to be available as of right. When the register is so indorsed any person can acquire the right to exploit the patent as a licensee on such terms as he may agree with the proprietor, or failing such agreement as may be determined by the Controller.

Compulsory licences. Three years after date of publication of grant any person may apply to the Controller for a licence under a patent. There are a number of grounds on which an application may be granted and most require evidence that the invention is not being exploited to a reasonable extent in the light of the demand of the public or industry or commerce. The threat of compulsory licences is an incentive to patentees to exploit inventions themselves and very few compulsory licences are granted.

28. The proprietor of a patent (either the original applicant or someone who has taken an assignment of the patent) has the right during the life of the patent to prevent any third party who does not have his consent doing anything in the Republic of Ireland which infringes the patent.

Infringing acts include:

(a) making, offering, putting on the market or using a product which is the subject matter of the patent, or importing or stocking the product for any of those purposes (s40 (a));

(b) using a process which is the subject matter of a patent or offering the process for use (s40 (b));

(c) offering, putting on the market, using or importing, or stocking for any of those purposes, the product of a process obtained directly by a process which is the subject matter of a patent (s40 (c));

(d) supplying the means, other than staple commercial products, of putting the invention into effect (s41).

29. A proprietor cannot prevent any of the acts which would otherwise be infringements if:

(a) the acts are done for private and non-commercial purposes;

(b) the acts are done for experimental purposes relating to the subject matter of the invention; or

(c) what is concerned is the extemporaneous preparation of a medicine by a pharmacist in accordance with a prescription.

30. When deciding whether an act infringes a patent what is considered is whether the act complained of come within the terms of the specification. In *Rawls v Irish Tyre and Rubber Services Ltd (1960) (I)* the court said:

   'The claims in the specification are to be construed in their ordinary natural meaning like any other document, but it may be found that words or phrases used in the claims have been in some way defined in the body of the specification: in which case it is permissible to look at the body of the specification in order to see in what sense the words or phrases have been used.'

31. Only a valid patent can be infringed and it is open to a defendant to challenge the validity of a patent. If his defence fails, and an infringement is judged to have taken place, the patentee is entitled to a declaration that his patent has been infringed and may seek an injunction, damages, surrender of any products infringing the patent, or all of these. He is also entitled to an account of any profits made by the infringer from the unauthorsied exploitation of the patent.

Revocation of patents

32. A person sued for an infringement may seek the revocation of a patent. The grounds for seeking revocation are broadly as follows:

   (a) the subject matter is not a patentable invention;

   (b) the specification does not disclose the invention clearly and completely enough for it to be performed by a person skilled in the art;

   (c) the matters disclosed in the specification extend beyond that disclosed in the application as filed;

   (d) the protection afforded was extended by an amendment;

   (e) the original applicant was not entitled to make the application under the Act (ie he is not the inventor, his successor in title or an employer of an inventor).

Employee inventions

33. As a general rule inventions made by employees in the course of their employment will be the property of their employer and it will be the employer who has the right to apply for the patent.

Short-term patents

34. Part III of the Patents Act 1992 makes provision for short-term patents. Such patents are granted for a period of ten years. There is no necessity for a search report. An invention will be granted a short-term patent if it is new and susceptible of industrial application, provided it is not clearly lacking an inventive step.

International conventions

35. The Patents Act 1992 enables Ireland to satisfy the European Patent Convention and the Patent Co-operation Treaty. Under the European Patent Convention a European Patent can be granted by the European Patents Office in Munich, which is equivalent to an Irish patent. Under the Patent Co-operation Treaty, an applicant in any treaty country can make an application to his local

patent office designating the countries in which patent protection is required. These provisons are an alternative to the country by country applications which were previously necessary to gain international protection.

• Copyright

36. The law of copyright is designed to make it possible for the authors or makers of works to have the benefit for themselves of the exploitation of their creative work. The owner of the copyright in a work has the sole right to do, or authorise others to do, certain acts, such as copying or publishing the work. The Copyright Act, 1963, as amended by the Copyright (Amendment) Act, 1987 and modified by the European Communities (Term of Protection of Copyright) Regulations, 1995, regulates copyright in Ireland. Certain rights relating to performances are regulated by the Performers Protection Act, 1968.

37. There is no protection in copyright law for ideas, it is only the material expressions of those idea that are protected. In the case of any particular work it must be first established which category under the Act it falls into before one can determine what acts are restricted in respect of the work.

38. Works which enjoy protection can be divided into two types according to their classification in the Act ie original works (Part II of the Act) and derived works (Part III of the Act).

39. Unlike patent law there is no need or novelty in order that a work enjoy copyright protection. What is required is originality' which in this context means that the work is a result of the author's mental processes or creative skill rather than a slavish copy of another work. Thus, a compilation of a selection of known mathematical questions was held to be original and copyright work - *University of London Press v University Tutorial Press (1916)*.

40. In what follows it should be borne in mind that where 'reproduction' is prohibited the form of what is produced is important. It is axiomatic that 'a rabbit pie is not a reproduction of the recipe', nor is a knitted sweater a reproduction of the pattern. Where there is a difference in form there may not be a reproduction. It was held in the last century that a tableau vivant, the recreation on a stage of a painting using people in the postures and clothing of the figures depicted in a painting, did not breach the copyright in the painting as it was not a reproduction. However, to engrave copyright text on a monument is to reproduce it and to print it on t-shirts and sell them is to publish it.

Scope of the 1963 Act

41. The Copyright Act 1963 protects the works of Irish individuals and bodies, works made in Ireland or first published here. Under international conventions (such as The Berne Copyright Convention) Ireland has agreed to grant reciprocal protection to persons and bodies from convention countries.

Formalities

42. There are no formal requirements in Irish law in respect of copyright, and, except in the case of sound recordings, there is no special marking required. The ubiquitous copyright mark©, dating and such statements as 'All Rights Reserved' are part of the international copyright regimes and are outside the scope of this text which is dealing with Irish national law.

Types of Works Protected

(A) Original works (Part II of the Act)

43. *Original literary works.* This category not only includes what we would normally consider to be 'literature' but also any work in a literary form. A recipe for a pie or a shopping list is literary work in this context. The essential characteristic to qualify is that it is expressed in a literary form.

   Original dramatic works. What is included here is the written version of any dramatic work, be it a script, stage directions, written instructions for choreography, mime or any entertainment. The scenario or script for a film are also included.

   Original musical works. Here again it is the written version of the work that is protected, whatever notation is used to express it. The work as audible music is protected under other provisions in the Act.

44. Under section 8 of the 1963 Act, copyright exists for each of these types of work, whether they have been published or not.

45. *Duration of copyright in literary, dramatic and musical works.* Literary, dramatic or musical works are protected by copyright for the lifetime of the author and a further 70 years starting at the beginning of the year after his death – Regulation 3 of the European Communities (Term of Protection of Copyright) Regulations 1995 (the 1995 Regulations). Where the work is anonymous or pseudonymous and the identity of the author has not been revealed or is in doubt then the period is 70 years from the date when the work was first made available to the public. Works which remain unpublished and not made available to the public are protected for a period of 70 years from the date of creation of the work.

46. *The acts restricted in relation to literary, dramatic and musical works.* The owner of the copyright in a literary, dramatic or musical work can prevent others doing any of the following in respect of the work, or a substantial part of it:

   (a) *reproducing the work*, or an adaptation of it, in a material form. This covers such things as including a work in a record or a film;

   (b) *publishing the work* by issuing reproductions of the work or an edition of it to the public;

   (c) *performing the work in public* which includes any visual or sound representation of the work. A person who broadcasts a work on air or via a cable system is not performing the work. However, a person who has a TV or radio receiving the work where it will be heard or seen by the public, such as in a cafe or pub, is causing the work to be performed;

   (d) *broadcasting the work* on radio or television;

   (e) *diffusing the work* over a cable system;

   (f) *making an adaptation of the work*, which includes translating the work to another language, making a dramatic work out of a literary one or visa versa or making a picture book version of the work. Arrangements or transcriptions of musical works are also restricted under this category.

(B) Artistic works (section 9 of the 1963 Act)

47. The works under this heading are grouped into three categories:

(a) paintings, sculpture, drawings, engravings & photographs;

(b) works of architecture, being either buildings or other structures or models of buildings; and

(c) other works of artistic craftsmanship. In this category there is a requirement that the work not only be one of craftsmanship but that it also have some artistic quality. A piece of original furniture, which would be a work of craftsmanship, would only be protected under this category if it could also be said to be artistic: *(George Hensher Ltd v Restawhile Upholstery (Lancs) (1976)*. In *Merlet v Mothercare plc (1986)*, the plaintiff lost her case when she sued Mothercare for copying a baby's rainhood and cape which she had designed in order to protect her infant rather than with artistic considerations in mind.

48. *Duration of copyright in artistic works*. In general the protection for artistic works is the lifetime of the author and a further 70 years starting at the beginning of the year after his death - Regulation 3 of the 1995 Regulations. Works which remain unpublished and not made available to the public are protected for a period of 70 years from the date of creation of the work.

49. *Acts restricted in relation to artistic works*. Acts restricted by the copyright in an artistic work are:

(a) *reproducing the work in a material form*, which includes producing a version of the work by converting it into a three dimensional form, or if it is already three-dimensional by converting it into a two-dimensional form;

(b) *publishing the work*, by issuing reproductions of the work to the public;

(c) *including the work in a television broadcast*;

(d) *causing a television programme which includes the work to be transmitted on a cable system*.

(C) Derived works (Part III of the Act)

50. In addition to and independent of any copyright that exists in works under the earlier headings copyright can exist in works such as recordings or films derived from them. It should be borne in mind that acts which fall outside the restrictions imposed in respect of these Part III works might still infringe the restrictions imposed under Part II.

(D) Sound recordings (section 17 of the 1963 Act)

51. A sound recording in this context is the embodiment of sounds in any disc, tape, perforated roll or other device so as to be capable of being automatically reproduced from the device with or without the aid of some other instrument. Thus vinyl records, audio cassettes and CDs are sound recordings in this sense. The sound tracks of films are excluded from the definition of sound recordings under the Act.

52. *Duration of copyright in sound recordings*. This is 50 years from the beginning of the year after the sound recording was made, if it remains unpublished. If it is published or communicated to the public then the period is 50 years from the beginning of the year in which the recording was published or communicated - Regulation 7 of the 1995 Regulations.

53. *Acts restricted in relation to sound recordings*. Acts restricted by the copyright in sound recordings are:

(a)   making a record embodying the recording;

(b)   causing a published recording or any reproduction of it to be heard in public, or to be broadcast, or to be transmitted over a cable system, without the payment of equitable remuneration to the owner of the copyright;

(c)   causing an unpublished recording or any reproduction of it to be heard in public, or to be broadcast, or to be transmitted over a cable system.

The prohibitions at (a) and (b) above do not apply if the recording was previously legitimately published without the record or its container being marked with the year in which it was first published.

The question of what is equitable remuneration can be referred to the Controller of Industrial and Commercial Property, under section 31 of the Act, provided the person causing the recording to be heard undertakes to pay the amount that will be determined by the Controller.

54.   *Right to issue recordings of previously recorded musical works.* Under section 13 of the Act a manufacturer of records can issue records of a musical work, or an adaptation of it, if he has given the prescribed notice to the owner of the copyright and pays a fair royalty fee, provided that records of the work, or a similar adaptation, were previously made or imported for sale in Ireland.

(E)   Cinematograph films (section 18 of the 1963 Act)

55.   A cinematograph film is any sequence of visual images recorded on a material, whether translucent or not, in such a way that they are capable of being shown as a moving picture or of being recorded on another material by which they can be shown. Video tapes and video disks are regarded as being cinematograph films in this context.

56.   *Duration of copyright in cinematograph films.* This is 50 years from the end of the year in which copies of the film was first sold, let or hire, or offered for sale or hire, or for showing by any means to the public.

57.   *Acts restricted in relation to cinematograph films.* Acts restricted by the copyright in cinematograph films are:

(a)   making a copy of the film, be it a print or a negative, or a tape or other article on which the film or part of it is recorded;

(b)   causing the film or its soundtrack to be seen or heard in public;

(c)   broadcasting the film;

(d)   causing the film to be transmitted on a cable system.

(F)   Sound and television broadcasts made by RTE (section 19 of the 1963 Act)

58.   Broadcasts made by RTE from anywhere in the State are protected by copyright for fifty years from the end of the year when they were first broadcast by RTE.

59.   The following prohibitions apply to such broadcasts:

(a)   making, otherwise than for private purposes, a film or a sound recording of the broadcast material or part of it;

(b)   causing the pictures or sound in a television broadcast to be seen or heard in public by a paying audience;

(c)   rebroadcasting a sound or television broadcast.

(G) Published editions of literary, dramatic or musical works (section 20 of the 1963 Act)

60.   The publisher of an edition of one or more literary, dramatic or musical works who is not simply reproducing the typographical arrangement of a previous published edition of the work(s) is entitled to copyright protection for 25 years from the end of the year in which the edition was published.

61.   The one act restricted in respect of such editions is the making of a reproduction of the typographical arrangement of the edition. Thus a modern edition of a work in the public domain such as a play of Shakespeare's is protected in so far as the page layout and typographical arrangements of the work are concerned.

(H) Computer programs

62.   Computer programs enjoy protection as though they were literary works under the provisions of the European Communities (Legal Protection of Computer Programs) Regulations 1993.

(I) Digital works

63.

> It cannot be assumed that works in a digital form, such as computer output recorded on a disk, will be treated for copyright purposes exactly as though it were analogous to its apparent equivalent as provided for in the 1963 Act.

(J) Miscellaneous protected categories

64.   These are:
(a)   the Central Bank has perpetual copyright in legal tender notes;

(b)   the Minister for Finance has perpetual copyright in Irish coins and in the artistic work defining the design of any such coins;

(c)   government publications which would not otherwise be copyright are so by virtue of section 51 of the 1963 Act;

(d)   works emanating from the United Nations and other international organisations have copyright under Section 44 of the 1963 Act.

Ownership of copyright

65.   As a general rule it is the author of a work who owns the copyright in it (section 10 of the Act).

There are some special situations however:
Press employees: Works made in the course of employment by a proprietor for the purpose of publication in a newspaper, magazine or other periodical belong to the employer for the purpose of that publication, but to the employee for all other purposes.

Commissioned works: Where a person commissions the taking of a photograph, the painting or drawing of a portrait, or the making of an engraving and agrees to pay money or money's worth for it, the work belongs to the person who commissioned it (section 10 of the 1963 Act).

The typographical arrangements of published works. These belong to the publisher.

The first publisher of a previously unpublished literary, dramatic, musical or artistic work, sound recording, broadcast or cinematograph film has rights equivalent to the rights of a copyright owner in respect of the work for a period of 25 years after the publication.

In each case these provisions apply unless there is an agreement to the contrary.

The Controller of Industrial and Commercial Property

66. The Controller of Industrial and Commercial Property has powers under the Copyright Act 1963 to adjudicate on disputes concerning reasonable remuneration and fair royalties and can adjudicate on disputes arising between licensees and licensing bodies.

Remedies for breach of copyright

67. Breach of copyright is a criminal offence under the 1963 Act. It is an offence to make, sell, let for hire, exhibit or import articles infringing copyright.

The owner of a copyright has a right of action against anyone infringing the copyright and is entitled to claim:
(a) damages in respect of loss suffered;

(b) an injunction to prevent further infringement;

(c) an account of profits made; and

(d) delivery up of infringing articles and any appliance with or from which the copies were made as though they were his property.

Fair dealing and other exemptions

68. The restricted acts in relation to a literary, dramatic, musical or artistic work can be done without infringing the copyright if what is done is a fair dealing with the work:

(a) for the purposes of research or private study;

(b) for criticism or review, whether of that work or another work,.accompanied by a sufficient acknowledgment;

(c) for the purpose of reporting current events in a newspaper, magazine or similar periodical, accompanied by a sufficient acknowledgement; or

(d) for the purpose of reporting current events in a broadcast or film.

69. *Fair dealing*: There is no definition of what constitutes a fair dealing. It is something that would have to be assessed in light of all the circumstances. To photocopy a readily available text in its entirety for the purpose of private research or study, as a alternative to purchasing it, could hardly be a fair dealing, but to make a single photocopy of an entire text for those purposes in circumstances where it was difficult to get one's own copy could conceivably be a fair dealing.

70. *Sufficient acknowledgment*: This is an acknowledgment identifying the work in question by its title or other description and also identifying the author.

Copyright in functional designs for commercial products

71. Section 1 of the Copyright (Amendment) Act, 1987 amended section 7 of the 1963 Act to provide that, except in respect of works of architecture, production of three dimensional objects with the shape, configuration or pattern appearing in the work does not infringe the copyright in two dimensional artistic works, if that which is reproduced is wholly or substantially functional and the owner of the copyright, or his licensee, has manufactured and made commercially available more than fifty such identical objects.

- Design registration

72. New or original designs to be applied to goods can be registered under section 64 of the Industrial and Commercial Property (Protection Act), 1927. In order to qualify for registration a design must not have been previously published in the UK prior to the foundation of the State or in Ireland since then. Publication of a description of the design or the exhibition of goods bearing it at an industrial or international exhibition in the six months prior to an application for registration does not disqualify the applicant from registration provided certain formalities have been observed.

73. In the Industrial and Commercial Property (Protection) Act, 1927 section 3, a design:

   'means only the features . . . applied to any article by any industrial process or means . . . which in the finished article appeal to and are judged solely by the eye, but does not include any mode or principle of construction, or anything which is in substance a mere mechanical device'.

74. A registered design enjoys copyright protection by virtue of its registration for a initial period of 5 years from the date of registration. This period can be further extended, on application and the payment of fees to a total of 15 years.

75. The copyright protection afforded by design registration is in addition to and independent of such copyright as may exist in the design as a artistic work.

Protection afforded to a registered design

76. It is unlawful for anyone other than the owner of the design to apply the design, or any fraudulent or obvious imitation of it, to goods for the purpose of sale or to publish or expose such goods for sale.

77. Remedies available to the proprietor are:

   (a) an injunction; and/or

   (b) damages; or

   (c) a limited monetary amount under the Act.

• Trade marks

78. The law governing trade marks in Ireland is contained in the Trade Marks Act 1963 and Trade Marks Rules 1963 - 1968. The trade mark legislation provides for a system of registration of marks which distinguish the goods of particular traders.

    It should be borne in mind that at the time of writing of this text, February, 1996, a new Trade Marks Bill is pending before the Dail.

79. In the modern world where marketing is a significant part of business activity the concept of brand recognition is a substantial part of goodwill and traders go to considerable lengths to ensure that their goods are recognised by the public as coming from them and associating those goods with the claims for quality, value and efficacy that they are making for them. The use of trade marks to identify goods as being from a particular source, to distinguish them from other goods of the same class and to foster brand loyalty, has long been a feature of business.

80. Section 2 of the 1963 Act defines a trade mark as:

    '. . . a mark used or proposed to be used in relation to goods for the purpose of indicating, or so as to indicate a connection in the course of trading between the goods and some person having the right either as proprietor or as registered user to use the mark, whether with or without any indication of the identity of that person . . .'

    A trade mark may be a brand, heading, label, ticket, name, signature, word, letter, numeral or any combination of these.

The register of trade marks

81. Under the system of registration the register is divided into Part A and Part B. And a trader registers his mark for use in connection with classes of goods.

    Part A marks:
    In order to register a mark in Part A of the register the mark must be distinctive and adapted to distinguish one trader's goods from those of another. Further, it 'must contain or consist of at least one of the following essential particulars pursuant to section 17 of the 1963 Act:

    (a) the name of a company, individual or firm represented in a special or particular maner;

    (b) the signature of the applicant for registration or some predecessor in his business;

    (c) an invented word or invented words;

    (d) a word or words having no direct reference to the character and quality of the goods, and not being, according to its ordinary specification, a geographical name or a surname;

    (e) any other distinctive mark, but a name, signature or word other than those covered by (a) to (d) above, shall not be registrable except upon evidence of its distinctiveness' (s9).

    Part B Marks:
    In order to be registered in Part B a mark must be 'capable of distinguishing' the relevant goods. This has been interpreted by the Irish Courts as meaning 'capable in fact' in *Waterford Trade Mark (1984)* where the word WATERFORD was allowed registration for crystal glass products.

    It is therefore easier to register a mark in Part B of the register but the protection afforded by Part A registration is greater.

Registrable trade marks

82. A trade mark is a mark used or proposed to be used in relation to goods so as to indicate a connection in the course of the trade or business between the goods and the proprietor or registered user of the mark, whether with or without any indication of the identity of that person. 'Mark' includes devices (eg the Mercedes three-cornered star), names (eg 'Gillette'), words known or invented (eg 'Crest', 'Kodak'), letters (eg 'BP') and numerals (eg '4711'). Some three-dimensional marks have been registered eg the Rolls Royce; Spirit of Ecstasy Silver Lady. The signatures of the applicant or of a predecessor in business may also be registered.

83. Section 19(2) goes on to say that a mark will only be regarded as distinctive if it is 'adapted to distinguish' the owner's goods from those of other traders.

84. It is not permissible under section 19, Trade Marks Act 1963, to register a mark which might be deceptive or confusing. For example, it would not be permissible to register a mark which might imply that the goods so distinguished are of a higher quality, or made of better materials, than in fact they are.

Defensive trade marks

85. Under section 35 of the Trade Marks Act 1963, a 'defensive' trade mark can be registered. Owners of very well-known invented word marks may obtain a registration of that mark to cover goods in which they do not intend to trade, when use of the mark on those other goods would suggest to the public a trade connection with the trade mark owner. Thus 'Kodak' may be defensively registered for a large number of goods allied to the photographic field.

Certification trade marks

86. Section 45, Trade Marks Act 1963 provides for the registration of 'certification trade marks'. Certification trade marks are granted to owners who do not actually trade in the goods themselves, but allow or authorise others to use the mark as a certificate of compliance with certain standards. Examples are the pure wool and wool-blend marks, and the Harris tweed mark. Registration is in Part A of the register.

Infringement

87. The exclusive right given to the owner of a mark is infringed if any other person, without the owner's consent, uses the mark itself or a mark closely resembling it in the course of trade (s12). The infringement will occur if the offender uses the mark either as a trade mark applying to his own goods, or in less blatant circumstances.

Case: Bismag v Amblins Chemists Ltd 1940
The defendants were a firm of chemists. They published a catalogue in which they listed in one column a number of well known proprietary pharmaceutical products, and in an adjacent column the corresponding products of their own manufacture. Many of the proprietary products in the first column were referred to by registered trade marks. In each case their own brand was shown to be cheaper than the rival product.

Held: the defendants were in breach of s4 TMA 1938 (UK provision similar to s12) as they were using the trade marks in the catalogue in the course of trade.

88. The exclusive use of a Part B mark is modified by section 13 of the Act which allows an effective defence to a person who can show that the use complained of is not likely to deceive or cause confusion or be taken as indicating a connection in the course of trade between the goods and some person having the right either as proprietor or as registered user to use the trade mark.

89. If the owner of a mark succeeds in his action against an infringement, he is entitled to an injunction and to damages or an account of profits for infringement and to an order for destruction or modification of the offending material.

90. A defendant faced with an action claiming a breach of a trade mark can challenge the registration on the grounds that the mark is not valid and should not have been granted. Part A marks cannot be challenged on this ground after 7 years on the register, unless at the time of the application there was fraud or there was then, and continues to be, a likelihood of confusion or deception.

91. It is not an infringement of a mark to make *bona fide* use of one's own name, business name or place of business or certain descriptions of the quality or character of one's own goods or services (section 16 of the 1963 Act).

92. A trader who has made use of a mark identical to or resembling a registered mark for his own goods and services from a date either before the registered mark was registered or, if the registered owner used his mark before that date, earlier than the registered owner began using his mark, cannot be restrained from continuing to use his mark or from registering it (sections 15 and 20 of the 1963 Act).

Use in connection with genuine goods and to indicate suitability

93. Once the proprietor of a mark has but goods into circulation it is not an infringement to use the mark in connection wih subsequent transactions involving the goods such as selling them second hand or marketing goods which have been imported.

It is also not an infringement to use a mark if it is in connection with goods that have been adapted to form part of or be accessories to other goods where the use is reasonably necessary to show that they have been so adapted. An example of this is the use of the IBM mark as part of a statement that particular software is compatible with IBM computers.

Comparative advertising

94. The practice of comparative advertising where one trader compares his goods to those of another may amount to an infringement where the trade marks owned by the other are used. In the case of *Gallager (Dublin) Ltd v The Health Educatioin Bureau 1982 (I)* the defendant who used a Part A mark belonging to the plaintiff in an anti-smoking campaign were found to have infringed the mark by using it in connection with cigarettes. A Part B mark could probably be used in comparative advertising provided care was taken to dispel any possible confusion and in a way that did not indicate a trade connection between the advertiser's goods and the trade mark owner.

● Service marks

95. There is no statutory regime under Irish law for the registration of 'service marks', ie marks to be used in connection with services rendered rather than goods. It was held in *Aristoc v Rysta Ltd 1945* that the fundamental idea of the function of a trade mark was to indicate the

origin of goods. Thus a mark applied to someone else's goods to show that you have rendered a service for them (repairing the goods, servicing them or such like) cannot be a trade mark, it is a service mark.

96. Where there are goods emanating from the supplier of the service there can be a trade mark registered in respect of those goods. The Irish Supreme Court allowed the registration of 'Golden Pages' as a mark on the grounds that the Act did not require the connection in the course of trade between the goods and the person using the trade mark to depend on that person selling the goods. Further unauthorised use of a service mark may give rise to an action for passing-off (see below at para 98).

Merchandise Marks Acts 1887 to 1978

97. It should also be noted in the context of trade marks and passing-off that the false attribution of identity to goods, false marking and counterfeiting goods is subject to criminal sanction under the Merchandise Marks Acts 1887 to 1978.

• Passing-off

98. Traders are entitled to protect the goodwill that they have built up in their business or their products by preventing others identifying their business, products or services with those of the owner of the goodwill. While there are similarities with what is sought to be achieved in this area of law with the law relating to the protection of registered trade marks the scope of the passing off action is much broader and will protect the trader against the use by others of:

(a) unregistered or un-registrable trade marks, service marks or names being used in the market which are associated in the public mind with his enterprise;

(b) get-up used in connection with goods, being distinctive packaging, colour schemes, labelling or product shape;

(c) use of his goodwill in a different area of enterprise where there is a likelihood that the public will associate the two enterprises.

99. The plaintiff in a passing-off action must establish that:

(a) because of the reputation attached to his goods or his business, there is a goodwill attached to the marks, names or get-up he uses;

(b) there is a likelihood that the defendant's goods or services will be mistakenly taken as being those of the owner of the goodwill or associated with his business; and

(c) he has, or is likely to, suffer damage to his business or goodwill.

There is no need to prove deception or even an intention to deceive.

100. 'Mere copying' is insufficient to found an action for passing-off.

Case: County Sound plc v Ocean Sound plc 1991
County Sound plc claimed to have established goodwill in the name of 'The Gold AM', a broadcast devoted to golden oldies. Ocean Sound subsequently copied the name and broadcast a programme under it. It was a deliberately provocative move.

Held: the elements to be proved were reputation (or goodwill), confusion and damage. To have reputation, the name must be distinctive, and not merely descriptive. It was held that the name 'The Gold AM' was descriptive and goodwill could only be acquired in it:

(i)   by the use of that name and none other; and
(ii) over a considerable period of time.

Neither of these was proved, so the plaintiffs failed to obtain an injunction against the defendants.

101. To exploit a market trend or a fashion, even one created or fostered by another firm's marketing is not actionable in itself provided there is sufficient to distinguish between the goods, however similar, coming from different sources.

Case: United Biscuits Ltd v Irish Biscuits Ltd 1971 (I)
The plaintiff and defendant companies both marketed similar biscuits, one called 'Cottage Creams' and the other 'College Creams', the packages in which they were sold were different in both design and colour.

Held: the similarity in the names and in the biscuits did not lead to a passing-off as the packaging distinguished the products. The Judge was of the view that similarities in the biscuits could not be passing-off as they were sold in packages.

Case: Reckitt and Colman Products Ltd v Borden Inc 1990
The plaintiffs had, since 1956, sold lemon juice in yellow plastic containers shaped like lemons under the brand name 'Jif.' In 1985 the defendants introduced a similar product in lemon shaped container which could be distinguished from the Plaintiff's product by the labelling, size and the colour of the cap.

Held: that the plaintiff had established such goodwill in their lemon-shaped containers that confusion would arise in the minds of shoppers wishing to buy lemon juice in a lemon-shaped container. The defendant had not taken sufficient steps to eradicate confusion and so an injunction was granted restraining the defendant from using the lemon shape.

102. *Case: Michelstown Co-operative Agricultural Society Ltd v Goldenvale Food Products Ltd 1985 (I)*
Both the plaintiff and the defendant had butter substitutes which were being marketed using separate registered trade marks. The plaintiff objected to the defendant marketing its product in a tub whose general colour scheme, shape, dimensions and overall printing resembled theirs and which had a yellow flower motif similar to theirs.

Held: an injunction would be granted.

103. *Case: C & A Modes v C & A (Waterford) Ltd 1976 (I)*
The defendant had used the name of the plaintiff who were a long established retail business in Belfast and the sign that they used was confusingly similar. The defendants were, however, in an entirely different area of enterprise.

Held: that the defendants were passing themselves off as being associated with the goods and services of the plaintiff, causing damage to the plaintiff's goodwill.

14: INTELLECTUAL AND INTANGIBLE PROPERTY

● **The tort of injurious falsehood**

104. The tort of injurious falsehood provides protection to a person against false statements being made which would injure him in his trade. It is not necessary to show that the misleading statement caused others to think less of him in his trade or of his goods or services.

105. What a plaintiff must show in order to succeed is:

    (a) the statements complained of were untrue;
    (b) that they were made malicously; and
    (c) that damage was suffered thereby.

In order to have a cause of action, where the statement was made orally rather than in writing or some other permanent form, it is necessary to show that the plaintiff has suffered actual pecuniary loss unless the statement can be shown to have been calculated to cause financial loss to the plaintiff in respect of any office, profession, calling, trade or business. Statements in writing are actionable without proof of actual financial loss.

Where a trader's goods have ben disparaged proof of general loss of business, rather than the loss of identifiable customers, is sufficient.

TEST YOUR KNOWLEDGE

Numbers in brackets refer to paragraphs in this chapter

1. In what circumstances will the Court prevent the revelation and use of information given in confidence? (4)

2. What are the necessary attributes that an invention must have before a patent can be obtained for it? (14)

3. What attribute must a written work have in order for it to enjoy copyright protection? (39)

4. My party piece is singing Sinatra's famous song 'My Way', can I issue recordings of it to the public? (54)

5. What are the benefits of registering a trade mark? (79)

6. What must a person who claims that another is passing-off their goods or services as his prove in order to succeed? (99)

Now try illustrative question 11 at end of the study text.

PART G
PARTNERSHIP

Chapter 15

PARTNERSHIP

Points covered in this chapter are:

- Partnership and types of partner
- Partnership agreement
- Relationship of partners to outsiders dealing with the firm
- Liability of incoming and outgoing partners
- The relationship of partners with each other
- Dissolution
- Companies and partnerships compared
- Limited partnerships

Purpose of chapter

Partnership is a particularly important topic for accountants since often that is the form of association chosen by professional people. The comparison with limited companies is also significant since this is an area where an accountant's advice is often sought.

• Partnership and types of partner

1. Partnership is the normal organisation in the professions but is less common is commerce. This is because most professions prohibit their members from carrying on practice through limited companies. Businessmen are not so restricted and generally prefer to trade through a limited company so that, if it becomes insolvent, they are not liable for its debts. A partner is personally liable for all the debts of the firm (incurred while he is a partner and sometimes even after he has ceased to be a partner).

2. Partnership law was codified by the Partnership Act 1890. In this chapter references to sections, eg 's5', denote sections of the 1890 Act unless otherwise stated. Partnership law has not changed substantially since 1890 but a knowledge of case-law which illustrates the statutory rules is useful.

3. The word 'firm' is correctly used to denote a partnership. It is not correct to apply it to a registered company (though the newspapers often do so). The word 'company' may form part of the name of a partnership firm, eg 'Smith & Company'. But 'limited company' or 'registered company' is only applied to a company incorporated under the Companies Act. You are advised to avoid using the word 'company' in connection with a partnership (and you should never use the words 'limited company' in that connection) as it may suggest to the examiner that you are unable to distinguish a partnership from a registered company.

15: PARTNERSHIP

What is a partnership?

4. In most cases there is no doubt about the existence of a partnership. The partners declare their intention by such steps as signing a written partnership agreement and adopting a firm name. But these outward and visible signs of the existence of a partnership are not essential - a partnership can exist without them. The main consequence of a partnership is that there is no separate legal person as distinct from its members.

5. A partnership exists whenever the facts satisfy the statutory definition (s1) which is:

> 'Partnership is the relation which subsists between persons carrying on a business in common with a view of profit'.

In *Pawsey v Armstrong 1881*, it was stated that the existence of a partnership is a question of fact to be determined by applying the above definition to the circumstances of each particular case. It will be noted that the above definition has three elements:

(i) there must be a business;
(ii) the business must be carried on in common;
(iii) and this must be done with a view to making a profit.

If the facts fit the definition there is a partnership even though those concerned did not realise it or expressly stated that their relationship would not be a partnership. Each of the points raised by the above definition is discussed below.

Partnership is a relationship between persons. There must be at least two partners. If therefore two men are in partnership, one dies and the survivor carries on the business he is a sole trader - there is no longer a partnership.

Carrying on a business

6. The next point in the statutory definition of a partnership is that the persons concerned are 'carrying on a business'. Business is defined to include 'every trade, occupation or profession': s45. But three points should be noted.

(a) A business is a form of activity. If two or more persons are merely the passive joint owners of revenue-producing property, such as investments or rented houses, that fact *of itself* does not make them partners: s2(1). If of course they combine shared ownership with some related form of activity, eg active management of property let to tenants, they may be partners.

(b) A business can consist of a single transaction. These situations are often described as 'joint ventures' - the partners associate solely for the purpose of completing one deal, such as a joint speculation in buying potatoes wholesale for re-sale: *Mann v D'Arcy 1968*. This can be a partnership.

(c) 'Carrying on' a business must have a beginning and an end. A partnership begins when the partners begin their business activity: it does not make any difference if they entered into a formal partnership agreement with effect from some earlier or later date. The Inland Revenue regard the opening of a partnership bank account as essential evidence of the commencement of a partnership. One cannot make a partnership exist retrospectively by agreement to that effect if there was no partnership business activity at the relevant time. The case below also illustrates the point.

Case: Spicer v Mansell 1970

M (the defendant) and another person (B) agreed to form a registered company to carry on a business. Before the company had been formed B ordered goods from S (the plaintiff) for the company. The company when formed later accepted the goods but failed to pay for them. As B could not pay S sued M alleging that until the company was formed M and B were in partnership and M was liable on the contract for goods supplied on the orders of B.

Held: in making preparations for the business to be carried on by the company later M and B were not carrying on any business themselves. Hence M was not liable for B's contract since without a business there was no partnership between them.

In common

7. To constitute a partnership the partners must also carry on business 'in common', that is by the partners themselves and/or by their agents. This causes each of the partners to be the implied agent of the other(s) for the purpose of the business and necessitates that the partners should be known to each other. Thus there can be no carrying on of a business 'in common' between strangers as this would be in conflict with that relationship of agency which is characteristic of a partnership.

With a view of profit

8. There is a partnership only if the persons associated in the business both:

   (a) intend the business to yield them a profit; and
   (b) are all entitled to a share of the profits.

   Both these points are discussed further below.

9. Traders sometimes agree to share risks (by mutual insurance) or expenses on the basis of contributing to a financial pool so much as is required to cover payments from it plus incidental expenses. This is not a partnership because there is no 'view' or intention of making a profit. But the test to be applied is one of intention. If persons enter into a partnership with a view to making profits but they actually suffer losses, it is still a partnership.

10. Unless a person is entitled to a share of the profits of a business the law is unlikely to treat him as a partner in the ordinary sense. Two issues have then to be considered:

    (a) what is meant by sharing profits;

    (b) is everyone who is entitled to a profit share to be treated as a partner liable for the firm's debts?

11. Profits are not defined. But profits are the surplus remaining after deducting from the revenue earned in a business all the expenses of running the business.

    The sharing of such net profit is *prima facie* evidence of the existence of a partnership. It is not conclusive evidence but gives rise to a presumption which places the burden of rebuttal on the party who denies the existence of a partnership. The sharing of gross returns, as distinct from net profits, is no indication of the existence of a partnership. Section 2 expressly provides that the sharing of gross returns does not *of itself* create a partnership. However, the Act does not state that such persons are never partners - they may be partners depending on the circumstances of each individual case.

Case: Cox v Coulson 1916
C agreed with M that M should put on a play in C's theatre. C was to have 60% and M 40% of the gross box office receipts. C paid the expenses of running the theatre and M paid the expenses of putting on the play. The plaintiff was a spectator who was injured when an actor in the play fired a revolver which by mischance was loaded with a live round instead of a blank cartridge. She sued C alleging that he must be liable jointly with M as M's partner.

Held: C was not a partner of M since they merely shared gross box office receipts; s2(2) expressly distinguishes this as not amounting of itself to partnership.

12. But there is profit-sharing (and can be partnership) even though the profit share is a fixed annual sum taken from the profits and not, as is more usual, a fraction of the profits such as one third or one half.

13. At one time it was considered that anyone who was entitled to a share of the profits of a business must automatically be treated as a partner in carrying it on. But s2(3) provides that receipt of a profit share does not *of itself* make the recipient a partner in each of five different situations:

    (a) a creditor who receives payment of his debt out of the profits;

    Case: Cox v Hickman 1860. A trader entered into agreements with a number of creditors whereby he was to carry on the business under their supervision, paying to them a portion of the profit by way of reducing his indebtedness.

    Held: that no partnership was of necessity created by this arrangement.

    (b) an employee who receives a share of the profits as reward for his services;

    The sharing of profits is *prima facie* evidence of partnership but this is not a conclusive test. S 2(3) and s 2(3)(b) of the Act expressly provide that a contract providing that an employee by remunerated by a share of the profits does not thereby make him a partner in the firm. It has been recognised ever since *Cox v Hickman* that the main rule to be observed in determining the existence of a partnership is that regard must be paid to the true agreement and the intention of the parties as appearing from the whole facts of the case.

    Case: David A O'Kelly v Austin Darragh 1988 (I)
    The High Court held that the receipt by a person of a share in the profits of a business is prima facie evidence that he is a partner in the business but the receipt of a share which varies with the profits of the firm does not of itself make someone a partner in the business. The Court will examine the arrangements between the parties as a whole.

    In this case the plaintiff was a key person in the defendant's drug testing unit operations but although he was entitled to a share in the profits there was insufficient evidence to hold that the plaintiff was a partner in the enterprise.

    (c) a widow or child or a deceased partner who receives an annuity out of the profits;

    (d) a person who advances money as a loan to another person engaged in a business on the basis that the lender shall receive a share of the profits instead of interest or shall receive interest at a rate varying with profits. But the terms must be expressed in a written document signed by or for them both;

    (e) a vendor of a business who receives a share of the profits as the price of the business goodwill which he has sold.

Persons in categories (d) and (e) rank as deferred creditors - sums owed to them are not paid (in insolvency) until the firm has paid its other creditors in full.

Partner by holding out

14. A person can become liable for the debts of a business as if he were a partner if (without receiving any share of the profits) he represents or allows someone else to represent that he is a partner: s14. The most common example of this situation is the 'salaried partner' - one who receives a set salary instead of a fluctuating profit share. It can arise on the retirement of a partner. But it can also result from any representation or holding out. This rule is an example of estoppel - if you mislead someone or know that someone has been led by others to believe that you are a partner and you leave him under that impression, you may not escape liability by denying it after he has acted on it.

Case: Martyn v Gray 1863
G went down to Cornwall to discuss a possible investment in a tin mine. His host introduced him to a creditor as 'a gentleman down from London, a man of capital'. The creditor later sued G as a partner of the miner.

Held: although it was oblique the introduction amounted to a representation that G was in partnership with the tin-miner and so he was liable for a debt incurred subsequent to the introduction. He should have made the true position clear by correcting the impression made.

15. A 'partner by holding out' is only liable for the debts of the business as if he were a partner. Within the firm he is not actually a partner and so he cannot claim any rights, eg to share in the profits or management of the business. He is only liable for money lent to the business or debts incurred after the representation has been made. He is not bound by any non-financial obligations of the firm as s14 refers to liability for 'credit given'.

Salaried partner

16. In professional firms it has been common practice to include in the list of partners on the firm's letterhead the names of professionally qualified employees who are not partners in the true sense and who do not usually receive any share of the profits. This is a representation that such employees are partners. It makes them liable for the firm's debts but it does not make them partners within the firm.

17. Alternatively it can happen that a true partner takes his share of the profits as a fixed annual sum. He is in this case a partner for all purposes.

Sleeping partner

18. A *sleeping partner* (which is a colloquial term not used in the 1890 Act) is a person who merely contributes capital and takes a share of the profits without participating in the management of the business. He is liable for the firm's debts as a partner even if that was not the intention. It is immaterial that he takes no part in the management of the business (provided that the business is carried on 'in common' for all the partners).

Firm name

19. A partnership is no more than a group of individual partners. Unlike a company it is not a separate entity distinct from its members, but the members in a partnership are known collectively as a 'firm' and may sue and be sued in the firm's name. Section 4 provides 'that persons who have entered into a partnership with one another are for the purposes of this Act called collectively a firm and the name under which their business is carried on is called the

firm's name'. The partners may select any name but it must not be too similar to that of another partnership or company otherwise it may be restrained by injunction. The provisions of the Registration of Business Names Act 1963, the purpose of which is to make public who is carrying on business under a given name, requires the partnership to register the business name, the nature of the business and the date of adoption of the name. Registration under the Business Names Act does not give a partnership any protection other than it may be used as evidence in a passing-off action.

● **Partnership agreement**

20. The agreement made between the partners is a species of contract and as such must be made in accordance with the general law of contract. Thus:

(i)   there must be a concluded agreement intended to create legal obligations;
(ii) the parties must have capacity to contract;
(iii) the agreement must not be illegal.

There is no legal requirement for a written partnership agreement. A partnership may be established without formality by oral agreement or even by conduct. But in practice there are advantages in setting down in writing (signed by the partners) the terms of their association. This is called a 'partnership agreement' or 'articles of partnership'. It fills in the details which the law would not imply - the nature of the firm's business, the firm name, and the bank at which the firm will maintain its bank account. Secondly, a written agreement serves to override terms otherwise implied by the Partnership Act 1890 which are inappropriate to the partnership. The Act for example implies (unless otherwise agreed) that partners share profits equally. But in many firms the older partners take a larger profit share than the younger ones.

The agreement may also be in the form of a deed under seal.

As regards capacity to contract, every person is presumed to be competent to enter into a partnership except minors and persons of unsound mind. 'Person' includes a corporation such as a registered company as well as a natural person, companies can therefore enter into partnership with each other or with individuals but such arrangements are not very common and partners are usually individuals.

The agreement may be void because of illegality. It may, for example, be illegal on account of the nature of the association (any association registered as a company cannot be also a partnership) or on account of the objects of the association. One should also note that the standard maximum number of partners permitted by law is 20: s 376 CA 63 as amended by s 13 C(A)A 82. The intention of this rule is that if more than 20 persons wish to carry on a commercial business they should form a registered company for that purpose. As professional practice cannot usually be carried on by a registered company, solicitors, and accountants are permitted to form partnerships with any number of partners. Section 13(2) C(A)A 82 permits the Minister for Enterprise and Employment by order to disapply the 20 partner limit to partnerships of a description specified in the order.

21. Some of the matters for which provision is required to be made in the Articles of Partnership are provided for by the Act. It is, of course, not strictly necessary to provide for such matters unless it is desired to exclude or modify the rules contained in the Act; however it is usual to include the provisions required to exclude the application of the Act and also to include matters covered by the Act where it is desired to make these particularly applicable. The form and content of the Articles will naturally vary in accordance with the type of business or profession concerned.

The articles are of an elastic nature and their terms may be varied from time to time though, until an agreement to vary is proved, they form the basis of the relationship of the partners to one another. In this connection, s 19 provides that 'the mutual rights and duties of partners, whether ascertained by agreement or defined by this Act, may be varied by the consent of all the partners and such consent may be either expressed or inferred from a course of dealing.'

An agreement to vary the terms of the articles may, therefore, be implied from the conduct of the partners, eg where the articles provide that profits are to be shared equally, evidence that they have in fact been shared unequally, will be accepted as proof of agreement to vary the terms of the articles. It should be noted that s 19 applies whatever form the articles may take. Thus articles which are in writing or *under seal* may be varied by consent of all the partners or by conduct of the partners in following a course of dealing which would estop them from denying the truth and validity of their acts.

In general the following matters are covered in almost all types of partnership agreement:

(a) The names of the partners.

(b) The date on which the partnership began and its expiry date (or how much notice must be given to terminate an agreement of unspecified duration).

(c) The nature of the firm's business, its firm name and principal place of business.

(d) How much capital each partner is to contribute, how profits or losses are to be shared (including 'interest' on capital and 'salaries' for working partners as allocations of profit), at which bank the firm is to maintain its bank account, partners' authority to sign cheques, how much each partner may draw monthly as an advance against his share of profits, and provision for retaining profits in a tax reserve account.

   It should be noted that *prima facie* all partners are (i) entitled to share the assets (after payment of partnership debts and returns of capital) equally although they may have contributed to the capital unequally: s 21 and s 44 and (ii) entitled to share profits and losses equally unless there is agreement, express or implied, to the contrary: s 24(1).

(e) The taking and keeping of accounts to show how the firm stands with third parties (ie outsiders) and how each partner stands with the firm, particularly as regards drawings.

(f) Auditors to the partnership.

(g) A list of the principal assets, such as office premises, which are partnership property.

(h) Powers and duties of partners in the management of the partnership. In the absence of agreement to the contrary, s 24 provides that each partner is entitled to take part in the management of the business.

(i) Whether the partners are to work full-time and any limits imposed on their business interests and activities outside the firm.

(j) Partners' meetings (including matters on which a unanimous not a majority decision is required).

(k) Acts which partners cannot do without the consent of the other partners.

(l) The effect of retirement or death of a partner, eg the partnership not to be dissolved but to continue between the surviving partners; the former partner to be repaid his capital, with interest pending repayment, by instalments over a period.

(m) Dissolution of the firm - provision for dissolution in the absence of agreement between the partners.

(n) Powers of expulsion - s 25 prohibits a majority of partners from expelling a partner unless power to do so has been expressly provided for.

(o) Valuation of shares and goodwill on the death or retirement of a partner, or on the introduction of a new partner or on any other partnership changes.

(p) Introduction of new partners - this must be specifically agreed upon as, under the Act, partners cannot be forced to accept a new partner.

(q) Pensions to retiring partners, annuities to spouses of deceased partners.

(r) Provisions dealing with transfers of interests to third parties.

(s) Provision for submission of disputes between partners to private arbitration (to avoid damaging publicity in a law suit).

● **Relationship of partners to outsiders dealing with the firm**

Power of a partner to bind the firm

22. Partnership is really nothing more than an extension of the law of agency and even before the Partnership Act the common law had endowed each partner with authority to bind the firm (ie himself and his fellow partners) by acts done in the usual course of the partnership business.

The law of agency distinguishes *actual* authority of an agent, which is exercised where an agent makes a contract which he is authorised to make and *apparent or ostensible* authority which is an authority which the agent appears to others to hold.

The Partnership Act 1890 defines the apparent authority of a partner to make contracts as follows:

> 'Every partner is an agent of the firm and his other partners for the purpose of the business of the partnership; and the acts of every partner who does any act for carrying on in the usual way business of the kind carried on by the firm of which he is a member bind the firm and his partners, unless the partner so acting has in fact no authority to act for the firm in the particular matter, and the person with whom he is dealing either knows that he has no authority, or does not know or believe him to be a partner': s 5.

The Act also states that the partnership is only bound by acts done by a partner in the firm's name and not apparently for the partners personally; ss 6 and 7.

23. The latter part of s 5 quoted above makes it clear that the partners can restrict the authority of an individual partner to less than it would otherwise be provided that they give notice of the restriction. If for example the partners give a mandate to their bank which requires that cheques exceeding a specified amount should be signed by at least two partners that express restriction overrides the normal apparent authority of a single partner to sign cheques of any amount. But if the partnership agreement imposes such a restriction and no notice of it (by mandate, production of the agreement to the bank or otherwise) is given to the bank the bank is entitled to rely on the partner's apparent authority to draw cheques of any amount even though (unknown to the bank) his actual authority is more restricted.

24. Although s 5 may seem very wide it does in fact restrict a partner's apparent authority as agent in certain respects:

    (a) what he does must be related to 'business of the kind carried on by the firm'; and

    (b) it must be what a single partner usually does in 'carrying on in the usual way' business of that kind; and

    (c) he must act in the firm's name not his own: s6.

25. Sometimes a single partner enters into a transaction which the other partners wish to repudiate on the ground that it is outside the limits of the kind of business which the firm has agreed to carry on. It is indeed usual to specify in a partnership agreement what is the nature of the firm's business. But unless the person with whom a partner deals is aware of the agreed limits he may hold the firm bound by an transaction which would appear to him (and other outsiders) to be the kind of business which such a firm ordinarily carries on.

Case: Mercantile Credit Co Ltd v Garrod 1962
Two partners had entered into a partnership agreement for the business of letting of garages and repairing cars. The agreement expressly excluded the buying and selling of cars. One partner, without the knowledge of the other, purported to sell a car, to which neither he nor the partnership had any title, to the plaintiff for £700, which was in fact paid into the partnership account. The plaintiff claimed that the partnership was liable as the 'sale' of the car was an act done within the scope of the partnership business.

Held: the partnership was liable because, in selling the car, the partner 'was doing an act of a like kind to the business carried on by persons trading as a garage', despite the express clause in the agreement.

What a single partner has apparent authority to do

26. The second test of s5 is that a partner is agent of the firm in carrying on the firm's business 'in the usual way'. What is usual in any particular business must always depend partly on the general practice of businesses of a similar type and size. In particular a distinction is made between commercial firms which trade in buying and selling goods and non-commercial firms (including of course professional partnerships) which do not do so. Judicial decisions warrant the view that a single partner of either type of firm (acting on behalf of the firm and within the apparent limits of its kind of business) is deemed to have the authority of the other partners to engage in any of the following transactions:

    (a) to sell the goods on chattels of the firm;
    (b) to buy on account of the firm goods of a kind necessary for or usually employed in its business;
    (c) to receive payment of the debts due to the firm and give receipts or releases therefor;

(d)   to engage employees to work in the firm's business; it may be that a single partner may only dismiss an employee with the consent of his co-partners;

(e)   to employ a solicitor to defend actions taken against the firm; it is not certain whether a single partner may engage a solicitor to take an action on behalf of the firm;

(f)   to sign cheques drawn on the firm's bank account.

27.   In addition to the above powers, a single partner in a commercial partnership would normally have apparent authority to engage in any of the following activities:

(a)   to draw, issue, accept, transfer and endorse bills of exchange and other negotiable instruments in the name of the firm (such apparent authority would also extend to a partner in a non-commercial partnership, such as a banking partnership, where it would be usual for a partner to have such power). It was *held* in *Higgins v Beauchamp 1914* that the acceptance by a partner of an inchoate bill of exchange, lacking the drawer's name, was sufficiently unusual to put such acceptance beyond the usual way of carrying on business so that the firm was not bound;

(b)   to borrow money on the credit of the firm;

(c)   to pledge the firm's goods as security:

Case: Higgins v Beauchamp 1914
B and M carried on business in partnership as cinema proprietors. B was a sleeping partner. The partnership agreement expressly prohibited a partner from borrowing on the credit of the firm. M borrowed money from H in breach (unknown to H) of that restriction. H sued B to recover the money.

Held: the business was not a commercial or trading business since it did not buy and sell goods. M therefore had no apparent authority to borrow money for the firm. M was not the agent of B and hence H could not recover from B.

(d)   to create an equitable mortgage by deposit of the title deeds of the firm's land and/or buildings to secure any borrowings.

28.   No partner, whether in a commercial partnership or not, has apparent authority to do any of the following:

(a)   to bind his firm by deed in the absence of express authority under seal, ie a power of attorney executed by all the partners. Thus, in the absence of a power of attorney, a single partner has no power to execute a legal mortgage in respect of partnership property;

(b)   to bind the firm by giving, in the firm's name, a guarantee of another's debt;

(c)   to accept shares in a company, even if fully paid up, in satisfaction of a debt owed to the firm;

(d)   to bind the firm by the submission of a dispute to arbitration.

With regard to (a) above, the position at common law is that an agent cannot bind his principal by the execution of a deed unless authorised to do so by deed executed by his principal and by virtue of s6, this rule applies to partners who are agents of the firm so that the firm will not be bound by a deed executed by one partner unless he has been duly authorised to do so. *Harrison v Jackson 1797* is authority for stating that the fact that the partnership agreement itself is under seal will not suffice. However, there are exceptions where the firm will be bound by deeds executed without power of attorney:

(i)   where it has been executed by authority and in the presence of all the partners, they will be estopped from denying their consent;

(ii) where the transaction need not have been made by a deed.

It should be observed that there is no converse rule that a firm is the agent of the individual partners, thus payment to the firm will not operate to discharge a debt due personally to a partner unless he has authorised the firm to receive the payment on his behalf.

Liability of the firm for contracts entered into on its behalf

29.   The liability of the firm and partners as the result of the acts of a partner is governed by sections 6 to 9. The fundamental rule is laid down in s 6 which provides that: 'An act or instrument relating to the business of the firm and done or executed in the firm-name, or in any other manner showing an intention to bind the firm, by any person thereto authorised, whether a partner or not, is binding on the firm and all the partners.'

Beckham v Drake 1841
Two partners of the firm entered into a written agreement to employ the plaintiff.

Held: that a third sleeping partner could be sued along with the active partners for breach of the agreement.

There is a proviso to s 6 which preserves the general rule of law relating to the execution of deeds or negotiable instruments and is discussed in para 28 above.

Section 7 provides that a firm will not be bound where a partner pledges the credit of the firm for a purpose apparently not connected with the firm's ordinary course of business unless the partner is in fact specially authorised by the other partners. Thus a firm will not be bound by where eg a partner gives a negotiable instrument or other security in the name of the firm to raise money for his private use or to pay a private debt to the knowledge of the party providing the money.

Case: Shirreff v Wilks 1800
Two of the partners in a three partner firm accepted a bill of exchange in the name of the firm in respect of a debt incurred before the third partner had joined the partnership.

Held: the third partner was not bound because the transaction was tantamount to the situation where a single partner pledges the firm's credit for his private purposes.

However, if the outsider knows the transaction in question is not for a partnership purpose he cannot recover from the firm.

Case: Kendall v Wood 1870
The plaintiff's partner, without authority, appropriated £1,000 of partnership funds to the payment of a private debt owed to the defendant.

Held: the defendant could not retain the money as the plaintiff had neither authorised the payment nor led the defendant to suppose that his partner had the necessary authority to so use partnership money.

Section 8 provides that where an outsider dealing with the firm has notice of an agreement between the partners which places a restriction on the power of any of them to bind the firm, the firm will not be bound by an act done in contravention of such agreement.

If a firm is fixed with liability, eg as a result of an act of a partner, then the rule in *Kendall v Hamilton 1879* impose on all the partners a joint obligation to discharge that liability except in the case of a partner who has died, in which event his estate is also severally liable. This rule was given statutory effect by s 9.

Liability of the firm in tort

30. Section 10 sets out the general rule governing the liability of the firm in tort.

   'Where, by any wrongful act or omission of any partner acting in the ordinary course of the business of the firm, or with the authority of his co-partners, loss or injury is caused to any person not being a partner in the firm, or any penalty is incurred, the firm is liable therefor to the same extent as the partner so acting or omitting to act.'

   Where the wrongful act is authorised by all the partners the firm will be primarily liable for the loss or injury resulting from that wrongful act. However, where a partner does a wrongful act without the authority of his fellow partners then the firm will not be liable unless the wrongful act was done 'in the ordinary course of the business of the firm' - a question of fact to be decided in each case.

   Case: Hamlyn v Houston & Co 1903
   Unknown to his sleeping partner, the active partner in a firm bribed a clerk in a rival firm to disclose confidential information.

   Held: both partners were liable. It was not illegal for a firm to seek information about a competitor and such activity would be in the ordinary course of business for a firm. The firm was liable because the active partner had used a wrongful means of doing what he was otherwise entitled lawfully to do in the ordinary course of business and it did not matter that he had no authority to act as he did.

   The extent to which a wrongful act will be considered to have been done in the ordinary course of business will depend on the facts of the case in question.

   Case: Meekins v Henson 1964
   A letter defamatory of the plaintiff was published on an occasion which was protected by qualified privilege. The letter had been signed by partner A on behalf of himself and his two partners, B and C. C had been motivated by malice on the occasion.

   Held: A and B were not liable to the plaintiff. Because liability was personal to the partners, C alone was held to be liable.

   It may be observed that a firm may be held liable for the wrongful act of a partner whether or not it benefitted by the act.

   Whereas s 10 is of general application, s 11 is concerned specifically with the misapplication of money or property received for or in the custody of the firm. Section 11 provides that the firm is liable to make good the loss (a) where one partner, acting within the scope of his apparent authority, receives the money or property of a third person and misapplies it, and (b) where a firm, in the course of its business, receives money or property of a third person and it is misapplied by one or more of the partners while it is in the custody of the firm.

   In sub-section (a) it is the *same* partner who is responsible for receiving the money or property and for its misapplication before it has come into the custody of the firm, whereas sub-section (b) covers a misapplication by *any* partner of money or property after it has come into the custody of the firm.

In (a) the liability of the firm depends on whether or not the partner was acting within the scope of his apparent authority when he received the money or property. It may be observed that receipt by a partner acting within the scope of his apparent authority will normally constitute a receipt by the firm in the course of its business so that in practice there will be little difference between the situations envisaged in (a) and (b).

Case: Blair v Bromley 1847
A client of a firm of solicitors handed over a sum of money to be invested in specific securities to one of the partners who in fact misappropriated it to his own use. His fellow partner was quite unaware of this transaction.

Held: the 'innocent' partner was liable to make good the loss because it had been established that it was within the ordinary course of business for a solicitor to receive money to invest in specific securities.

Where, however, money has been received with a general discretion about its investment, the firm may escape liability.

Case: Harman v Johnson 1853
A client gave money to one partner of a firm of solicitors with general instructions to invest it for him. The partner misappropriated the money. His fellow partner was unaware of the transaction.

Held: the 'innocent' partner was not liable as it was not within the ordinary course of business of a firm of solicitors to receive money for the purpose of general investment.

The court indicated in *Harman v Johnson* that if it had been shown that the money was given to the defaulting solicitor for the purpose of its being invested in some specific security, his partner would have been liable. This principle was recognised in *Earl of Dundonald v Masterson 1869* where the court *held* that it was 'surely within the ordinary everyday practice of a firm of solicitors . . . to receive money for any specific purpose connected with the professional business which they have in hand.'

It should be noted that an 'innocent' partner may escape liability if he can show that the injured party had dealt with the defaulting partner in his personal capacity and not as a partner in the firm.

Case: British Homes Assurance Corp. v Paterson 1902
A third party, having been informed that the solicitor with whom he had been dealing, had taken another solicitor into partnership, chose to ignore the existence of the partnership and insisted in dealing with him only.

Held: the firm was not liable as the third party had elected to deal with the defaulting partner as principal and not as an agent for the firm.

Note that even though the act in question may be outside the apparent authority of a partner or unconnected with the ordinary course of business, this will not necessarily give automatic exemption from liability.

Case: Polkinghorne v Holland 1934
A client of a firm of solicitors lost his money when, on the advice of one of the partners, he invested it in the shares of two companies.

Held: the firm was liable. The court accepted that solicitors had no special skill in the valuation of shares and that it was not in the course of their professional duties to advise on such matters. However the court indicated if a solicitor is consulted on a matter outside his expertise he ought to make this clear to the client and make such inquiries and take such outside professional advise as may be necessary to as to be able to furnish the client with such facts and information as will enable him to form a judgment of his own in the matter.

Section 12 provides that every partner is liable jointly with his co-partners and also severally for everything for which the firm, while he is a partner therein, become liable under either s 10 or s 11. What this means is that a victim of a tort may sue any or all of the partners, in separate actions if necessary, until he recovers the entire amount of compensation to which he is entitled. This joint and several liability of the partners in tort may be contrasted with their joint liability in contract (the rule in *Kendall v Hamilton*) where there is only one cause of action and thus if the plaintiff has sued one partner and recovered judgment, he is precluded from bringing a subsequent action against any other partner if the judgment remains unsatisfied.

• Liability of incoming and outgoing partners

31. The general rule is that a person is only liable in respect of partnership liabilities incurred while he is a partner, ie he is not liable for things done before he became a partner or after he has died or retired from the firm.

There are three events to be considered here - (i) death of a partner (ii) retirement of a partner and (iii) the admission of a new partner.

32. The <u>death of a partner</u> may itself dissolve the partnership (s33 so provides unless otherwise agreed) but it is usual to avoid this inconvenient result by expressly agreeing that so long as there are two or more surviving partners the partnership shall continue between them - though the deceased partner ceases to be a partner. The estate of a deceased partner is liable for debts of the partnership incurred before but not after his death.

Case: Meagher v Meagher 1961 (I)
Where partnership assets increase in value after the death of a partner and before realisation such increase is profit and the deceased partner's personal representatives are entitled to an appropriate share thereof.

Retirement

33. Section 17(2) provides that a partner who retires remains liable for partnership debts or obligations incurred *before* his retirement. Section 17(3) envisages a situation whereby a retiring partner can be freed from such liabilities. It provides that 'a retiring partner may be discharged from any existing liabilities, by an agreement to that effect between himself and the members of the firm as newly constituted and the creditors, and this agreement may be either express or inferred as a fact from the course of dealing between the creditors and the firm as newly constituted.' Such an agreement is referred to as a contract of *novation* and must be supported by valuable consideration unless it is by deed under seal.

An agreement between the retiring partner and the partners in the newly constituted firm (ie the continuing partners plus any new ones) that the latter will assume liability for the firm's existing obligations will not give any right to a creditor to recover from the new partners or deprive him of a right to recover from the partners in the old firm (including the retiring partner) unless the creditor has agreed to accept the new firm as his debtor and to discharge the old firm from its liability to him.

Case: Bilborough v Homes 1876
A banking firm originally consisting of two partners, advised its customers that two new partners were joining the firm. Subsequently one of the original partners died, a fact which was known to the depositors who continued to receive interest on their deposits. The firm went bankrupt and depositors sought to recover from the estate of the partner who had died.

Held: the course of dealing between the depositors and the firm after the death of the partner amounted to a 'complete novation' and they could not recover from the deceased partner's estate for the loss of their deposits.

34. As regards the liability of a retiring partner for partnership debts or obligations incurred *after* his retirement, section 36(1) provides that 'where a person deals with a firm after a change in its constitution he is entitled to treat all apparent members of the old firm as still being members of the firm until he has notice of the change.' Section 36(2) provides that a notice in *Iris Oifigiú il* of his retirement will be effective against persons who have had no previous dealings with the firm and section 36(3) provides that a retiring partner will not be liable to a person dealing with the firm who was not aware that he was a partner (before his retirement).

The leading case in this area is:

Case: Tower Cabinet Co v Ingram 1949
The firm consisted of two partners, A and B. The partnership was dissolved with B's retirement and A continued the business under the firm of 'Merry's' and undertook to notify customers that B had retired. In fact no notice was published in the London Gazette and no alteration was notified to the Registrar of Business Names, but new notepaper was printed which omitted B's name. Some months after B had retired, the plaintiffs, who had had no previous dealings with Merry's, received an order which, in error, was written on the old notepaper, which of course listed B as a partner.

Held: B was not liable to the plaintiff because (a) he was not known to the plaintiff as a partner prior to the date of his retirement and was therefore under no obligation to give notice in any form to those who might learn, after his retirement, that he had been a member of the firm - s 36(3) applied; (b) he had not knowingly allowed A to hold him out as a partner under s 14 and (c) the fact that his name still appeared in the Business Names Register was irrelevant because the plaintiff had not searched the register.

35. To avoid being still an 'apparent member' of the firm after his retirement the retiring partner should give notice of his retirement:

    (a) to creditors who had dealings with the firm while he was a partner, he should give actual notice of his retirement. This need not been an express notice. If for example the firm reprints its letterhead to omit him from the list of partners and writes a letter on the new letterhead to a creditor that is sufficient notice to the creditor of the change;

    (b) to persons who may have known that he is a partner (before his retirement) but who begin to have dealings with the firm for the first time after his retirement, the retired partner cannot easily give actual notice since he does not know (at his retirement) who they may prove to be. But sufficient notice is given to them if he advertises the fact of his retirement in the Iris Oifigiú il: s36(2). They are then deemed to have notice even if they have not read the advertisement.

But *Tower Cabinet* is authority for stating that a creditor, who has not had previous dealing with a firm or knowledge of its constitution, cannot hold a retired partner liable for debts incurred by the firm after he has retired, even if no notice, in any form, of his retirement is given. The fact that a creditor may subsequently learn that a person had been a partner is irrelevant because the date from which s 36(3) operates is from the date the person retired from the firm. 'If at the date of the dissolution the person who subsequently deals with the firm had no knowledge at or before that time that the retiring partner was a partner, then sub-section 3 comes into operation, and relieves the person retiring from liability.'

36. The normal procedure when a partner retires is that the retiring partner, the continuing partners and any new partner agree that the continuing and new partners will assume liability for all outstanding debts (but this does not affect the rights of creditors unless they agree) that they will indemnify the retired partner and that the necessary action will be taken to give notice of his retirement. He is not liable for what they may do without his knowledge and consent.

Case: Williams v Harris 1980 (I)
The partnership agreement provided that if one partner retired his shares should be purchased by the other partners in proportion to their stake in the business. It also provided that the shares should belong to the remaining partners from the date of retirement. The plaintiff retired in 1976 and his shares were not evaluated until 1978. The retiring partner claimed interest on the value of his shares from the date of his retirement.

Held: the Supreme Court took the view that the provisions of the partnership agreement superseded any provisions in the 1890 Act. The agreement made no provision for interest payment in the event of a delay by the partners in buying out the shares and therefore the court had no power to award interest.

37. A new partner admitted to an existing firm is liable for debts incurred after he becomes a partner. Section 17(1) provides that a new partner will not be liable to creditors of the firm for anything done before he became a partner. Of course he may agree with the old partners to make himself liable but a creditor could not rely on such an agreement to recover from the new partner unless there is a contract of novation, ie where the creditor has agreed with old and new partners to accept the newly constituted firm as his debtor in place of the old.

● **The relationship of partners with each other**

38. The rights and duties of partners *'inter se'* (ie between themselves) depend mainly upon the terms of their agreement as defined in the articles of partnership, but in the absence of agreement to the contrary, s 24 of the Act regulates the internal affairs of the partners.

39. Management - subject to contrary agreement every partner is entitled to access to partnership books (s 24(9)) and may take part in the management of the business: s 24 (5). At common law there is an implied obligation on each partner to participate in the management of the firm and a partners' failure to do so may be a ground for dissolution: *Airey v Borham 1861*.

In the absence of agreement to the contrary, a partner is not entitled to remuneration for acting in the partnership business: s 24(6).

Interpreting s 24(5) and (6), the courts have held that a partner's right to share in profits is not normally conditional upon the due performance by him of his duties to the business and that a partner cannot claim compensation for extra work done by him because of the inattention to the business by another partner. However it has been held that inattention to business may be a ground for dissolution and that upon dissolution the aggrieved partner may be entitled to compensation for extra work performed by him.

Decisions on ordinary matters connected with the partnership business are by a majority of the general partners. If there is a deadlock the view of those opposing any change will prevail, but unanimity is required for matters relating to the constitution of the firm, for example to change the nature of the partnership business or to admit a new partner: s 24(8).

40. <u>Profits and losses</u> - are shared equally in the absence of contrary agreement. However if the partnership agreement states that profits are to be shared in certain proportions then, prima facie, losses are to be shared in the same proportions: s 24(1).

    No interest is paid on capital except by agreement: s 24(4). However, a partner is entitled to 5% interest on advances beyond his original capital: s 24(3).

41. The firm must <u>indemnify</u> any partner against <u>liabilities</u> incurred in the ordinary and proper conduct of the partnership business, or in doing anything necessarily done for the preservation of the partnership property or business: s 24(2).

    No person may be introduced as a partner without the consent of all existing partners: s 24(7).

Partnership property

42. Whether or not property is partnership property is a question of fact dependent upon the precise circumstances of each case; but s 20 specifies 3 tests which may be expressed as follows :

    (a) was the property originally brought into the partnership stock?
    (b) was it acquired on account of the firm?
    (c) was it acquired for the purposes and in the course of the firm's business?

    If any one of these questions can be answered in the affirmative the property is partnership property but the answers must depend entirely upon the particular circumstances of each case.

    The *initial* property of the partnership is that which the partners expressly or impliedly agreed shall be partnership property. It is quite possible that property used in the business is not partnership property but is the sole property of one of the partners; it depends entirely on the intention of the partners.

    Property *afterwards* acquired is governed by the same principle, but property bought with partnership money is *prima facie* evidence that it is purchased on account of the firm: s 21.

    Case: Miles v Clarke 1953
    A photographer had a business with premises and equipment and he decided to take in a partner. After some time difficulties arose which necessitated dissolution.

    Held: that all the assets, excluding the stock of films used in the business, remained those of the partner bringing them in.

Expulsion of a partner

43. In the absence of agreement to the contrary, no partner can be expelled from the firm without his consent. Section 25 provides that 'no majority of the partners can expel any partner unless a power to do so has been conferred by express agreement between the partners.' Where the majority have been given such power it must be exercised in good faith and it may be restrained by injunction if used for an ulterior motive.

Case: Blisset v Daniel 1853
The articles empowered a two-thirds majority to expel a partner and also gave the remaining partners a right to buy his share at a certain valuation.

Held: it was not a *bona fide* exercise of the power to expel a partner merely in order to buy up his share.

Where it is intended to expel a partner he must be given a reasonable opportunity to defend himself.

Partners' shares and assignment

44. A partner's share or interest is defined as 'the proportion of the then existing partnership assets to which he would be entitled if the whole were realised and converted into money and after all the then existing debts and liabilities of the firm had been discharged.' A partner's share is an asset which may be assigned in which event the position of the assignee is as follows:

    (a) He does not thereby automatically become a partner as s 24(7) provides that a new partner cannot be introduced without the consent of all existing partners.

    (b) He is not entitled to interfere in the management of the firm or require accounts or inspect the books - only on dissolution is he entitled to an account from the date of dissolution for the purpose of ascertaining his share of the assets.

    (c) He is bound by the partnership articles and also by any subsequent agreements between the partners.

    Case: Re Garwood's Trusts 1903
    The firm had 3 partners, none of whom received a salary. One partner charged his share to trustees. The remaining partners then agreed that each of them should receive a salary and that the partner who had allowed his share to be charged should receive no salary. Trustees sought to have the payment of salaries set aside.

    Held: that the payments were in order and binding on the trustees for s 31 provides that an assignee cannot interfere in the management or administration of the business.

    (d) He is entitled to the assignor's share of the profits and his share on dissolution of any distribution of capital. The assignee usually promises the assignor to be responsible for the latter's liabilities both to the firm and to outsiders.

Good faith

45. A partnership agreement is one of those contracts where the duty of utmost good faith *(uberrimae fidei)* is required of the parties to it, ie good faith and mutual trust is essential to the relationship between partners. The duties of partners in this regard are found in ss 28, 29 and 30 of the Act.

    By s 28 partners are bound to render *true accounts* and full information on all matters affecting the partnership to any partner or his legal representatives.

    By s 29 a partner being an agent of the firm must not make a *secret profit* out of the firm's transactions and is accountable for any benefit obtained by him, without the consent of the other partners, from using the firm's property, name or trade connections.

Case: Pathirana v Pathirana 1967
The plaintiff and his brother were Caltex petrol retailers. A disagreement arose and one of the brothers served 3 months notice of dissolution and requested Caltex to change the agency to him alone. He then proceeded to trade in his own name.

Held: the defendant was obliged to account to his brother for the profits so made and the plaintiff was entitled to his share.

Case: Bentley v Craven 1853
Bentley and Craven were partners in a firm of sugar merchants. Craven was also in business on his own account as a sugar refiner and this was known to his partner who made no objection.; Craven was employed by the firm to buy sugar for the firm and without the knowledge of his partner he sold his own sugar to the firm at the market price and made a considerable profit.

Held: defendant must account to the firm for the profit made.

Section 30 provides that a partner cannot compete in a business of the same nature with that of the firm without the consent of his partners. To be in breach of this section the business must be of the same nature as that carried on by the firm and it must actually compete with the firm's business.

● Dissolution

46. Basically there are 3 ways to dissolve a partnership:

    (a) by mutual agreement;
    (b) by operation of law;
    (c) by order of the Court.

Mutual agreement

47. The partnership agreement will usually provide for dissolution but the agreement may be overridden by mutual agreement (s 19) and thus the partnership may be dissolved at any time by the consent of all the partners.

Operation of law

48. Section 32 provides that subject to any agreement between the partners, a partnership is dissolved:

    (a) if entered into for a fixed term, by expiration of that term;
    (b) if entered into for a single adventure or undertaking, by the termination of that adventure or undertaking;
    (c) if entered into for an undefined time, by any partner giving notice to the other partner(s) of this intention to dissolve the partnership.

In (a) the partnership will end without any positive or formal act by any of the partners but it may end sooner by eg the death of a partner or if the partnership agreement provides for prior determination. Partners who continue in business after the expiration of a fixed term become partners at will (s 27) and any partner may give notice to terminate at any time (s 26).In (c) the partnership is dissolved as from the date of dissolution mentioned in the notice, or if no date is mentioned, as from the date of communication of the notice.

Case: McLeod v Dowling 1927
Two solicitors formed a partnership for a fixed term of 7 years. The term expired and the partnership continued without any new agreement. Plaintiff sought to dissolve the partnership by giving notice under s 32(c) to his partner who died before receiving it.

Held: the partnership was dissolved by the death of the partner and not by the notice with the result that the plaintiff was entitled to the entire business and goodwill as provided for in the partnership agreement instead of being confined to an equal share on dissolution which would have been the case had the notice taken effect.

Section 33 provides that, subject to any agreement between the partners, every partnership is dissolved by the death (see *McLeod v Dowling*) or bankruptcy of a partner. The partnership may also be dissolved, at the option of the other partner(s), if a partner suffers his share of the partnership property to be charged under the Partnership Act for his separate debt.

Section 34 provides that a partnership is dissolved by the happening of any event which makes it unlawful:

(a) for the business of the firm to be carried on; or
(b) for the members of the firm to carry it on in partnership.

Situation (a) could occur, eg where a partner is an enemy alien in time of war; (b) envisages the situation where the business may be lawful in itself but those who are partners must comply with certain requirements or possess certain qualifications.

Order of the Court

49. Section 35 permits a partner, but not a creditor, to apply to the court for a decree of dissolution of the partnership. The section provides six grounds on which the court may, in its discretion, give such decree:

(a) insanity of a partner (but not if he is a limited partner unless his share cannot be ascertained by any method other than dissolution);
(b) when a partner, other than the partner sueing, becomes in any other way permanently incapable of performing his part of the partnership contract;
(c) when a partner, other than the partner sueing, has been guilty of such conduct as, in the opinion of the court, regard being had to the nature of the business, is calculated to affect prejudically the carrying on of the business;
(d) when a partner, other than the partner sueing, wilfully or persistently commits a breach of the partnership agreement, or otherwise so conducts himself in matters relating to the partnership business that it is not reasonably practicable for the other partner(s) to carry on the business in partnership with him;
(e) when the business of the partnership can only be carried on at a loss;
(f) whenever in any case, circumstances have arisen which, in the opinion of the court, render it just and equitable that the partnership be dissolved.

The conduct envisaged in (c) may relate to the business itself.

Case: Essel v Hayward 1860
Held: that, where one partner in a firm of solicitors had become liable to a criminal prosecution for embezzling trust moneys, his co-partner was entitled to have the partnership dissolved although the partnership was not one at will.

Also envisaged in (c) is conduct which may have no direct connection with the business but nonetheless may affect it, eg where a partner is convicted of some criminal offence, unrelated to the business, but which makes it impossible or undesirable for his continuance as a partner.

The following situations have been held sufficient to justify a dissolution under (d): the keeping of erroneous accounts and the failure to enter receipts into the partnership books *(Cheesman v Price 1865);* refusal to meet on matters of business, continued quarrelling and such a state of animosity as precludes all reasonable hope of reconciliation and friendly co-operation *(Baxter v West 1858).*

With regard to (e), it is not necessary to show that the firm is approaching insolvency, it is sufficient to show that, to all intents and purposes, the business cannot generate a profit, the expectation of which must be implied into partnership. However the fact that the partnership assets will be insufficient to repay the partners after paying off the firm's debts and outside liabilities would not be, in itself, a ground for applying to the court to have the partnership dissolved.

It is impossible to specify all the acts and circumstances which would enable the court to order dissolution on the wide ground that it is 'just and equitable' to do so: 'the court ought not to fetter itself by any rigid rules; and any case in which it is no longer reasonably practicable to attain the object with a view to which the partnership was entered into or to carry out the partnership contract according to its terms will, it is apprehended, be within this section' ie s 35(f): *Lindley on Partnership.* See Chapter 11 for cases where registered companies, which were, in substance, partnerships, were ordered to be wound up pursuant to the corresponding provision:s 213(f) CA 63.

Notification of dissolution

50. Apart from a partner's right to notify those dealing with the firm that he or another partner has ceased to be a member of it (s 36), s 37 confers on each partner the right, on dissolution of the partnership to notify the public of that fact and to require the other partner(s) to do whatever is necessary and proper to bring this about, eg by signing notices.

Continuing authority of partners for the purposes of winding-up

51. Section 38 provides that after dissolution the authority of each partner to bind the firm, and the other rights and obligations of the partners, continue so far as may be necessary to wind-up the affairs of the partnership, and to complete transactions begun but unfinished at the time of the dissolution, but not otherwise. Thus in the case of a partnership dissolved by death the surviving partner has the right to do all such acts as are necessary to wind up the partnership, eg to continue the business, to borrow money and to sell assets:

Case: Re Bourne 1906
A partnership was dissolved on the death of a partner and the surviving partner continued the business and deposited the title deeds to the premises owned by the partnership to secure a bank overdraft. The personal representatives of the deceased partner claimed that the deposit of the deeds was void and that they had a right in preference to the bank.

Held: the bank had the prior claim as the deeds had been deposited in order to wind up the affairs of the partnership.

Application of partnership property

52. Section 39 gives to each partner the right to have the property of the partnership applied to the payment of the debts and liabilities of the firm and to have the surplus assets after such payment applied in payment of what may be due to the partners respectively after deducting what may be due from them as partners to the firm; and for that purpose any partner (or his representative) may, on termination of the partnership, apply to the court to wind up the business and affairs of the firm.

    The rights of partners to be paid what is due to them out of surplus assets is in the nature of an equitable lien.

    Partners are free to make whatever arrangements they wish for the disposal of partnership assets on dissolution. They may, eg agree that some of them will take over the business on agreed terms or that in the event of a complete dissolution that the assets available for distribution among the partners will be distributed in a particular way. Irrespective of what partners may agree to, the rights of creditors remains unaffected.

Final settlement of accounts

53. Subject to whatever may have been agreed by the partners or in the absence of agreement, s 44(b) provides that the assets of the firm (including the sums, if any, contributed by the partners to make up losses or deficiencies of capital) shall be applied as follows:

    (i)   in paying the debts and liabilities of the firm to persons who are not partners therein;
    (ii) in paying to each partner rateably what is due from the firm to him for advances (ie loans) as distinguished from capital;
    (iii) in paying to each partner rateably what is due from the firm to him in respect of capital;
    (iv) the residue to be divided among the partners in the proportions in which profits are divisable.

    As might be expected creditors take priority in the matter of repayment. Costs incurred if the court has been involved are payable out of the assets and rank after claims of creditors and partners' advances but before the latter in respect of capital repayments. It should be observed that capital is not a debt in the legal sense until such time as the amount is settled by taking accounts pursuant to s 44.

    Case: Green v Hertzog 1954
    In an action during the life of the partnership to recover money lent by a partner to the partnership as capital it was *held* that the plaintiff must fail as there was no right of action at common law. The money could only be recovered as a claim when accounts were finally settled.

54. Subject to any agreement between the partners, s 44(a) provides that losses and deficiencies of capital shall be paid first out of profits, next out of capital and lastly, if necessary, by the partners individually in the proportions in which they were entitled to share profits. The operation of s 44(a) is best understood by means of examples.

    Example: A, B and C contribute £12,000, £7,000 and £2,000 respectively as capital. A also made an advance of £3,000. On dissolution the assets realise £30,000 and the debts of the firm amount to £13,500. The net assets available for repayment of capital to the partners are computed so:

Assets realised on dissolution		£30,000
Less: Creditors	£13,500	
Advance to A	£3,000	£(16,500)
Net assets		£13,500

Loss of capital = £21,000 - £13,500 = £7,500. Subject to any agreement to the contrary, s 24 provides that profits and losses are shared equally and thus the loss of capital of £7,500 is shared equally, ie each partner bears a loss of £2,500. The capital accounts of the 3 partners are computed as:

A:	£12,000 less £2,500 =	£9,500
B:	£ 7,000 less £2,500 =	£4,500
C:	£ 2,000 less £2,500 =	£(500)
		£13,500

Note that C has a deficiency of capital which he must make up from his private resources.

Note also that if the partners had agreed to share profits in proportion to the capital contributed, the loss of capital would be apportioned to A, B and C in the proportions 12:7:2:, ie A, B and C would bear 12/21, 7/21 and 2/21 respectively of the £7,500 loss, ie £4,286, £2,500 and £714 respectively, so that the share out of the net assets would then be:

A:	£12,000 less £4,286 =	£7,714
B:	£ 7,000 less £2,500 =	£4,500
C:	£ 2,000 less £714 =	£1,286
		£13,500

Rule in *Garner v Murray 1904*

55. If on a dissolution one partner has a deficiency of capital (as C has in the first example above) and is moreover, insolvent and unable to make up his deficiency from his private resources, such a deficiency is regarded as a debt due to the solvent partners as individuals and not to the firm as such. Consequently the loss is borne, not in the proportion in which profits and losses are normally shared, but by the solvent partners in proportion to their respective capitals as last agreed. The 'last agreed capitals' will normally be the capitals as shown on the last balance sheet.

See the solution to question 33 at the end of the study text.

Section 43 provides that, subject to any agreement between the partners, the amount due to a former partner (or his estate) in respect of his share is a debt which accrues at the date of dissolution or death. Section 43 therefore has the affect of converting the partners's share (hitherto a contingent right) into a debt.

Return of premiums

56. Section 40 provides that where one partner has paid a premium to another on entering into a partnership for a *fixed* term, and the partnership is dissolved before the expiration of that term (otherwise than by the death of a partner), the court *may* order the repayment of the premium, or of such part thereof as it thinks just, having regard to the terms of the partnership agreement and to the length of time during which the partnership has continued; *unless* (a) the dissolution is, in the judgment of the court, wholly or chiefly due to the misconduct of the partner who paid the premium; *or* (b) the partnership has been dissolved by an agreement containing no provision for a return of any part of the premium.

Note that if no fixed term has been agreed, the partner has no entitlement to a return of premium paid:

Case: Atwood v Maude 1868
A solicitor took a premium of £800 from an inexperienced partner in a partnership expressed to last for 7 years. After 2 years he sought a dissolution because of his partner's incompetence.

Held: that the partner seeking the dissolution was not entitled to retain the whole premium.

Unless there has been a total failure of consideration the court will normally order the repayment of such part of the entire premium as is proportionate to the fraction which is still unexpired of the original term; eg in *Atwood v Maude* a refund of 5/7 might be expected but the court is not precluded from using some other formula where that formula would not produce a fair result.

Right to share profits made after dissolution

57. Section 42 provides that where partners continue to carry on the business without any final settlement of accounts as between the firm and a former partner (or the estate of a deceased partner), then, in the absence of any agreement to the contrary, the former partner is entitled to such share of the profits made since dissolution as the court may find attributable to the use of his share of the partnership assets *or*, at the option of the former partner to interest at 5% per annum on the amount of his share of the partnership assets.

The former partner must choose one or other of the options available; he would not be entitled to claim both profits and interest or eg a mixture of profits and interest.

The Court stated in *Manley v Sartori 1927* that there is a presumption that profits should be apportioned to the share of assets continued to be used in the business, the onus being on the surviving partner(s) to rebut this presumption by showing that the profits earned since dissolution have been earned wholly or partly by means other than the utilisation of the assets, including goodwill.

The alternative of opting for interest on his share of the partnership assets suffers from the disadvanage of an unrealistic interest rate but it has the merit of simplicity and is usually the preferred choice on that account.

The provision just discussed is subject to the proviso that where the partnership agreement gives an option to surviving or continuing partners to purchase the interest of a deceased or outgoing partner and that option has been duly exercised, the former partner (in his estate) is not entitled to any further or other share of profits.

Fraud or misrepresentation

58. Where a partner has been induced to enter a partnership by fraud or misrepresentation he is entitled, in addition to any other rights he may have, eg a common law right to damages in tort for deceit under the rule in *Derry v Peek 1889* to the following remedies provided by s 41:
    (a) to have a lien on the surplus assets for any sum paid for his share in the firm or for any capital contributed by him;
    (b) the right to be subrogated to the position of creditors of the firm for any payments made by him in respect of partnership liabilities;
    (c) to be indemnified by the partner(s) guilty of fraud or misrepresentation against all the debts and liabilities of the firm.

Goodwill

59. Goodwill is very difficult to define but in essence it is the reputation of the firm, which may have been built up over many years by hard work, which brings in custom. It is the one thing

which distinguishes a long-established business from a newcomer. On dissolution, each partner is, in the absence of agreement to the contrary, entitled to have the firm's assets, including goodwill, sold and the proceeds used in the manner provided for in s 39. If the business is sold, then in the absence of agreement to the contrary, the following rules apply:

(a) the purchaser alone has the right to represent himself as carrying on the business;

(b) the vendor may carry on a similar business in competition with the purchaser under a new name, provided he does not represent himself as continuing or succeeding to the business he has sold;

(c) the vendor may publicly advertise his business but he cannot solicit customers of his old firm;

(d) the sale carries the exclusive right to use the name of the old firm but subject to the qualification that the vendor is not thereby exposed to liability.

Other points to be noted are:

(i)   while the purchaser has the right to trade as the vendor's successor, he has no right to hold out the vendor as being still involved in the business;

(ii) a sale of goodwill carries with it the benefit of any covenant by a partner not to carry on a competing business;

(iii) in the absence of express agreement to the contrary, goodwill does not survive for the benefit of continuing partners.

● Companies and partnerships compared

60. The main differences between companies and partnerships are as follows.

(a) A company is created by registration under the Companies Act. A partnership is created by the express or implied agreement of the partners, no special form being required, although writing is usually used.

(b) A company is an artificial legal person with perpetual succession. It may own property, make contracts and sue or be sued. It has a legal personality distinct from its members. In contrast, a partnership is not a separate legal person although it may sue and be sued in the firm's name. The partners own the property of the firm and are liable on its contracts. A partnership is terminated by the death or bankruptcy of a partner.

(c) Shares in a public company are freely transferable whereas a partner cannot transfer his share without the consent of all of his partners. He may assign the right to his share of the profits but the assignee does not become a partner.

(d) A company must have at least two members (seven if a plc) and there is no upper limit on membership except for a private company where the limit is 50. A partnership must not consist of more than twenty persons although there are some exceptions, for example solicitors and accountants.

(e) Members of a company must not take part in its management unless they become employees or directors, whereas all partners are entitled to share in management unless the partnership agreement provides otherwise.

(f) A member of a company is not an agent of the company and he therefore cannot bind the company by his acts. A partner however is an agent of the firm, therefore it will be bound by his acts.

(g) The liability of a member of a company may be limited by shares or by guarantee. The liability of a general partner is unlimited although it is possible for one or more partners to limit their liability provided there remains at least one general partner. The advantage of limited liability is unlikely to be real for many small companies since lenders will usually require a personal guarantee of their loan from the directors and/or majority shareholders.

(h) The powers and duties of a company are closely regulated by the Companies Acts and the company can only operate within the objects specified in its Memorandum of Association although these can be altered to some extent by a special resolution of the company. In contrast, partners may carry on any business they wish and they may make their own arrangements with regard to the running of the firm, subject to compliance with the Partnership Act 1890.

(i) Creditors of a company generally have no right of action against individual members personally whereas if a firm defaults the creditors have rights against the individual partners.

(j) The memorandum and articles of a company are public documents, partnership agreements are not open to the public.

61. The table below may help you to remember these important points.

	Company	*Partnership*
Creation	Registration under Companies Act	Express or implied agreement
Legal status	Artificial legal entity	Not a separate legal person
Transfer of rights	Shares freely transferable	Transfer requires other partners' consent
Membership	At least 2	Upper limit of 20 (sometimes relaxed)
Management	Members may participate only if directors or employees	All partners entitled to share in management
Agency	Member not an agent	Partner is an agent
Liability of owners	Limited	Unlimited
Regulation	Statutory	Minimal

• Limited partnerships

62. Generally the liability of a partnership is unlimited but there is a special type of partnership known as a *limited partnership* which is provided for by the Limited Partnership Act 1907.

    Section 4 of that Act provides that a limited partnership must consist of 'one or more persons called *general partners* who shall be liable for all the debts and obligations of the firm and one or more persons called *limited partners* who shall, at the time of entering into such partnership, contribute thereto a sum or sums as capital or property valued at a stated amount and who shall not be liable for the debts or obligations beyond the amount so contributed.' Section 4(3) provides that a limited partner shall not during the continuance of the partnership, either directly or indirectly, draw out or receive back any part of his contribution, and if he does so, he shall be liable to contribute a sum, not exceeding the amount withdrawn, in order to discharge the debts or obligations of the firm.

    Section 5 provides that the 'limited partnership' must be registered in order to enjoy the protection of the Act. It should be noted that the use of the word 'limited' in this context does *not* confer a separate legal existence on the firm.

    A limited partner is precluded by s 6(1) of the Act from taking part in the management of the firm; if he does so, he will be liable for all the debts and obligations incurred by the firm during the period he takes part in the management as though he were a general partner.

    The Act does not define what amounts to taking part in the management and it is difficult to suggest the proper test to apply in view of the proviso in s 6(1) which allows a limited partner to 'advise with the partners' on 'the state and prospects' of the business.

    Section 6(2) provides that 'a limited partnership shall not be dissolved by the death . . . of a limited partner.' Clearly if there is more than one limited partner, the death of one of them will not operate to dissolve the partnership, but if there is only a single limited partner and he dies, then, on the authority of *Lindley on Partnership,* since there cannot be a limited partnership without at least one limited partner (s 4), the partnership must necessarily be dissolved on the death of that partner. *Lindley* suggests that, until the law is clarified by decisions of the courts, if it is desired that a partnership should not come to an end on the death of the single limited partner, the partnership agreement should provide for someone else to become a limited partner in his place should the single limited partner die during the continuance of the partnership.

    Section 8 provides that particulars of the firm-name, nature of business, place of business, full names of each partner, the terms of the partnership, and other matters must be registered and Section 9 provides that any change in the particulars required to be registered must be registered within 7 days.

    It should be noted that a new partner may be introduced without the consent of the 'limited partner(s).' Also a 'limited partner' cannot dissolve the partnership on notice. The rights and duties of the partners among themselves are governed by the partnership agreement but, in the absence of agreement to the contrary, they are governed by s 24 of the Partnership Act 1890. The Partnership Act 1890 applies to a limited partnership insofar as it is not expressly excluded.

Investment limited partnerships

63. In 1994, the Investment Limited Partnership Act was passed, which created a new vehicle for collective investment, such as managed funds. These investment limited partnerships are based on an American concept and were designed to attract American fund managers to the International Financial Services Centre in Dublin. They are a highly specialised form of limited partnership.

TEST YOUR KNOWLEDGE

(Numbers in brackets refer to paragraphs in this chapter)

1. How is partnership defined? (5)

2. What is (a) the minimum and (b) the maximum number of partners allowed by the law? (5, 20)

3. What must be present for a partnership to be confirmed as being conducted 'with a view of profit'? (8)

4. Which persons who take profits are not partners by that fact alone? (9–13)

5. What is 'holding out'? (14) For what debts is a partner by holding out liable? (15)

6. Name six terms which are typically found in a partnership agreement. (21)

7. How is a partner's apparent authority as agent defined? (22)

8. For what acts does a single partner in a commercial firm have authority? (26,27)

9. What effect do (a) death of a partner, (32) (b) retirement of a partner, (33–36) and (c) a new partner, have on the firm? (37) What are their liabilities?

10. What duties does the requirement of good faith impose on partners? (45)

11. When may dissolution of the partnership occur? (46)

12. State five main differences between a partnership and a company. (60)

13. Who is a limited partner? (62)

Now try illustrative questions 18 to 22 at the end of the study text.

KEY SECTION NUMBERS

(All references are to the Partnership Act 1890 unless otherwise stated)

s 1	Definition of partnership	(5)
s 2	Rules for determining existence of partnership	(11)
s 5	Power of partner to bind the firm	(22-25)
s 6	Partners bound by acts of the firm	(29)
s 10	Liability of the firm for wrongs	(30)
s 11	Misapplication of money or property	(30)
s 12	Liability for wrongs joint and several	(30)
s 14	Persons liable by holding out	(14,15)
s 17	Liabilities of incoming and outgoing partners	(33-37)
s 19	Variation of terms of partnership	(21,47)
ss 20,21	Partnership property	(42)
s 24	Rules as to interests and duties of partners subject to special agreement	(21,38,39,40,41)
s 25	Expulsion of partner	(21,43)
s 28	Duty of partners to render accounts	(45)
s 29	Accountability of partners for private profits	(45)
s 30	Duty of partners not to compete with the firm	(45)
s 32	Dissolution by expiration or notice	(48)
s 33	Dissolution by bankruptcy, death or charge	(32)
s 35	Dissolution by the court	(49)
s 38	Continuing authority of partners for purposes of winding up	(51)
s 39	Rights of partners as to application of partners' property	(52,59)
s 40	Appointment of premium where partnership prematurely dissolves	(56)
s 44	Rules for distribution of assets on final settlement of accounts	(53,54)
s 44	Distribution of assets	(21)
	Limited Partnership Act, 1907:	
s 4	Definition of limited partnership	(62)
s 4(3)	Restriction on withdrawal of capital by a limited partner	(62)
s 6(1)	Limited partner precluded from taking part in management of firm	(62)
s 36	Liability of partner for debts incurred after his retirement	(34,35)
s 376 CA 63}*	Maximum number of partners	(20)
s 13 C(A)A 82}		

* as amended

PART H

EUROPEAN COMMUNITY LAW

Chapter 16

EUROPEAN COMMUNITY LAW
LEGAL AND INSTITUTIONAL STRUCTURES

Points covered in this chapter are:

- The Constituent Communities of the European Community
- The Single European Act
- The Treaty on European Union (Maastricht Treaty)
- The Institutions of the European Union
- Legal acts of the Community
- Supremacy of European Community Law

Purpose of chapter

One of the effects of Ireland's membership of the EC/EU was to import into Irish law, laws made by the EC/EU, thus knowledge of this source of law is very important.

● The Constituent Communities of the European Community

The European Coal and Steel Community

1. The first of the three Communities which comprise the European Community to be established was the European Coal and Steel Community which was established by the Treaty of Paris in 1951. Its primary functions were to control the production and marketing of coal and steel in member states and in particular regulate the fixing of minimum and maximum prices. As between member states restrictions, levies and tariffs on imports/exports of coal or steel were eliminated creating a free market within the community of member states. A common set of tariffs *vis a vis* non-member states was created.

Euratom

2. The Treaty establishing Euratom was signed in Rome in 1957. This treaty has as its principal objective the speedy establishment and growth of nuclear industries.

European Economic Community

3. The EEC Treaty was signed in Rome in 1957 and its primary objectives are the harmonisation of social and economic policies amongst member states with the gradual elimination of customs tariffs and the free movement of goods, persons, services, and capital within the community area. The Community also promotes the harmonisation process by implementing common policies in various areas of common interest, eg transport, competition rules, agriculture and fisheries.

4. Ireland joined the European Community in 1973. Since 1995 there are 15 member States; Austria, Belgium, Finland, Netherlands, Luxembourg, France, Italy, Germany, Ireland, Denmark, UK, Greece, Spain, Sweden and Portugal. Various other countries have formally applied for membership such as Malta and Cyprus.

• The Single European Act

5. The Single European Act, passed after a referendum in 1987, is essentially an updating of the three treaties which together form the EEC's Constitution. Originally, the Government did not call a referendum on the Act, but the Supreme Court held that a referendum was legally necessary: *Crotty v Attorney General 1987 (I)*.

    This Act was designed to speed up decision-making and enable the Council of Ministers to avoid as far as possible crises and all night negotiating sessions which had become characteristic of its processes. The Act also gave specific treaty status to a number of important policies, such as measures to bridge the prosperity gap between the richer and poorer regions of the Community, the protection of the environment and such like matters which were not specially provided for in the original treaties.

    The Act also included provisions on what is known as European Political Co-Operation and the process by which the member states endeavour to co-ordinate foreign policy. It enhanced the political and social dimensions of the Community which was traditionally considered an economic force since its inception.

    The Single European Act introduced into the EEC Treaty new articles on monetary co-operation, social policy, regional policy (called 'economic and social cohesion'), the environment, and technological and research development.

    The Act also allowed for the establishment of inferior tribunals for the hearing of certain categories of cases from which there would be a right of appeal to the Court of Justice. It strengthened the role of the Parliament and introduced a 'co-operation procedure' to replace the old consultative procedure which existed under the Treaty. The Act stipulated that 1992 was the latest date for the attainment of the free internal market in services, capital, persons and goods.

• The Treaty on European Union (Maastricht Treaty)

6. This Treaty was signed in Maastricht in February 1992 and eventually came into force in November 1993. The Treaty is intended to facilitate the development of the EC into a political, economic and monetary union. Effectively, it gives the Community more powers, and it accelerates decision making by substituting majority decisions for unanimous ones. In addition the European Parliament acquires more democratic rights.

    The principal changes are as follows:

    -   Institutional changes. There will be a system of 'Co-Decision making' between the Parliament and the Council. The Community will act in accordance with the principle of subsidiarity, ie that member States should be free to make decisions as appropriate at national, local or regional level. There will be a new concept of European citizenship, a new Committee of the Regions, and a new EU Ombudsman.

    -   New or widened areas of action. These include public health, the environment, culture, consumer protection, industry, research and development, education, vocational training and youth.

- Monetary union. It is proposed that there will be a single European currency by 1999. A European Central Bank will be established.

- Foreign policy and defence. There will be more inter-governmental co-operation in these areas and there may eventually be a common defence policy.

- There are provisions governing police and judicial co-operation, immigration policy and asylum.

There is a special Protocol in the Treaty, and a Solemn Declaration, which deal with Ireland's constitutional protection of the right to life of the unborn.

● The Institutions of the European Union*

7. There are five central Institutions of the European Union: The Council of Ministers, the Commission, the Parliament, the Court of Justice and the Court of Auditors. They now serve all three Communities (ECSC, Euratom and EEC) since the Merger Treaty, 1965 and carry out the tasks entrusted to the Communities and act within the limits of the powers conferred upon them by the relevant Treaty. The Single European Act (SEA) and the Maastricht Treaty (MT) retain these basic institutions but have extended their powers. The principal functions of each will be considered before briefly looking at the inter-relationship between the institutions.

It should also be noted that there are various other EU institutions, apart from these five central ones. Examples include European Council (which is when the Heads of Government and Heads of State meet to decide on major matters of EC policy), and a European Investment Bank which was set up to facilitate the financing of projects which contribute to the balanced development of the Union.

The Commission

8. The Commission is similar in its functions to a national central administration of a member State. It can be described as an executive which also has the role of initiation of action. The Commission exists primarily to protect the interests of the Union. There are 20 Commissioners nominated by governments of member States. The President of the Commission is appointed in advance of the appointment of other members and plays an active part in the allocation of portfolios as between the new appointees who hold office for a term of five years. At present, there are two Commissioners from France, Germany, the United Kingdom, Italy and Spain and one from each of the other ten member States. An out-going Commissioner is eligible for re-appointment.

9. The Commission acts by a majority of its members. The decision-making process takes place either by the circulation of proposed decisions to members prior to meetings which if unopposed at the subsequent meeting of the Commission when reached for discussion is deemed to be adopted unanimously - the so-called 'written procedure' or by being raised and debated at a Commission meeting and voted through by a simple majority.

---

* *For simplicity, the European Community/Union is referred to in this text as the European Union in accordance with Commission's preference.*

10. The Commission's functions are four-fold and will now be considered.

    Firstly, the Commission must act as 'watchdog' to detect breaches of the various treaties and to take remedial action. Article 213 empowers it to collect information and carry out any enquiries or checks, eg by way of statistical analysis. Other Articles empower it to inspect the origin of goods to ensure that the rules on competition and the rules on free movement are complied with of goods and to curtail fraud.

    The Commission has power to punish breaches of certain Treaty provisions, particularly those relating to competition and to transport. The Commission will take action against a member State in a case where a member state breaches a Treaty provision. Article 169 of the Treaty lays down the procedure to be followed. Initially, the Commission will issue a 'reasoned opinion' on the matter and direct it to the offending member State. If the state persists in non-compliance, the Commission can then institute proceedings before the Court of Justice to establish infringements of the Treaty or of any secondary legislation.

11. Secondly, the Commission is empowered by Article 155 of the Treaty to formulate recommendations or to deliver opinions if the Treaty expressly so provides or if the Commission considers it necessary. This power is quite significant insofar as it gives the initiative to the Commission as to when it should act in giving an opinion or making recommendations and is used to enable the Commission to have an input into the formulation of binding acts and legislation. The Commission may also exercise powers conferred upon it by the Council. This has occurred extensively in relation to the development of agricultural policy.

12. Thirdly, the Commission's executive functions require it to act as agent of execution of the Treaty. In principle it is the Council which must ensure that the objectives of the Treaty are attained and to this end it has power to take decisions. Normally the Council leaves these tasks to the Commission. Article 155 enabling the Commission to exercise the powers conferred on it by the Council for the implementation of the rules laid down by the latter is the only provision for delegation by the Council contained in the Treaties themselves.

    In a number of cases the Commission can act on its own initiative, eg in setting agricultural levies under market organisation regulations. Other provisions may require the Commission to liaise with member States or seek the opinion of a committee - normally a *Management Committee*. Management Committees are chaired by a member of the Commission and comprised of representatives of member States. They were first introduced by Regulation 19/1962. They facilitate the relationship between the Commission and the Council. The Commission submit a draft implementation measure to the relevant Management Committee for its opinion. Its opinion is not binding on the Commission. If there is a conflict between the Management Committee and if the Management Committee gets a qualified majority of 45 votes, then the matter must be referred to the Council. The Council then has one month within which it may reverse the Commission's decision if it wants to.

    The Commission also has power to establish the customs union and powers in relation to competition under the Treaty.

13. Finally, the Commission takes an active part in the shaping and development of measures taken by the Council and by the Parliament. Article 155 specifically provides for such participation. In very many instances the decision-making power of the Council can only be exercised on the basis of proposals submitted to it by the Commission. As such, the Commission can be described as the major initiator of the Community decision-making process.

The Council

14. The Council consists of representatives of the member States, each government delegating one member to it. Normally, the Council consists of a meeting of the foreign ministers of each member State. But it can also take the form of a meeting of the finance ministers, the agriculture ministers, the labour ministers etc. The Council of Ministers takes the key decisions. It can, however, only act in response to a proposal by the Commission, except in exceptional cases. If the Council wishes to amend a proposal put forward by the Commission, it can only do so by unanimous decision. There is a convention, referred to as the 'Luxembourg Compromise' that member States will act unanimously and thereby endeavour to find a solution acceptable to all whenever a decision threatens the vital interests of one or more member States. This compromise is nothing more than a 'gentleman's agreement' but it has had a significant political influence on the Council since it was evolved in 1966.

Sometimes the Council acts by what is known as a *qualified majority*. In such a situation, voting for each member State is weighted and a total of 62 votes of 87 in total is required in order for a decision to be made. The weighted voting system operates as follows:

France, Germany, Italy and UK	have	10 votes each	=	40
Spain	has	8 votes	=	8
Belgium, Netherlands, Greece and Portugal	have	5 votes each	=	20
Ireland, Denmark and Finland	have	3 votes each	=	9
Luxembourg	has	2 votes	=	2
Austria and Sweden	have	4 votes each	=	8
		Total votes		87

The proceeding of the Council are prepared by the Committee of Permanent Representatives – COREPER. This is referred to in Article 151 of the Treaty and was given firm status by Article 4 of the 1965 Merger Treaty. Depending on the Treaty Article to be applied, the Council acts by simple majority or by qualified majority or unanimously.

Coreper consists of permanent representatives of the member States and is responsible for preparing the work of the Council of Ministers and to carry out the tasks assigned to it by the Council. The Treaty does not allow for delegation by the Council of its responsibilities. *Coreper* tries to find solutions to problems. When this is done it must be confirmed by the Council.

Functions of the Council

15. Article 145 lays down the two primary functions of the Council:

   (1) *Co-ordination of the general economic policies of the member States*
   The Article gives to the Council a residual power of co-ordination where no specific legislative power is given to it.

   (2) *Power to take decisions*
   The Treaty empowers the Council to enact legislation - this covers all types of legislation - Regulations, Decisions, Directives. Only the Council can conclude International Agreements - although it is the role of the Commission to negotiate them.

The Parliament

16.   The Treaty provides for a system of direct elections to be carried out by means of a uniform procedure in all member States. Direct elections were first held in 1979. Members are elected for a 5-year term.

The composition of the Parliament is as follows:

Germany	99 members	=	99
United Kingdom, Italy, France	87 members each	=	261
Spain	64 members	=	64
Netherlands	31 members	=	31
Greece, Belgium, Portugal	25 members each	=	75
Denmark and Finland	16 members each	=	32
Ireland	15 members	=	15
Luxembourg	6 members	=	6
Sweden	22 members	=	22
Austria	21 members	=	21
	Total members		626

Ireland's 15 seats are distributed as follows

Connacht-Ulster	3
Dublin	4
Leinster	3
Munster	5

17.   The powers of the Parliament were originally somewhat limited. However, the SEA and MT have substantially extended Parliament's powers and this trend is expected to continue in the future development of the Union. Article 137 of the EEC Treaty provides that the Assembly shall:

'exercise the advisory and supervisory powers which are conferred on it by this Treaty'.

Parliament has 4 main powers:

(a)   Legislative powers
(b)   Motions to Censure
(c)   Budgetary powers
(d)   Power of appointment

18.   <u>Legislative powers</u>. The parliament had originally only consultative powers. It was generally consulted by the Council on proposals put forward by the Commission. In practice this occurred even when not required by the Treaties. It was, however, given consultative capacity though the Council is not obliged to take its advice.

Under Article 149, as long as the Council has not acted on a proposal, the Commission may alter such proposal, in particular where Parliament has been consulted on it.

Case: Roquette Freres v Council 1979, Maizena v Council 1979
In both cases the role of Parliament in legislative matters was considered. The Commission had put forward a proposal to the Council to amend a regulation in relation to the Common Agriculture Policy. The Council consulted Parliament but enacted the regulation before the Parliament had given its opinion.

Held: the consultative process provided for in Article 43 was a means of allowing Parliament to play an effective part in the legislative process of the Community. Although limited, it reflects at Community level the fundamental democratic principle that people should take part in the exercise of power through the intermediary of a representative assembly. Consultation was an essential procedural requirement and failure of the Commission to comply with it gave grounds for declaring that the action of the Commission was void under the procedure for annulment.

In response to criticism that the Parliament could not determine Community laws (the so-called 'democratic deficit'). The SEA which came into force in 1987 granted greater powers to it. A co-operation procedure was introduced allowing Parliament the right to reject or amend the Councils proposals, but with the draw-back that the final decision rested with the Council. In addition, the same Act gave Parliament the right to approve or reject treaties for accession or association of non-member countries. The MT further extended the powers of Parliament. It was now granted the right of co-decision in many areas of decision making. Effectively, Parliament now has the right to amend or reject Council's decisions. Further, Parliament was also given the limited right to initiate proposals by majority decision to the Commission on specific matters.

19. Censure Motion and other powers. These include: Motion to Censure the Commission; Under Article 144 there is a provision whereby the Parliament may pass a vote of censure (an open vote carried by a 2/3rds majority) on the Commission in which circumstances the entire Commission must resign. This has never in fact happened though it has been threatened. There are also procedures whereby oral and written questions may be put to the Commission, the Council and meetings of the conference of Foreign Ministers. The Commission is obliged to answer by the provisions of the Treaty. There is a growing trend towards consultation between the Parliament, Council and Commission which has increased since the introduction of direct elections in 1979. Article 40 provides that a member of the Commission may attend the Parliament sittings and can be heard if required and can give oral or written replies. The Council is heard by Parliament in accordance with rules made by the Council. Normally the President of the Council addresses the Parliament.

20. Budgetary Powers. These are perhaps the most extensive powers of the Parliament. Article 203 of the Treaty requires the Parliament to draw up an estimate of its own expenditure. It can also propose amendments to the Commission's proposals for expenditure. Parliament has power to amend non-compulsory expenditure. Council can only accept or reject Parliament's amendments in these cases. In the case of compulsory expenditure Parliament can only accept or reject. If compulsory expenditure does not result in an increase in total expenditure, Parliament may make amendments under different headings. If there is to be an increase in the total expenditure, however, any proposal to alter this by the Parliament must have the express approval of the Council. Since 1975 Parliament adopts the Budget and can reject it by a 2/3rd majority of votes cast and has done so in 1979, 1982 and 1984. Parliament also scrutinises expenditure during the year. It examines the implementation of the Budget and gets a Report on that from the Commission.

21. Power of Appointment. Parliament always had the right to sack the Commission, provided it had a sufficient majority (2/3 majority) to pass a censure motion. It never used this power. With the passing of the MT, the nature of the relationship between Parliament and the Commission has fundamentally changed. Now Parliament has an important role to play in the appointment of the Commission. The President will continue to be unanimously nominated by the Member States but will now have to consult Parliament on their nominee. Further the President and the other nominated members of the Commission will be subject as a body to a vote of approval by

Parliament and only then appointed unanimously by the member States. The MT also empowered Parliament to appoint an ombudsman to deal with complaints of mal-administration in the activities of the Union institutions.

The Court of Justice

22. Membership of the Court: There are 15 judges. Each member State provides one judge and an additional judge is provided in rotation by Britain, France, Germany and Italy. The judges are assisted by 9 Advocates-General. An advocate-general is not a member of the court but in effect is of equal standing with the judges. Both judges and the advocates-general are appointed for terms of six years and are eligible for re-election. They are nominated by member States and are appointed by the common accord of all the member States.

23. Jurisdiction of the Court. There are a number of areas where the court has jurisdiction to hear cases:

    (a) Direct Actions. These are normally actions involving member States or the institutions. They can arise under Articles 169, 170, 171 of the Treaty:

        (i) Article 169: these involve actions by the Commission against a member State for failing to fulfil an obligation under the Treaty;
        (ii) Article 170: these involve actions by one member State against another member State. Before such an action is commenced there is a preliminary procedure whereby the member state seeking to bring such an action must first refer the matter to the Commission which must deliver a reasoned opinion before the member State can proceed against another member State;
        (iii) Article 171: this arises where a member State fails to comply with a judgment of the Court. In such circumstances a fresh action can be taken under this Article.

    (b) Unlimited Jurisdiction. Article 172 provides for unlimited jurisdiction of the Court. It can therefore fix penalties without limit. Actions under this heading can be brought by natural or legal persons. Actions in the area of Competition are often brought under this Article. It is also available for non-contractual liabilities of the Community, ie actions claiming damages.

    (c) Review of the failure to act of the Council/Commission or Review of the legality of an act. Such proceedings may be brought at the request of a member State or one or other of the institutions. In certain circumstances, set out in Articles 173-176 natural or legal persons may also bring such proceedings.

    (d) Preliminary rulings. Article 177 deals with this mechanism whereby cases are referred from courts of member States for clarification of Community Law on a particular point. There have been several referrals from Ireland in the *Campus Oil Case*, the Supreme Court has laid down rules regarding the right to appeal references from the High Court.

    (e) Compensation for damages caused by the Institutions. These actions can be taken against the Community by a member State or a natural or legal persons and the procedures are laid down in Articles 178 and 215.

    (f) Other situations. The court can also deal with disputes between the Community and its staff and with claims under Article 184 which deals with exceptions to the plea of illegality and under Article 181 it has jurisdiction where contracts created by or on behalf of the Community and governed by private/public law confer jurisdiction in relation to any dispute on the Court. The MT empowered the COJ, acting on a Commission proposal to impose a financial penalty on any Member State which, after a Court ruling that it has infringed

Community law, refuses to comply with the Court's judgment despite reminders from the Commission that it must do so.

The SEA provided for the establishment of inferior tribunals for the hearing of certain categories of cases. The new Court known as the Court of First Instance (COFI) also comprised of 15 judges appointed for 6 years, began operating in October 1989. Essentially its jurisdiction is narrow, hearing cases brought by individuals or businesses in competition matters, those stemming from production quota system in the steel industry and cases claiming damages arising in any of these matters. There is a right of appeal on a point of law to the Court of Justice.

The Court of Auditors (COA)

24. The MT elevated the COA to the institutional status of the other institutions. The COA is not a judicial court. Its responsibility lies solely in examining the Community's financial affairs. Its elevated status reflects the Community's concern about the increasing squandering of funds and general financial irregularities. It is hoped that by highlighting these matters, moral pressure for reform will be exerted. The COA consists of 15 members, one from each member state. Members should have a strong background in financial control of public funds. The COA's work consists of financial audit and assessment of financial management.

The balance of power between the Institutions

25. Certain powers are specifically granted to the Council and the Commission under the Treaty. These are known as Powers of Attribution. Apart from these where it appears that Community action is needed to achieve an objective of the Treaty such additional powers derive from Article 235 which gives power to the Council, acting unanimously on a proposal from the Commission and after consulting the Assembly, to take the necessary measures.

26. *Case: Commission v Council 22/70 (ERTA Case)*
This case concerned international agreements on Road Transport and Article 235. The Council adopted a regulation in relation to drivers' hours of work. The Commission disagreed with the policy adopted by the Council and member States and contended that as it was a Community matter and an international agreement the Commission had power to negotiate it. The Commission therefore brought an action against the Council seeking annulment under Article 173 of the Council's decision. The Council objected that such an action was inadmissible as the matter being objected to by the Commission was a discussion and not a binding act.

The court gave a verdict in principle to the Commission but the Council was not punished for what it had done. The court held that it was necessary to look at the Treaty as a whole to decide who had power to negotiate and enter into such agreements. It looked at Articles 3 and 5 of the Treaty and found that in the light of them, member States could not act outside the framework of the Community Institutions in this sphere. The court held that since Article 75 related to Transport therefore the matter was a Community matter and the Commission should have been involved in the negotiations.

• Legal acts of the Community

27. The basic point of reference is Article 189 which provides that in order to carry out their tasks under the Treaty the Council and the Commission shall, in accordance with the Treaty:

(a) make Regulations;
(b) issue Directives;
(c) take Decisions;

(d)   make Recommendations; or

(e)   deliver Opinions.

Regulations

28.   Regulations have general application, are binding in their entirety and are directly applicable in all member States. It creates rights and obligations for those to whom it is addressed. A Regulation is directly applicable, ie it takes immediate effect and it is not necessary for the legislative institutions of the member State to take any action or step to put a Regulation into effect.

Directives

29.   These are binding as to the aims to be achieved. However, the member State has the choice as to the form and method to achieve this within the framework of their national legal system. Some Directives may be very precise as to the results to be achieved, giving little discretion to the member State whereas others may be more liberal and give much more freedom. The status of a Directive needs legal process in two stages:

(i)   the result the Directive aims to achieve is imposed as an obligation on the addressee of the Directive. The addressee is then legally bound to achieve that result. A Directive can only be addressed to a member State – never to a private individual;

(ii)   the substance of the obligation laid down in the Directive must be transposed into national law but within that framework the member State has freedom as to the form and content in the mode it chooses to implement the Directive.

Case: Lee v Minister for Agriculture, 1979
A Directive on Agriculture was implemented by Ireland via an Administrative Procedure by the Minister for Agriculture and no appeal was available. This was challenged in the Irish Courts and referred therefrom to the European Court which upheld the measure as valid. Even where directives have not been implemented, they may still confer rights on individuals even at national level. The term usually applied to such is that they have 'direct effect.'

Case: McDermott & Cotter v The Minister for Social Welfare, 1987 (I)
This case concerned a Social Welfare Directive 79/7/EEC which entitled women to benefits under the same conditions as men. The Plaintiffs were claiming that existing Irish legislation was invalid as infringing the Directive. The High Court referred the matter to the European Court which held that where the provisions of the Directive appear to be unconditional and precise individuals may rely on those provisions, in the absence of implementing measures adopted within the prescribed period, as against a national provision incompatible with the Directive.

Decisions

30.   Decisions are binding in their entirety on those to whom they are addressed. Addressees may be:

(i)   member States;

(ii)   natural person(s);

(iii) legal person(s).

A Decision addressed to a natural or legal person provides the Community with a means of regulating a particular situation. It provides the Community Institutions with suitable legal instruments for performance of their executive function.

31.   A Decision has individual application. If there are a number of addressees it may not be necessary to name them all. It is sufficient that they can be identified.

Case: Toepfer v EC Commission 1963
This case held that it is sufficient if on the day the Decision is published there is a distinguishable group of addressees which cannot be added to later.

It is sufficient if it is addressed to an identifiable number of people. A Decision is binding in its entirety and this distinguishes it from Recommendations and Opinions. Whether a measure is a Decision or Regulation is of importance in that a private person can challenge a Decision but cannot challenge a Regulation.

Recommendations and Opinions

32. The addressees of such are invariably member States. In exceptional cases, however, it may be a person, group of persons or an undertaking. Normally a Recommendation emanates from a Community Institution which has made it. Its objective is to recommend a particular course of conduct to the addressees without legally binding them thereby.

33. Opinions are given in consequence of an initiative from elsewhere. They contain either:

    (i) general appraisal of certain processes; or
    (ii) contribution to the preparation of further legal acts.

    While not legally binding Opinions may give rise to indirect legal effect if they create conditions necessary for further measures of which Community Institutions which drew them up bind themselves, a consequence of which may be to create a situation of 'legitimate expectation.'

34. Legitimate expectation. This is a principle to be found in Community law which operates by providing that one party by its conduct may create an expectation in another and may be estopped (prevented) from acting in a way that is contrary to those legitimate expectations.

• Supremacy of European Community Law

35. If there is a conflict between European Community law and national law, the EC law prevails. This was stated by the European Court of Justice in the *Van Gend en Loos* case 1962. In that case the Court emphasised that the EC constitutes a new legal order in international law, for whose benefit the States have limited their sovereign rights, albeit within specific fields. In Ireland, there have been three constitutional amendments which clarify this. The result is that Article 29.4.3 of our Constitution states that no provision of the Constitution invalidates laws enacted which are necessitated by our membership of the EC and that no provision of the Constitution prevents laws enacted by the EC from having the force of law in the State. See also the European Communities Acts, 1972 and 1973 which provide that Ministers may make Regulations to enable the EC Treaties and the Acts of the EC institutions to have full effect. These regulations have statutory effect. There is a special committee called the Joint Oireachtas Committee on the Secondary Legislation of the European Communities which monitors these regulations.

Direct effect

36. EC law also has a concept of 'direct effect', which is very important if someone is trying to enforce EC law in their domestic courts. If a provision of EC law is classified as being 'directly effective', then an individual can rely on that provision in their national courts. There are three tests which are used to decide whether a particular provision is directly effective namely:

(a) it is clear and precise;

(b) it is conditional; and

(c) it requires no implementing measures by member States (or there is very little discretion left to member States as to the implementation of the provision).

TEST YOUR KNOWLEDGE

Numbers in brackets refer to paragraphs of this chapter

1. What are the functions of the Commission? (8-13)

2. Describe the legislative powers of the Parliament. (18)

3. Define and distinguish between Regulations, Directives and Decisions. (28-31)

4. What reforms were initiated by the Single European Act?
and Masstricht Treaty (5,6)

Now try illustrative questions 23 to 26 at the end of the study text.

PART I
COMPETITION LAW

Chapter 17

COMPETITION LAW

Points covered in this chapter are:

- Irish competition law
- EU competition law
- Article 85
- Undertakings
- *De minimis* rule
- Enforcement
- Block exemptions
- Article 86

Purpose of chapter

In order to ensure free trade it is often necessary for the legislature to make laws to give effect to this. This chapter looks at Irish legislation and the law of the EU on this matter.

- **Irish competition law**

1. After the end of World War II when normal Trade began to return many groups of traders began engaging in restrictive practices such as limited entry and price fixing. As the general policy was to move towards a more open economy these practices had to be tackled, hence the need for legislation. In Ireland the response was the Restrictive Trade Practices Act 1953 which established a Fair Trade Commission.

2. The following are the main Irish statutes in this area:

   (a) Restrictive Practices (Amendment) Act 1987 (as amended);
   (b) Mergers, Take Overs and Monopolies (Control) Act 1978 (as amended);
   (c) Competition Act 1991.

Competition Act 1991

3. The primary purpose of this is to prohibit anti-competitive practices and agreements and the abuse of dominant positions in the market place. These provisions are based on Articles 85 and 86 of the Treaty of Rome and apply to all undertakings within the State engaged in trade in goods and services.

   Section 4 of the Act is generally parallel to Article 85 and Section 5 of the Act is parallel to Article 86 of the Treaty of Rome.

The Act introduces a new concept prohibiting anti-competitive activity which replaces the 'control of abuse' system on which the existing legislation was based. There is direct access to the Courts for anyone who is adversely affected by anti-competitive activity which is prohibited under the Act.

Where arrangements have the effect of restricting competition but are beneficial to economic activity, it is possible to seek an exemption from the Rules of the Competition Act. These exemptions, which take the form of a licence, may be granted by the Competition Authority.

To qualify for an exemption licence bodies or groups affected by the Act are required to notify their agreements and decisions or concerted practices to the Competition Authority.

It is also open to the Competition Authority to find that a specific agreement, decision or concerted practice does not in fact offend against the rules of competition as found in the Competition Act and the Competition Authority in such a case can issue a Certificate of Negative Clearance to this effect.

Competition Act 1991 - Anti-Competitive Rules

4. Section 4, which is based on Article 85 of the Treaty of Rome and on the Sherman and Clayton Acts of the USA, prohibits, in the interests of the common good, the prevention, restriction or distortion of competition and the abuse of dominant positions in trade within the state.

    It is a new approach and it replaces the 'control of abuse' system on which the existing legislation dealing with the Restrictive Practices Acts and Orders were based. Rather than relying on the lengthy and cumbersome system of investigation, reporting, the formulation of Orders and confirmation by an Act of the Oireachtas Section 4 applies a straightforward system of prohibition with access to the Courts for anyone affected by the anti-competitive activity prohibited under the Act.

5. Section 4 prohibits all agreements between undertakings, decisions by associations of undertakings and concerted practices which have as their object or effect, the prevention restriction or distortion of competition within the State.

    The Section gives specific examples of such conduct.

    (a) Directly or indirectly fixing purchase or selling prices or any other trading condition.

    (b) Limiting or controlling production, markets, technical development or investment.

    (c) Share markets or sources of supply.

    (d) The application of dissimilar conditions to equivalent transactions with other trading parties, thereby placing them at a competitive disadvantage.

    (e) Making the conclusion of contracts the subject to acceptance by the other parties of supplementary obligations which, by their nature or according to commercial usage have no connection with the subject of such contracts.   Note: this list is not exhaustive and maybe, and has in fact, (see Woodchester case) been expanded.

Section 4 introduces into Irish Law a new category of void contracts. Any agreement which offends Section 4 is automatically void. The Competition Authority in its very first decision entitled *Nallen and O'Toole, 1992* considered the meaning of 'undertaking'. The meaning of this term was important because it effectively defines the jurisdiction of the Competition Authority. Section 3 of the CA 1991 states that 'undertaking' means any person being an individual, body corporate or unincorporated body of persons engaged for gain in the production, supply or distribution of goods or the provision of a service.

The Competition Authority came to the view that an 'undertaking' is any entity carrying on any economic or commercial activity. In doing so the Competition Authority essentially adopted the same position as that in the European Community competition law.

Somewhat later, the Supreme Court in the case of *Deane and Others v The VHI 1992* came to the conclusion that the defendant, established by statute to provide health insurance and prohibited by law from making profit, was engaged for gain in the carrying out of its activities and was therefore an 'undertaking.'

Dominant position

6. Section 5 follows Article 86 of the Treaty of Rome and prohibits the abuse of a dominant position by undertakings in trade for goods or services. It should be noted that Section 5 does not prohibit a dominant position *per se*, it is only the abuse of a dominant position which is prohibited by the Section.

The concept of 'dominant position' has been defined in the European Courts in the decision of Continental Can in 1972 as follows:

'Undertakings are in a dominant position where they have the power to behave independently, which puts them in a position to act without taking into account their competitors, purchasers or suppliers. That is the position when because of their share of the market, or their share of the market combined with the availability of technical knowledge, raw materials or capital, they have the power to determine prices or to control production or distribution for a significant part of the products in question. This power does not necessarily have to derive from an absolute domination permitting the undertakings which hold it to eliminate all will on the part of their economic partners, but it is enough that they be strong enough as a whole to ensure those undertakings in overall independence of behaviour, even if there are differences in intensity in their influence on the different partial markets.'

Dominant position has been more recently defined as 'a position of economic strength enjoyed by an undertaking which enables it to hinder the maintenance of effective competition on the relevant market by allowing it to behave to an appreciable extent independent of its competitor and customers and ultimately of consumers': *Michelin v Commission 1983*.

It remains to be seen whether the Irish Courts adopt this definition of the concept of a dominant position.

Section 6 of the Act provides that any person who is aggreived by actions which are prohibited either under Section 4 or 5 of the Act shall have the right to bring an action to the High Court or Circuit Court to seek relief.

Competition Authority

7. Section 10 provides for the establishment of the Competition Authority replacing the Fair Trade Commission. This new authority is empowered to discharge the functions of the Fair Trade Commission which have not been completed at the date the Act comes into force. The Competition Authority has the power to issue a Licence Exemption in certain circumstances, from the new rules of competition and also to issue a Certificate of Negative Clearance which will certify that there is no offence against the rules of competition contained in the Act by a named undertaking. To qualify for a Licence or Certificate an undertaking must notify the Competition Authority. In the application of Esso Solus and Related Agreements, 1991, the CA considered the

nature of the solus agreement (see Irish Business Law chapter 11, para 25) which provided in this case for the exclusive purchase by independent dealers of Esso petrol and the giving by Esso in return of equipment and financial loans and found that Esso was entitled to an exemption from the competition rules under the CA 1991 and granted a licence.

Mergers and take-overs

8. The 1978 Act provided that no proposal for a merger or takeover of a certain size is valid unless the Minister for Enterprise and Employment has been notified and has given approval in advance. The Act will normally apply where in the most recent financial year the value of the assets of each of two or more enterprises involved is at least £5m or the turnover of each is at least £10m. Sections 16 to 19 of the Competition Act, 1991 amend the existing legislation on mergers and takeovers. The new concept of 'abuse of a dominant position' replaces the existing concept of 'monopoly' which is defined in the Mergers Takeovers and Monopolies (Control) Act 1978. The new concept is a flexible mechanism permitting case by case analysis of market position. It also empowers the Minister to prohibit the continuance or require the adjustment of the 'dominant position' in the interests of the common good. Section 22 provides for the repeal in total of the Restrictive Practices Act, 1972 and those sections of the Restrictive Practices (Amendment) Act 1987 which relate to restrictive practices and fair trade. In *Woodchester Bank Ltd and UDT Bank Ltd 1992*, the Competition Authority considered whether the s4 provisions of the Competition Act 1991 applied to mergers and takeovers which restrict competition. In this case, Woodchester acquired the entire issued share capital of UDT Bank Ltd. The agreement contained certain restrictive convenants on the part of UDT, which were to continue for three years. The Competition Authority said that mergers and takeovers which restrict competition come within s4 of the Competition Act 1991 and would therefore be void unless notified to and then licensed by the Competition Authority.

9. The Minister may refer the proposed merger or takeover to the Director of Consumer Affairs and Fair Trade who will report and give his opinion. The Minister may make an order prohibiting the proposal and may make certain conditions.

Monopolies

10. Under the 1978 Act the Minister may request an inquiry into a monopoly. Sections 13, 14 and 15 of the Competition Act 1991 changes the requirements for notification and provision of information in relation to proposed mergers. The trigger for notification of share acquisitions is reduced from 30% to 25%.

- **EC competition law**

11. Part III of the EEC Treaty deals with Policy of the Community and the first title in this part deals with the Common Rules. Chapter one of this title is the chapter dealing with Competition and the relevant articles of the Treaty are 85-94. Articles 85 and 86 are considered the key articles in this area.

- **Article 85**

12. This Article prohibits certain activities as being incompatible with the Common Market, these include:

    (a) all agreements between Undertakings;
    (b) decisions by associations of Undertakings;
    (c) concerted practices which:

      (i)   may affect trade between member States; and

      (ii)   have as their object or effect the prevention, restriction or distortion of competition within the Common Market.

In particular concerted practices and certain types of horizontal agreements are prohibited where they:

(a)   directly or indirectly fix purchase or selling prices or any other trading conditions;

(b)   limit or control production, markets, technical development or investment;

(c)   apply dissimilar conditions to equivalent transactions with other trading parties, thereby placing them at a disadvantage;

(d)   limit markets or sources of supply;

(e)   make the conclusion of contracts subject to the acceptance by the other parties of supplementary obligations which, by their nature or according to commercial usage, have no connection with the subject of such contracts.

The requirement that an agreement to violate Article 85, must be one which may affect trade between member states is illustrated by the case:

Case: Consten v Grundig, 1964
Grundig entered into an agreement with Consten whereby Consten would be its exclusive dealer in France, giving Consten exclusive territorial rights in France and Grundig dealers from other EEC member States were not allowed to sell in France. In return, Consten agreed not to handle any competing products and to promote Grundig's products. Other French companies purchased Grundig products in Germany and imported and sold them in France. Consten took proceedings in France against those companies. The case was referred to the Commission which held that Consten's agreement with Grundig infringed Article 85 and the Court upheld this saying: 'What is particularly important is whether the agreement is capable of constituting a threat, direct or indirect, actual or potential, to freedom of trade between member States, in a manner which might harm the attainment of the objective of a single market between member States. The fact that an agreement encourages an increase, even a large one, in the volume of trade between member states is not sufficient to exclude the possibility that the agreement may affect trade between member States.'

13.   Not withstanding the provisions of Article 85 there are certain exceptions and the provisions set out at paragraph 12 above may be held inapplicable in the case of:

(a)   any agreement or category of agreements between undertakings;

(b)   any decision or category of decisions by associations of undertakings;

(c)   any concerted practice or category of concerted practices provided:

      (i)   they contribute to improving the production or distribution of goods; or

      (ii)   promote technical or economic progress while allowing consumers a fair share of the resulting benefit and which does not:

            (1) impose on the 'undertaking' concerned restrictions which are not indispensible to the attainment of these objectives; and

            (2) afford such undertakings the possibility of eliminating competition in respect of a substantial part of the products in question.

●   **Undertakings**

14.   This is a very broad concept in European terms. It includes any allocation of resources to carry out economic activity, ie limited companies, partnerships, individuals. In certain cases it can

include inventors and artists insofar as they exploit the relevant invention or performance: *Aoip-Beyrard 1976* (owner of patents for components for electric motors). It is also possible to have a group of companies treated as a single 'undertaking'. This is because the activities of a subsidiary may be imputed to its parent company. In a case involving *Johnson & Johnson (I)* the Commission imposed fines jointly and severally on a parent company its subsidiaries and a sub-subsidiary. Because subsidiaries are part of the same entity, there can be no 'competition' between them in the sense of Articles 85 and 86: *Christiani & Nielsen 1969*.

15. Companies outside the Common Market may be guilty of an infringement of Community rules. There may be such companies involved in trade with the Community and may have agreements that fall foul of Article 85 (1) (such companies may also be guilty of a breach of Article 86). These Articles relate only to obstructions between member States and accordingly if a company within the Community has a contract which tends or attempts to obstruct trade outside the Common Market, such an agreement does not breach the treaty.

● Article 85(1)

16. With regard to agreements or concerted practices there are certain conditions that have to be met before it falls foul of the Article:

   (i) they must have the possibility of affecting trade between member States; and
   (ii) they must have either as object or effect the prevention, restriction or distortion of competition within the Community.

   So, if an agreement cannot affect trade between member States or if it does not prevent, restrict or distort competition within the Commission it does not fall foul of Article 85.

17. The Court of Justice has held that certain agreements between undertakings, even if the undertakings are within the same member State will not necessarily mean that they won't or can't affect intra community trade and such may fall foul of Article 85.

   Case: Quinine Cartel, 1969
   The cartel had a contract of fixing prices and quotas for the whole of the world but specificially excluding the EEC. However, the parties entered into a 'gentleman's agreement' enforceable by artibration, to extend its application to the EEC.

   Held: it was an agreement within Article 85 and such agreements did not have to be in writing.

   Case: BP Kemi, 1979
   An agreement had been drawn up but never signed. It was held to constitute an 'agreement' within the meaning of Article 85 since it had been implemented by the parties.

18. Concerted practices can be extremely difficult to prove. The activities of companies in the same field may be very similar but may not result from an agreement between them. For example, oil companies often increase/decrease prices and it is difficult to ascertain whether there is some agreement or concerted practice or whether each company is individually reacting to market factors.

   Case: ICI v EC Commission 1972
   There had been price increases on three occasions by producers and there was evidence that they had met and there was other circumstancial evidence of collusion. It was held that on the evidence a form of concerted action existed which was contrary to Article 85(1). The Court went on to hold that for a few firms in a concentrated market to take account of each other's market behaviour did not amount to a concerted practice. It also established that Article 85

distinguished concerted practices from agreements and decisions. It offered an explanation for this being that it extended competition rules to any 'form of co-ordination between undertakings which, without having reached the stage where an agreement properly so called had been concluded, there is knowingly substantial practical co-operation between them protecting from the risks of competition.' 'Consciously parallel behaviour does not of itself constitute a concerted practice but concerted practices may be inferred if the parties have been in communication about their market behaviour.'

19. Clearly every producer is entitled to chance his prices and when he does so he may have regard to the price levels fixed by other competitors in that market. What Article 85(1) prohibits is the existence of any agreement or understanding or any acting together by producers so as to effectively rule out competition between them to a substantial degree.

- **The *de minimis* rule**

20. The so-called *de minimis rule* applies in the field of competition, though not in other areas of trade such as the free movement of goods. This rule provides that if the effect of an agreement is very minor it will be disregarded even though it strictly infringes the competition rules of the Treaty.

   Case: Volk v Vervaecke, 1969
   Volk made less than 1% of all washing machines produced in Germany. It concluded an agreement with Vervaecke for the exclusive distribution of the machines in Luxembourg and Belgium. The Court held that '. . . an exclusive dealing agreement, even with absolute territorial protection, may, having regard to the weak position of the persons concerned in the market in the products in question in the area covered by the absolute protection, escape the prohibition laid down in Article 85(1)'.

21. If an agreement has the characteristics which are prohibited by Article 85(1), then it will be automatically void and the parties cannot rely upon it. This may create difficulties for parties relying upon contracts since it may be pleaded by the other party that the agreement is void. The issue may have to be decided by the Commission if the dispute is brought to its notice. There is a provision for the provisional validation of certain agreements. If they are notified to the Commission certain of the consequences of being found void may be avoided. Where an agreement is found to be contrary to Article 85 the 'undertaking'(s) will be liable to pay very heavy fines - often millions of pounds. The Commisson is primarily concerned with very large undertakings with huge budgets. Often it is difficult to prove violations of Article 85.

- **Enforcement**

22. Where an agreement is suspected of being void then it should be referred to the Commission. The Commission will investigate the matter and if it finds a case against a party it will commence proceedings. The case is heard firstly by the Commission and can be appealed to the Court of Justice.

23. The rules on competition stem from Article 3(f) of the Treaty which deals with the activities of the Community and in particular provides: 'The Institution of a system ensuring that competition in the common market is not distorted.'

   Article 9 of Regulation 17 authorises the Commission to terminate breaches of Articles 85 and 86. The Commission has power to impose fines of up to 10% of turnover for the preceeding year of an 'undertaking' that has infringed either of the Articles. The fines are imposed in Units of Account (UA). In the *Pioneer Case* the Commission imposed fines of 4.35 million UA (ie £3 million approx).

24. The enforcement procedure is provided by the Competition Directorate called DG 4 of the Commission in Brussels. The Commission has power:

    (a)   to fine undertakings for infringement of the rules on competition;

    (b)   to collect information to ascertain if an infringement has occurred;

    (c)   to grant exemptions under Article 85(3);

    (d)   to take interim measures to bring damaging behaviour to an immediate halt - this is similar to an interlocutory injunction.

This last power is used in situations, eg where a small business is refused supplies by a large manufacturer and there is a risk that it will become insolvent whilst awaiting the outcome of the Commission's findings. The Commission can order that the business be supplied by the manufacturer pending its decision.

25. Procedure of the Commission: There is a procedure for notification for exemption or negative clearance.

Negative clearance arises where on the basis of information supplied to it, the Commission will say it is of the opinion that the agreement does not fall foul of the competition rules. However, that is only on the basis of the information with which it has been furnished and if it should later transpire that the information was inadquate or incomplete, the Commission can act in relation to this.

Where a block exemption (see below at paragraph 26) has been obtained the parties to such an agreement must ensure that its provisions do not go outside the terms of the Block Exemption.

Complaints must be formally made to the Commission and the complainant may be:

    (a)   one of the parties to the agreement; or

    (b)   some other party; or

    (c)   the Commission itself carrying out an investigation; or

    (d)   a member State.

The Commission can request information from the parties and if it does not get co-operation it can take a formal Decision under Regulation 17 requiring the undertakings to furnish certain information to the Commission under pain of fines or periodic penalties. The Commission has a number of investigative bodies with very wide powers to inspect premises, examine files etc, without notice or warning (so called 'dawn-raid' powers). If the undertaking fails to co-operate and supply the information sought to the investigators it can be subjected to severe fines.

After the Commission has fully investigated the complaint it will give, to the 'undertaking' complained against, a full statement of the complaint - called The Statement of Objections. The 'undertaking'/company may then wish to defend the claims set out in the Statement of Objections and it has two months within which to do so. After it makes its response it can seek an oral hearing and such hearings are held under the control of a hearing officer. After the oral hearing the Commission must consult the Advisory Committee on Restrictive Practices and Dominant Positions which is comprised of representatives of all member States though the Commission is not bound to follow that Committee's recommendations.

After all these steps are taken the Commission comes to a final decision:

    (i)   if an infringement is found to exist the Commission will order the 'undertaking' to stop immediately - a Cease and Desist Order is made;

(ii)   if the 'undertaking' has already ceased the Commission may declare that the conduct complained of was in fact an infringement;

(iii)   the Commission can order positive action by the 'undertaking' ie that it should supply certain parties. As already outlined it can impose fines and heavy penalties for breaches.

- **Block exemptions**

26.   A number of Regulations have come to be called the Block Exemption Regulations. These relate to the application of Article 85(3). Initially, to get an exemption from the application of Article 85 a separate application had to be made to the Commission. This resulted in a large number of agreements being submitted and the Commission was unable to examine them all. It therefore adopted 'Block Exemption Regulations' to specify certain areas and types of agreements that, once it was shown they complied with the rules relating to that type of agreement, get automatic exemption.

27.   A party to a contract can be faced with a plea that the contract is contrary to Article 85(1), eg if a manufacturer appoints an exclusive distributor in a member State - Ireland - and he is precluded by the terms of the contract from selling outside Ireland. If the distributor, in breach of that agreement does proceed to sell outside of Ireland and the manufacturer tries to sue, the distributor may raise the defence that this term of the agreement infringes Article 85(1).

The existing Block Exemption Regulations in relation to distributorship agreements indicate that it is possible to restrict a distributor by preventing him from canvassing for sales outside his territory, but he cannot be prohibited from selling outside it. If a manufacturer is looking for an exemption for an agreement of such a type, the presence of an export ban would probably mean that the Commission will not grant the exemption.

- **Article 86**

28.   Article 86 deals with abuse of a dominant position in the market.

'Any abuse by one or more undertakings of a dominant position within the common market, or in a substantial part of it, shall be prohibited as incompatible with the common market insofar as it may affect trade between member States'.

Such abuse may, in particular, consist in:
(a)   directly or indirectly imposing unfair purchase or selling prices or other unfair trading conditions;
(b)   limiting production, markets or technical development to the prejudice of consumers;
(c)   applying dissimilar conditions to equivalent transactions with other trading parties, thereby placing them at a trading disadvantage;
(d)   making the conclusion of contracts subject to acceptance by the other parties of supplementary obligations which, by their nature or according to commercial usage, have no connection with the subject of such contracts.'

The concept of the 'undertaking' appears frequently in community law and especially in the field of competition law. Neither the Treaty nor Regulation 17, the main implementing Regulation, defines 'undertaking'. The cases of the court indicate that to be an 'undertaking' a body must have legal capacity and may be a limited liability company, a partnership or a sole trader. It must have an economic aim, it can be engaged either in the production or distribution of goods or in the provision of services. It need not be profit-making.

29. In practice the process of establishing whether a dominant position exists in a particular case normally involves two distinct stages; firstly, the definition of the relevant market and secondly, the assessment of the strength of the 'undertaking' in question in that market. The term 'Relevant Market' is used to designate the field of competitive forces within which the 'undertaking' operates in either satisfying, or obtaining satisfaction of, a certain demand. One has to consider the extent of the range of products in question and the geographical distribution. A dominant position is not confined to a monopoly or quasi-monopoly but can also be found in cases like that of *United Brands case* (considered below) where the company's market share was 40%.

30. In the recent Irish case entitled *Masterfoods Ltd v HB Icecream Ltd 1992 (I)* the High Court examined alleged breaches of Articles 85 and 86 of the Treaty of Rome as well as alleged breaches of the restrictive practices legislation. Essentially the facts of this case are as follows:

    HB Icecream, a major player in the Irish icecream market, entered into a number of agreements with a large number of retailers whereby *HB* would supply to these retailers the freezer cabinet for the purposes of storing icecream products. A term in these agreements (referred to in court as 'an exclusivity term') excluded the retailers from stocking icecream products of rival firms in these freezer cabinets which had been supplied and owned by HB. It was claimed by *Masterfoods Ltd* that in view of *HB's* position in the Irish icecream market, including its dominant market share, its range of products, the number of freezer cabinets which they supplied to retailers, and its position of economic strength generally that these agreements either alone or in combination with others were in breach of Article 85 of the Treaty. *Masterfoods* claimed that these agreements essentially constituted agreements between undertakings or alternatively constituted concerted practices which affected trade between member States and which had as their object the prevention restriction or distortion of competition within the Common Market established by the Treaty. It was further alleged by *Masterfoods* that the activities of *HB Icecream Ltd* constituted abuse of its dominant position in a substantial part of the Common Market contrary to Article 86 of the Treaty.

    The court came to the conclusion that the agreements did not infringe Article 85. The court was also satisfied that the agreement and practices carried out by *HB* did not constitute an abuse of their dominant position and accordingly did not contravene Article 86 of the Treaty. In effect then the court decided that these agreements and practices did not prevent, restrict or distort competition and were in effect legitimate business strategies.

    The court also noted that Sections 4 and 5 of the Competition Act 1991 essentially reflected the wording of Articles 85 and 86 of the Treaty. Presumably the court would have come to a similar conclusion if it has been asked to decide whether on the facts of this case the agreements and practices indulged in by *HB* contravened Sections 2 and 3 of the 1991 Act.

    It should be noted that the proceedings in this case had been brought to court before the commencement of the Competition Act 1991.

31. The field in which Article 86 is applied has been considerably extended owing to the prevailing tendency to reduce the degree of market strength necessary for establishing the existence of a dominant position. Decisions show that the objectives in applying Article 86 amount to the elimination of abuses concerning price differentials within the Community, refusal to sell, overcharging and discriminatory treatment of suppliers and consumers.

32. Product Market

   Case: United Brands (Chiquita Banana Case) 1976
   The Commission found that the company was abusing its dominant position in the market because it charged different prices in the various states of the Community based on the price that it thought each market could bear. The Commission found that there was no justification for these discriminatory prices. On appeal to the Court, the Court upheld the Commission and held that the banana as a fruit had special characteristics which effectively meant that it had to be examined as a separate market (ie unlike most fruits it did not have fluctuations in seasonal availability) in its own right, and not in conjunction with the entire fresh fruit market. The interchangeability of bananas and other fresh fruit was so limited as to mean that the banana market had to be examined on its own as a separate market.

33. Geographical Market. Article 86 makes it clear that an abuse of a dominant position must take place within the Common Market or a substantial part of it, but it does not define what 'a substantial part' of the Common Market means. In the case of *Cadbury Ireland Ltd v Kerry Co-Operative Limited, 1982 (I)* it was held that County Kerry could not be considered a 'substantial part' of the Common Market.

34. The existence of a dominant position is also tested by reference to the product market in question. This market extends to cover all competing products and substitute products: *ICI and Commercial Solvents v EC Commission 1973*. Further, the court will draw a distinction between the market in raw materials and the market on which the ultimate product is sold: *Commercial Solvents* (above).

35. It is essential to be clear that a dominant position is not *per se* prohibited by Article 86, it merely provides that the firm or 'undertaking' which holds a dominant position must not abuse it. In the case of *Eurofix-Bauco/Hilti, 1988* the Commission imposed a fine on Hilti (a company which specialises in the manufacture of nail guns used in the construction industry) because it had acted to prevent independent producers of nails for Hilti nail guns from entering the nail market.

36. *Case: ICI and Commercial Solvents v EC Commission, 1973*
   The company had refused to supply a small pharmaceutical competitor with certain raw materials. The company pleaded that this did not affect trade with member States since 90% of the final product was exported to countries outside the Common Market.

   Held: 'when an 'undertaking' in a dominant position within the Common Market abuses its position in such a way that a competitor in the Common Market is likely to be eliminated it does not matter whether the conduct relates to the latter's exports or its trade within the Community once it has been established that this elimination will have repercussions on the competitive structure within the Common Market.'

   This case is authority for the proposition that an abuse under Article 86 can take place where an 'undertaking' in a dominant position takes over a competitor and thus strengthens its position to a point where the degree of domination thus achieved represents a substantial obstacle to competition, leaving in existence only firms which in effect have their actions dictated by the dominant 'undertaking.'

Mergers

37. <u>Mergers and concentrations between undertakings.</u> Article 86 includes mergers, take-overs or concentrations between undertakings though there is no express provision or mention of this in the Treaty. The *Continental Can Case* illustrates this principle whereby the Court and the Commission lean against the excessive concentration of a particular market activity in one or a very few undertakings.

Case: Europemballage and Continental Can v EC Commission, 1972
The Commission found that the take-over of a Dutch packaging firm by a subsidiary of Continental Can amounted to an abuse of the dominant position which this American firm enjoyed through its German subsidiary. The Commission felt that the takeover amounted to an unacceptable strengthening of the company's position on the markets concerned. The Court on appeal annulled the Commission's decision as being too narrow but it endorsed the Commission's view that a take-over could constitute an abuse of a dominant position and set out the concept of 'limited interchangeability' and spoke of the essential significance of defining the relevant market because 'the possibilities of competition can only be judged in relation to those characteristics of the products in question by virtue of which those products are particularly apt to satisfy an inelastic need and are only to a limited extent interchangeable with other products.'

Consequences of prohibition

38. An infringement of Article 86 does not give rise to any consequent nullity nor is there any possibility that an 'undertaking' can seek an exemption from the prohibition. The Commission can make a 'Cease and Desist Order' as outlined above at paragraph 25. It can make an order under Regulation 17 Article 3 compelling an 'undertaking' to supply to a customer or manufacturer. This power is used regularly.

Industrial and commercial property

39. Patents, trademarks and copyright, because of their protective nature, have been a source of litigation in EC competition law.

Case: Deutsche Grammophon v Metro 1970
DG manufactured certain records in Germany which it sold to its subsidiary, Polydor, in France. Such records were acquired by Metro in France which sought to re-import them into Germany. DG sought an injunction to prevent Metro selling these records in Germany.

Held: 'If a right related to copyright is relied upon to prevent the marketing in a member State of products distributed by the holder of the right, or with his consent, on the territory of another member State on the sole ground that such distribution did not take place on the national territory, such a prohibition, which would legitimise the isolation of national markets, would be repugnant to the essential purpose of the Treaty which is to unite national markets into a single market.'

The exercise of its industrial property rights by DG was incompatible with the Treaty.

40. *Case: Centrafarm v Sterling Drug, 1974*
The purpose of a *patent* was considered in this case. There were widely divergent prices for similar drugs on the Dutch and English markets. The English prices being far cheaper. Centrafarm bought the drug 'Negram' in England and re-sold it in Holland. ('Negram' was a trade mark). Negram's patent was owned by Sterling Drug, a US company. Sterling Drug took action in the Dutch Courts to prevent parallel imports from England into Holland of Negram by Centrafarm.

Held: derogations from the principles of the Treaty are permitted under Article 36 of the Treaty only where such derogations are justified for the purpose of safeguarding rights which constitute the specific subject matter of the property. The Court stated 'in relation to patents, the specific subject matter of the industrial property is the guarantee that the patentee, to reward the creative effort of the inventor, has the exclusive right to use an invention with a view to manufacturing industrial products and putting them into circulation for the first time either directly or by the grant of licences to third parties, as well as the right to oppose infringements.' It also said: 'A derogation from the principle of the free movement of goods is not justified where the product has been put onto the market in a legal manner by the patentee himself, or with his consent, in the member State from which it has been imported, in particular in the case of a proprietor of parallel imports.'

41. The exhaustion of trade mark rights was also considered by the Court. The specific subject matter of a trademark itself was considered in the case: *Centrafarm v Winthrop, 1976*. This case also concerned the drug 'Negram' but only the *trade mark* aspect of it. The trade mark in both Holland and England was owned by Sterling Drug's subsidiary Winthrop.

Held: the specific subject-matter of a trade mark is 'a guarantee that the owner of the trade mark has the exclusive right to use that trade mark for the purpose of putting products, protected by that trade mark, into circulation for the first time. Therefore it is intended to protect him against competitors wishing to take advantage of the status and reputation of the trade mark by selling products illegally bearing that trade mark.'

The Court concluded that it was incompatible with the principles of the free movement of goods enunciated in the Treaty to use a trade mark in one member state to prohibit the sale there of a product marketed by oneself with the consent of the owner in another member State.

42. The rules to be applied where two trade marks have a common origin were laid down in:

Case: Van Zuylen Feres v Hag, 1973
Prior to World War II a German company acquired trade marks in the name 'Hag' for coffee. The trade mark was regisered in Belgium, Germany and other countries. In 1944 the Belgian Government sequestered the assets of the Belgian subsidiary, including the trade mark, and sold it to a Belgian who later sold it to Van Zuylen Freres. So, although the trade mark had a common origin it came to be splintered and the German trade mark and the Belgian trade mark were owned by totally unconnected parties. The German company began marketing its product in the Belgian company's area. The Belgian company took proceedings to prevent this.

Held: 'One cannot allow the holder of a trade mark to rely on the exclusiveness of a trade mark right which may be a consequence of the territorial limitation of national legislation with a view to prohibiting the marketing in a member State of goods legally produced in another member State under an indentical trade mark having the same origin.'

The attempt to exclude the German-produced Hag from Belgium and Luxembourg was contrary to the freedom of movement of goods and Article 36 of the Treaty.

43. On the risk of confusion of consumers the case *Terrapin v Terranova 1975* is illustrative. Terranova was a German company which manufactured dry plaster and other building products. Terrapin was an English company manufacturing pre-fabricated buildings. Both trade marks were registered in England and Germany respectively. There was no connection between the two trade marks or between the two companies. Terrapin began marketing in Germany and Terranova took an action to prevent this on the grounds that the similarity in the products' names would cause confusion. The Court held in certain circumstances national laws could be used to protect industrial and commercial property rights even though it restricts the free movement of goods.

It held that in the present state of community law, an industrial or commercial property right legally acquired in a member State may legally be used to prevent its marketing in another member State, under Article 36 of the Treaty.

'The guarding of commercial and industrial property rights has to be reconciled so that protection is ensured for the legitimate use of the rights conferred by national laws and justified within Article 36 of the Treaty.' The marketing of Terrapin on Germany was prohibited to avoid consumer confusion between the two products.

44. The case *EMI Records v CBS 1975* also concerned trade marks. The trade mark 'Columbia' belonged to EMI in Europe and to CBS in the United States. The US company sought to import records with the 'Columbia' label into the Community and EMI took the proceedings to prevent this. The Court held that since CBS was a non-member State, Articles 30 and 36 of the Treaty did not entitle it to manufacture and market its product within the Community either by itself or through a subsidiary.

'The exercise of a trade mark right in order to prevent the marketing of products coming from a third country under an identical mark does not affect the free movement of goods between member States and thus does not come under the prohibition in Article 30 of the Treaty.'

TEST YOUR KNOWLEDGE

Numbers in brackets refer to paragraphs in this chapter

1. How has Irish legislation dealt with restrictive practices? (3-7)

2. What type of activity does Article 85 prohibit? (12)

3. What is meant by a 'Block Exemption'? (26)

4. When is an undertaking said to be in a 'dominant position'? (29, 33-35)

5. In what way can a use of a patent restrict competition? (40)

Now try illustrative questions 27 and 28 at the end of the study text.

MULTIPLE CHOICE QUESTIONS
AND SUGGESTED SOLUTIONS

MULTIPLE CHOICE QUESTIONS

Choose only one of the optional answers (A, B, C or D) to each question – only one is correct

Legal process and legal reasoning

Question 1

In considering whether he must apply a previous decision to the case actually before him, a judge of the High Court must:

1. decide whether the decision is binding or merely persuasive;
2. distinguish the *obiter dicta* from the *ratio decidendi* and apply the former to his reasoning;
3. decide if the material facts of the two cases are similar;
4. be satisfied that the decision was made by a court of higher status than the Circuit Court or the District Court.

A   1 and 3 only
B   2 and 4 only
C   1, 2 and 3 only
D   1, 3 and 4 only

Question 2

When called upon to decide what a section or a provision in a particular statute means and to decide whether or not it applies to a particular case, the court is *not* permitted to have regard to:

A   dictionary meaning of the words used in the statute;
B   the type of general problem which the Act was apparently designed to regulate;
C   the expressed intention of the Minister who introduced the Bill in the Dail;
D   interpretation of similar clauses in previous statutes dealing with the same subject matter.

Duress and undue influence

Question 3

In which of the following relationships will undue influence be presumed to have existed when there has been manifest disadvantage:

1. trustee and beneficiary;
2. parent and minor child;
3. husband and wife;
4. banker and customer;
5. solicitor and client.

A   2 and 3 only
B   1, 2 and 5 only
C   1, 4 and 5 only
D   1, 2, 3 and 4 only

MULTIPLE CHOICE QUESTIONS

Sale of goods contracts

Question 4

Heathcliff is in business as a supplier of spare parts and equipment for bicycles. He supplies such goods under a standard form contract which purports to restrict his liability should (a) his title to the goods sold prove defective and (b) the goods prove unfit for the purpose for which they are to be used.

He sells a number of gear-change mechanisms to a cycle shop. Within a short time the manufacturer who supplied the goods to Heathcliff takes action because he has not been paid for them and establishes to the satisfaction of a court that they were supplied under a contract with a retention of title clause and that ownership remains with him until the goods are paid for. The bicycle shop is also complaining that the mechanisms are not functioning properly. May Heathcliff rely on the exclusion clause?

	(a) Title of goods	(b) Fitness for purpose
A	Yes, if fair and reasonable	Yes
B	Yes, if fair and reasonable	Yes, if fair and reasonable
C	No	Yes, if fair and reasonable
D	No	No

Question 5

Donal bought a racing bicycle from John for £350, which unknown to John had been stolen from Ciaran Donal resold it to David for £400. Ciaran recovered his bicycle from David and it is estimated that it has depreciated in value by £100 since John sold it to Donal.

How much can (a) Donal reclaim from John? (b) David claim from Donal?

	(a)	(b)
A	£350	£400
B	£250	£400
C	£250	£300
D	£250	£300

Question 6

Peter, who is a building contractor, attends a liquidator's auction sale of contractors' equipment. He sees an air compressor entered by Paul in the sale and described in the auction catalogue as an AirCo Model A and stated to be 2 years old and in first class mechanical condition. On inspecting it Peter observes that it is in fact an AirCo Model B, a bigger and more powerful machine than the Model A. In the event he buys the machine and reckons he has got a bargain but later discovers its performance is unsatisfactory and on having the machine inspected by an expert it is discovered that it is in poor mechanical condition and over 4 years old.

Peter wonders whether he can sue Paul for breach of the condition that the machine should correspond with the description in the catalogue. In which of the following circumstances will he be *unable* to do so?

A   The contract contained a clause restricting liability for breach of description and that clause is clearly not 'fair and reasonable'.
B   The contract contained the phrase 'bought as seen'.
C   Where it is proved that, despite his inspection of the machine, Peter relied on the description.
D   Where it is proved that Peter relied on the description and the defects were not apparent.

MULTIPLE CHOICE QUESTIONS

Question 7

A sign in a shop states 'Goods bought during the sale will not be exchanged nor will refunds be made'. If a customer buys goods which prove to be of unmerchantable quality, the statement on the sign will be:

A   binding on him;
B   not binding on him if he can show its terms are not 'fair and reasonable';
C   void and not binding on him at all;
D   unenforceable.

Question 8

Larry contracts with Liz to supply her with a PC computer and a laser printer as selected by her from his shop. It is agreed that Liz will postpone the collection of both items until Larry has installed a maths co-processor in the computer which he has undertaken to do. In the absence of any express stipulation when does the property in the 2 items pass to Liz?

	Computer	Printer
A	When the contract is made	When the contract is made
B	When the co-processor is installed and Larry informs Liz of this	When the contract is made
C	When the co-processor is installed and Liz accepts delivery	When Liz accepts delivery
D	When Liz pays for it	When Liz pays for it

Question 9

A buyer is deemed to have accepted goods:

1.   if he has taken delivery of them;
2.   if he has informed the seller that he has accepted them;
3.   if after they are delivered to him he resells them;
4.   if he resells the goods with delivery made directly from the seller to the sub-purchaser;
5.   if after a reasonable period of time he retains the goods without informing the seller he has rejected them.

A   1, 2, 3, 4 and 5
B   1, 3 and 4 only
C   2, 4 and 5 only
D   2, 3 and 5 only

Question 10

Terry contracts to sell to Francis 100 widgets for £20,000 for delivery in 2 months time. Francis immediately contracts to sell the goods to a third party for £23,000. When the date for delivery arrives Terry fails to deliver and Francis has to buy substitute goods for £27,000 to fulfil his contract with the third party. How much is Francis entitled to recover from Terry?

A   £3,500
B   £4,000
C   £3,000
D   £7,000

Negotiable instruments and cheques

Question 11

Consider the following bills of exchange where Kelly fills in the details as to the *payee* and the *amount* and then gets Murphy, his employer, to sign them as drawer.

1. A bill expressed to be payable to Black, a person with whom Murphy has had no previous dealings. Kelly purports to 'indorse' the bill to White by forging Black's signature.
2. A bill expressed to be payable to Green, a person with whom Murphy has had dealings in the past but to whom he owes no money at present.
3. A bill expressed to be payable to the same Kelly who signs his name on the back of it.
4. A bill expressed to be payable to Brown who is in fact owed money by Murphy. Kelly 'indorses' the bill to White by forging Brown's signature.

Which of the above bills is an *order* bill?

A   1, 2 and 3 only
B   2 and 4 only
C   4
D   none of them

Question 12

Matthew draws a bill expressed to be payable to Mark and it is accepted by Luke. The following indorsements appear subsequently and it can be taken that all the indorsees gave value for the bill:

> 'Pay John or order, signed Mark'
> 'Pay Peter or order, signed John'
> 'Pay Paul or order, signed Peter'
> 'Pay Saul or order, signed Paul'
> 'Pay James or order, signed Saul'

James presents the bill for payment but it is dishonoured. Against whom may he claim payment if it be the case that Peter had lost the bill and the finder forged his signature and negotiated it to Paul?

A   Matthew, Luke, Mark, John, Peter, Paul and Saul.
B   Matthew, Luke, Paul and Saul only.
C   Matthew and Luke only.
D   Paul and Saul only.

Question 13

William draws a bearer bill for £1,000 and hands it to Elizabeth in payment for goods received. Zoe steals it from Elizabeth and gives it to Heathcliff as a present. What are the positions now of (a) Elizabeth and (b) Heathcliff?

	Elizabeth	Heathcliff
A	True owner	Holder in due course
B	No position	Holder for value
C	No position	Holder in due course
D	True owner	Holder for value

MULTIPLE CHOICE QUESTIONS

Question 14

Kish Bank has presented to it for payment an open cheque drawn on it by its customer Baily and expressed to be payable to Howth, to whom payment is duly made. It later transpires that Baily's signature had been forged by his accountant.

Kish Bank will be entitled to debit Baily's account:

1. by virtue of s60, Bills of Exchange Act, 1882;
2. by virtue of s80, Bills of Exchange Act, 1882;
3. by virtue of s1, Cheques Act 1959;
4. if Baily knew of the forgery but did not inform his bank.

A   1 only
B   4 only
C   1 and 3 only
D   2, 3 and 4 only

Question 15

In which of the following situations would a paying bank be without protection:

A   it pays a cheque in good faith and in the ordinary course of business of Browne even though the cheque is expressed to be payable to Brown and is indorsed 'Browne';
B   it pays, in good faith and without negligence, a generally crossed cheque to Black's bank and it later transpires that Black had stolen the cheque from the true owner and had forged a special indorsement to himself;
C   in good faith it pays cash over the counter to White on his presenting an open cheque expressed to be payable to Black without requiring it to be indorsed;
D   in good faith and in the ordinary course of business it pays a cheque to Green and it later transpires that Green had forged the required indorsement of the payee Black.

Question 16

Assuming a collecting bank acting in good faith gives value for a cheque, which of the following statements is true:

A   it becomes a holder for value where the customer presents for collection an order cheque with a forged indorsement;
B   it obtains a better right to the cheque than its customer even though it is crossed 'not negotiable';
C   it may not recover payment as holder for value from its customer;
D   it becomes a holder in due course and accordingly may resist a claim from the true owner if it has negligently collected the cheque for a person not entitled to it.

MULTIPLE CHOICE SUGGESTED SOLUTIONS

Question	Answer		Question	Answer
1.	A		9.	D
2.	C		10.	D
3.	B		11.	C
4.	C		12.	D
5.	A		13.	D
6.	B		14.	B
7.	C		15.	C
8.	B		16.	D

Comments

Question 1

A judge of the High Court is only obliged to follow a previous decision if it is binding on him and if the material facts are similar. To do this he must follow the *ratio decidendi* **not** the *obiter dicta* in the case (hence 2 is incorrect). Statement 4 is incorrect because it includes decisions of the High Court which are not binding on future decisions of the High Court. See Chapter 3 paras 1 to 12.

Question 2

The court is not entitled to consider the Minister's expressions of intent. The other 3 options refer to well-established principles of statutory interpretation: A describes the literal rule; B the mischief rule and D the *pari materia* rule. See Chapter 3 para 24.

Question 3

It is only in relationships 1, 2 and 5 that undue influence is presumed to exist - it can exist in the other relationships but this must be proved. See Chapter 4 paras 5 and 6.

Question 4

Because Heathcliff is selling in the course of business and the shop is buying in the course of business this is not a consumer sale even though the goods are of a type ordinarily supplied for private use or consumption: s3 Sale of Goods and Supply of Services Act, 1980 and s55, Sale of goods Act 1893 apply. See Chapter 6 paras 1 and 15.

Question 5

See Chapter 6 para 22.

Question 6

The inclusion of the phrase 'bought as seen' indicates that the sale is *not* one by description - see *Cavendish Woodhouse v Manley, 1984*. Chapter 6 para 26.

MULTIPLE CHOICE SUGGESTED SOLUTIONS

Question 7

There is an implied condition that the goods are of merchantable quality (s14(2)) and this condition cannot, in general, be excluded where the buyer deals as a consumer (s55) - see Chapter 6 paras 15 and 29 to 31.

Question 8

Both items are specific goods. In a contract for the sale of specific goods which must be put into a deliverable state (ie the computer) then in the absence of an express stipulation the property passes when the seller has done what he has undertaken to do and has informed the buyer: s18, Rule 2. Where there is a contract for the sale of goods in a deliverable state (ie the printer) the property passes when the contract is made: s18 Rule 1 applies. See Chapter 6 paras 52, 54 and 55. Neither acceptance of delivery nor time of payment affect these rules unless there is express provision on the time the property will pass.

Question 9

Mere delivery (1) does not amount to acceptance. The buyer is entitled to a reasonable time to examine the goods and indicate either expressly (2) or by implication (3 and 5) that he has accepted them: s34 and s35. If the buyer has not had an opportunity to inspect the goods (ie option 4), their resale will not amount to acceptance - see Chapter 6 paras 79 and 80.

Question 10

Williams v Agius 1914 is authority for the proposition that in such circumstances the buyer can claim for the difference between the contract price (here £20,000) and the price £27,000) at which the substitute goods had to be bought. See Chapter 6 para 105.

Question 11

Only the bill in option 4 fully satisfies the definition of an *order* bill even though it bears a forged indorsement. The other 3 bills are *bearer* bills: 1 is a non-existent payee; 2 is a fictitious payee and 3 has been transformed into a bearer bill by Kelly's indorsement in blank. See Chapter 10 paras 12. 13, 14, 35 and 36.

Question 12

Peter's forged indorsement breaks the chain of title so that the bill was not payable to Paul, when he had it, and he had no right to transfer it to Saul - the bill was still payable to Peter and required his signature to make it deliverable. So that Saul had no title to it and neither has James: s24, Bills of Exchange Act 1882, see Chapter 10 paras 24 to 26. However s55 provides that those who indorse the bill after the forgery (ie Paul and Saul) guarantee the genuineness of all prior indorsements, including the indorsement purporting to be Peter's - see Chapter 11 paras 24 to 26.

The net result is that James can recover from Saul or Paul provided he gives them notice of dishonour.

Question 13

When Heathcliff receives the bill as a present he is not a holder in due course because he has not himself given value for it, but because value has at some time been given for it. Heathcliff becomes a holder for value. However a holder for value who is not a holder in due course takes the bill subject to prior defects in title which means he is subject to Elizabeth's right to have the bill restored to her - she is still the true owner. See Chapter 10 para 38 and Chapter 11 paras 78 and 17.

MULTIPLE CHOICE SUGGESTED SOLUTIONS

Question 14

The bank will only be allowed to debit his account if he knew of the forgery and neglected to inform the bank. Section 60, Bills of Exchange Act 1882 and s1 Cheques Act 1959 have no bearing since the cheque is neither indorsed nor requires indorsement and s80 is only of relevance to crossed cheques. See Chapter 13 paras 9 to 11.

Question 15

The bank's failure to obtain Black's indorsement means that the payment was *not* made in the ordinary course of business and so the bank would not have the protection of s60, Bills of Exchange Act 1882 and s1 of the Cheques Act. Section 80 would not be available because it only applies to crossed cheques. In situation A the bank is protected by s1; in situation B it is protected by s80 and in situation D by s60. See Chapter 13 paras 8, 10 and 11.

Question 16

As a holder in due course the bank is in fact the true owner of the cheque and can resist any other person's claim. Statement A is not correct, because the transferor of the cheque was not the holder of it the bank cannot be a holder for value. Because of the 'not negotiable' crossing a transferee cannot obtain a better right than that of the transferor – this rule applies to a collecting bank as much as to any other transferee (statement B). Statement C is not correct, by giving value for the cheque the bank becomes a holder for value and may recover payment from its customer if eg the drawer stops payment. See Chapter 13 paras 24 to 26.

ILLUSTRATIVE QUESTIONS
AND SUGGESTED SOLUTIONS

ILLUSTRATIVE QUESTIONS

1. (a) Explain the difference between civil law and criminal law.

   (b) Whilst driving in the course of employment you cause damage to another vehicle and it is alleged that you are to blame. What legal proceedings may arise from the incident? In which courts would these proceedings take place? What is the possible outcome of these proceedings?

2. In recent years many disputes have been settled through administrative tribunals instead of through the courts.

   (a) Explain, with examples, what is meant by an administrative tribunal.
   (b) Why are such tribunals established?
   (c) What controls exist over their work and decisions?

3. What is meant by delegated legislation? Outline the forms that delegated legislation may take, its advantages and any controls that exist over its use.

4. What is meant by:

   (a) European Community Law; and
   (b) a Code of Practice?

   Explain in both cases the extent to which these are sources of Irish law.

5. Outline the sources from which a judge may draw the legal rules to apply in deciding a case.

6. In what circumstances may a person seek to set a contract aside on grounds of undue influence?
                                                      (ICSA Irish Business Law - December 1990)

7. Distinguish between a condition and a warranty in a contract for the sale of goods.

8. (a) Bill sells a car to Ben to be collected in three days. The day after the sale Bill sells the car to Bob. Ben wishes to recover the car from Bob and seeks your advice as to his legal rights. Advise him.

   (b) Ron sells his car to Con who pays by cheque. The cheque is dishonoured. As soon as Ron learns that the cheque has not been paid he informs the Gardái. Meanwhile Con sells the car to Brian who buys in good faith. Ron seeks to recover the car or its value from Brian. Advise Brian.

9. (a) 'Under a contract for the sale of goods risk passes with title.' To what extent is this true?

   (b) Murphy, a farmer, orders from the Co-Op five tons of fertiliser. In addition he asks the Co-Op if it will put the five tons on one side and store it for him until he is ready to take delivery. The Co Op accepts the order, complies with Murphy's request and writes to him informing him that 'five tons have been put aside and await collection'. Three days later the warehouse is burnt down and the fertiliser destroyed. Advise the Co-Op as to whether it is likely to succeed in recovering the fertiliser price.

10. (a) Discuss the rights of action which a seller has for breach of contract against the buyer personally.

(b) A flour miller agreed to buy 200 tons of wheat from a corn dealer at £100 per ton. The miller later refused to accept delivery as the market price of wheat had fallen to £20 per ton. The corn dealer is now claiming damages. Advise the miller.

11. Michael bought a caravan for £1,500 under a hire purchase agreement using finance provided by Leisure Finance plc. The agreement required Michael to make equal monthly payments over three years.

After six months Michael was made redundant and, although offered another job, he discovered that he would have to wait two months to begin the new employment. He therefore wrote to Leisure Finance plc requesting termination of the agreement. He received no reply. One month later, not having made the due payment, he has been sent a computerised letter from Leisure Finance plc advising him to make good the payment by return of post, failing which representatives of Leisure Finance plc will call to repossess the caravan. Michael cannot pay:

Advise Michael as to:

(a) his rights to terminate the agreement;   (10 marks)
(b) the options available to Leisure Finance plc if he defaults.   (10 marks)
                                                                              (AAT June 1988)

12. State, giving reasons, whether the following are valid bills of exchange:

(a) Pay on demand to Frank the sum of £500 provided he passes his driving test in June 19X9.

(b) Pay to John the sum of £5,000 from the proceeds of sale of the goods consigned to you.

(c) After a stag party, the best man finds he has left his cheque book at home. In a slightly inebriated state he writes in pencil on the back of an envelope 'To City Bank, Cork. Pay to the Green Dragon the sum of £40 or order.'

You may assume that in each case the bills are correctly signed and dated.

13. (a) Give examples of the following indorsements of a bill of exchange:

   (i)   an indorsement in blank;
   (ii) a special indorsement; and
   (iii) a restrictive indorsement.

(b) Declan, a junior clerk, without any authority so to do, indorses a bill of exchange on behalf of his employers and sends it to their bank for collection. What is the effect of such an indorsement?

ILLUSTRATIVE QUESTIONS

14. A draws a cheque for £50 payable to B. B indorses it in blank and negotiates it to C. C, without indorsing the cheque himself, negotiates it to D in good faith. A meanwhile stops payment of the cheque.

    D wishes to sue C for £50.

    (a) Advise D.
    (b) Would it make any difference if C knew that the cheque had been stopped?

15. (a) What is meant by a holder in due course of a bill of exchange?

    (b) Distinguish between a holder in due course and a holder for value.

16. Peter steals cheques to the value of £2,000 payable to Trading & Co. He pays them into his account, telling his bank that Trading & Co is the name of a company under which he sometimes trades. The bank accepts this explanation without enquiry, collects the £2,000 and credits his account. The theft is discovered and the bank is sued for the £2,000. Advise the bank.

17. Slurps Ltd after carrying out intensive market research commissioned a designer to design packaging for their new range of soft drinks. Their designer has come up with a distinctively shaped plastic container for the products which will be manufactured and printed in colours already associated with the company's product range. The company intends a market launch and advertising campaign which will focus on the product name and the shape of the container. The managing director of the company believes that the product will start a market trend and wishes to know what long term protection is available in law to maximise the return to the company from their investment and prevent others cashing in on the trend created.

18. (a) In what circumstances will dissolution of a partnership be ordered by the court?

    (b) By what circumstances other than an order of the court may a dissolution of partnership be effected?

19. Alex, Brian and Charles are partners. To what, if any, extent have Alex and Brian power without the consent of Charles to:

    (a) expel Charles from the partnership;
    (b) dissolve the partnership;
    (c) admit David as a partner; or
    (d) limit the authority of Charles to bind the partnership?

20. (a) Brian and Rory carry on business in partnership as plumbers. Brian has discovered that Rory also has an interest in a rival firm and has been diverting business to that firm. What action should Brian take?

    (b) What is the position if Brian also discovers that after paying off debts and outside liabilities of the partnership there will be insufficient partnership assets to repay the partners?

21. Richard and James are partners in a firm of merchants. They have a written agreement which provides that the partners shall devote their whole time and attention to the business and that profits and losses are to be shared equally. Richard is very interested in golf and spends a great deal of time at the golf club, claiming that he is thereby attracting business to the firm. In consequence a disproportionate share of the work falls upon James who has to work long hours.

    (a) Can James successfully claim any additional reward for his extra work?

    (b) If Richard draws more than his share of the profits from the firm so that its bank account becomes overdrawn how will the bank interest be treated?

22. What was decided in *Garner v Murray*?

23. Explain the structure and function of one of the following:

    (a) The Committee of Permanent Representatives

    (b) The Management Committees.

24. Outline the general procedures followed in an action under Article 169 of the EEC Treaty in proceedings brought by the Commission where it considers that a member State has failed to fulfil an obligation under the Treaty.

    If a member State complies with the requirements of the Commission just after the Commission has brought the matter before the Court of Justice, does this preclude a decision by the Court?

25. By what criteria does the Court of Justice of the European Communities determine whether a Treaty provision creates individual rights which national courts must protect?

26. What administrative acts of a binding nature can be made by the Council or the Commission under Article 189 of the EEC Treaty? Explain the distinguishing legislative characteristics of each and the means by which they are implemented in Ireland?

27. What is understood by an undertaking having a 'dominant position' in the Common Market? What criteria would you apply in determining whether a 'dominant position' exists?

28. Would the exercise of a trade mark right, for the purpose of preventing the marketing of goods coming from a third country under an identical mark, constitute a measure having equivalent effect to a quantitative restriction if the holder of the trade mark in the third country also owned the trade mark in one of the member States and imported the goods via that member State?

SUGGESTED SOLUTIONS

1. (a) Civil law exists to enable a person, be he an individual or a corporate body such as a company, to obtain redress or protection if their legal rights are infringed or threatened. Such proceedings are brought against the person alleged to be at fault. The usual result of successful civil action is the award of damages as compensation, or a court order instructing the defendant to do or to abstain from doing something. For example, a newspaper might be ordered not to publish a libellous statement or to pay damages if it has already done so.

   The action is brought in a civil court under civil procedure as a case between private persons to do justice between them. The rules of standard and burden of proof are different to those in criminal cases.

   A crime is an act prohibited by law in the interests of society, even though its immediate effect (eg in a case of manslaughter) is injury to a particular person. The state, through the Director of Public Prosecutions or the police, institutes a criminal prosecution with the object of obtaining a conviction and a suitable punishment by imprisonment, a fine or otherwise.

   Criminal proceedings are brought by the Director of Public Prosecutions in courts which have criminal jurisdiction, usually a District Court or (for serious offences) a Circuit Court. The accused person is presumed to be innocent until the prosecution proves by evidence beyond reasonable doubt that he is guilty. If the prosecution cannot prove his guilt he is entitled to be acquitted.

   (b) On the facts given, the driver may have been guilty of a driving offence ie a crime, such as dangerous driving or careless driving. If the investigating gardai decide that a driving offence has been committed they will prosecute the driver in the District Court. If found guilty the driver is likely to be fined and a record of his conviction will be endorsed on his driving licence; he may also be disqualified from driving for a specified period and if the case is sufficiently serious he could be given a prison sentence.

   The owner of the damaged vehicle (or, if it is insured, his insurers after compensating him) may sue the driver at fault in civil proceedings to recover damages. Unless the claim exceeds £30,000, the action would be brought in a Circuit Court. The claim would be based on tort, in this case, the tort of negligence (want of due care) by the driver at fault.

   Since the accident occurred while the driver was acting in the course of employment, the action could be brought against his employer under the principle of vicarious liability. The employer or his insurers would be able to pay the damages even though the driver perhaps could not do so.

2. (a) Administrative tribunals serve mainly to decide disputes between private persons and public officials or local authorities over decisions taken by the latter in administering the law. There are also tribunals which exist to decide disputes between private persons arising out of legal codes, such as the employment protection law. Administrative tribunals differ from ordinary courts in the narrow and specialised range of their activity which is related to detailed rules and particular claims rather than broad questions of law. Their procedure is usually less formal than that of the courts.

As an example, an individual whose claim for social security benefit has been refused may apply to a social security tribunal which will hear evidence of the facts and decide whether under the relevant rules the applicant is properly entitled to the payment which he claims. Such a tribunal consists of a legally qualified chairman and two other members. It must act within the powers conferred upon it and fairly and if it fails to do so it will be subject to judicial review in the High Court.

Other examples of administrative tribunals are the Employment Appeals Tribunal which hears claims relating to unfair dismissal and redundancy and the Labour Court which hears claims under the Anti-Discrimination (Pay) Act, 1974 and the Employment Equality Act, 1977.

(b) The reason for establishing these tribunals is that they can deal quickly and informally with claims which require a knowledge of law and practice, sometimes very complicated, in a particular area. The members of the tribunal rely to some extent on their general knowledge of past practice in the relevant matters. For example, the tribunal which hears a complaint by an employee that he was unfairly selected for dismissal as redundant will know what is general industrial practice in redundancy situations. It does not need to hear as much evidence as a court might require in reaching its decision.

Since there is a general informality in hearings before tribunals, the claimant is more willing to state his case in person or to bring a friend to do it for him. Employers sometimes retain lawyers to present their case but an employee will usually ask his trade union to represent him (unless he appears in person).

(c) The absence of legal procedures in tribunal hearings may result in errors, especially on legal points. In some cases there is an established appeal procedure. From a Rights Commissioner, for example, there is an appeal to the Employment Appeal Tribunal, with the possibility of further appeal to the higher appeal courts.

The High Court can be asked to review the proceedings of a tribunal (and possibly to quash the decision) by application for judicial review and an order of *certiorari*.

3. The Oireachtas gives delegated authority to make additional rules of law.

An Act of the Oireachtas begins as a Bill which must pass through a sequence of discussions (including consideration of the Bill clause by clause in Committee) in both the Dáil and the Seanad before the Bill receives the President's signature and becomes an Act. This procedure usually takes about six months (since the successive stages are taken at intervals) and absorbs several days of debate in each House.

In most Acts there is a section which authorises an appropriate person or body to make subordinate rules for specified purposes. In this way a Minister (in practice civil servants acting under his instructions) may prepare *statutory instruments* to fill in the details or to modify an Act. A local authority may similarly be authorised to make bye-laws in its area. A harbour authority may also be given power to make bye-laws. A professional body such as the Law Society may have power to make rules binding on its members.

The advantages of delegated legislation are that by this means the output of detailed law can be greatly increased, with speed, flexibility and effective definition of detail. Many statutory instruments, some very short but others rather longer, are issued every year. Parliament does not have time to deal with all this lawmaking. Delegated legislation is not put through the slow-moving parliamentary procedure of scrutiny and debate. It can be produced in a hurry when needed.

Insofar as delegated legislation fills in detail, which is its main purpose, it can be altered from time to time by making a new regulation. Many details are very technical, for example, some accounting practices applicable to company accounts. These are best discussed and agreed between the ministries and business and professional groups; TDs normally have neither the time nor the expertise to make such rules.

The standard method of control is to require (in giving authority to make delegated legislation) that the new rules shall either require positive approval (by a single vote) in the Oireachtas or, more often, shall be open to Parliamentary challenge for 40 days before coming into effect. Standing Committees of both Houses report on any delegated legislation laid before the House which requires debates etc.

Delegated legislation must be kept within the limits of the powers given by the relevant Act. If it appears to exceed those limits, anyone may challenge the rules in a court of law, asking for a declaration that the rules are *ultra vires* (in excess of the delegated lawmaking power) and void or repugnant to a provision of the Constitution.

4. (a) Ireland has been, since 1 January 1973, a member of the European Community and a party to the Treaty of Rome by which the European Community was established in 1957. It is also party to related treaties under which the European Coal and Steel Community and the European Atomic Energy Community were established. These three treaties were merged in 1965 and operate as binding obligations on member states.

    The treaties give powers to the Council of Ministers to issue regulations and directives to member states. *Regulations* are 'self-executing' - they are immediately effective as law, binding persons within (or even trading within) the territory of the Communities. The prohibition of restrictive practices in trade in manufactured goods is effected by regulations (issued mainly under Article 85 of the Treaty of Rome). An infringement of these regulations which apply to trade between member states, is punishable by fine imposed by EC authorities in Brussels even though no Irish law has been enacted to give them direct effect as law. Ireland did pass its own European Communities Act 1972 to bring treaties and regulations, then existing or yet to be made, into operation in the Republic of Ireland.

    The general programme of harmonisation of law throughout the Community is carried forward by the issue of *directives* which state in general terms the principles to which the national law of each member state should conform. The governments of member states then propose legislation, framed with due regard to their system of law, to bring their law into conformity with the EC directive.

The Council and the Commission of the Community may make *decisions* on particular issues which are binding on those to whom they are addressed. They may also issue advisory recommendations and opinions. The principles expressed in directives may be relied on in proceedings before national courts: *Van Duyn v Home Office 1974; McDermott & Cotter v The Minister for Social Welfare, 1987.*

In legal proceedings before national courts, a party may raise the question as to whether the local law conforms to a relevant provision of the EC law. The court may then seek an opinion from the European Court on the issue raised and will apply the ruling in the proceedings before it. One such case *Lee v Minister for Agriculture, 1979* sought a ruling on whether the farm modernisation scheme introduced by Council Directive EEC 72/159 encompassed grants for the construction of private dwelling houses.

(b) Codes of Practice do not have immediate effect as law. But if a court finds that a person did not conform to a code of practice it may take that fact into account in deciding the legal position of the person at fault, eg whether he behaved 'reasonably' or 'negligently'.

5. In presenting his case to the court a barrister specifies the rules of statute or case-law on which he relies. He usually reads the section of an Act of the Oireachtas or a passage from a judgment in an earlier case if he relies on it as part of his argument. He also develops his points by legal argument. The judge listens to both sides and then explains (in a judgment) the reasons for his conclusions.

If the dispute before the court depends on a statute (or delegated legislation made under powers given by an Act of the Oireachtas), the judge has to consider in the light of the arguments and any previous decisions (precedents) put to him by counsel what those statutory words mean.

A statute usually contains an interpretation section which sets out what certain defined expressions used in the statute are intended to mean. There is also a general Interpretation Act 1937 which provides, for example, that a singular word (such as 'person') also includes its plural (persons). Private Acts in particular contain preamble sections which set out the Act's overall objects.

There are a number of general principles on interpretation of statutes which the court may have to apply. The most basic and important of these rules is that usually any word should be given its literal meaning as found in a dictionary, in preference to a less obvious meaning (but an interpretation section of the statute can override that). There are subsidiary rules of interpretation such as the golden rule (make sense of it if possible) the contextual rule, the mischief rule and the *eiusdem generis* rule.

If the point at issue is related to delegated legislation the court may be asked to decide whether the 'statutory instrument' is invalid because it has been made in excess of (*ultra vires*) the delegated power to make it.

The counsel, in presenting their case to the court, are likely to cite 'precedents', which are earlier decisions on the same issue given in a previous case. The judge will decide whether these are genuine precedents to which he should turn for guidance.

When an earlier case is cited as a precedent it is necessary to extract from it the reason given for the decision in that case (called the *ratio decidendi*). Only that reason can be a precedent. The court will also consider whether the facts of the earlier case are so like those of the present case as to make the earlier decision a relevant precedent.

The court will also consider whether a relevant precedent is binding or only persuasive. A decision of the Supreme Court is binding on all lower courts. The High Court is not bound by earlier decisions of that court. If it is not a binding precedent the court will give it due attention as a persuasive precedent but need not follow it. Decisions of foreign courts, such as English or US, are persuasive only. Finally, if there is a ruling of the European Court on the point at issue, an Irish court would follow it.

6. Whenever one party is in a fiduciary position in relation to another, that party must act with extreme care when dealing with the weaker party or with the weaker party's property. Because of the relationship that exists the courts have feared that the stronger party may gain some advantage at the expense of the other and the courts have to protect against this.

A fiduciary relationship, or one of trust or confidence, is one where a considerable amount of influence is acquired by the very nature of the relationship that exists between the parties, eg a patient and his physician, or a solicitor and his client. In order to discourage victimisation and sharp practice, the courts developed the doctrine of undue influence.

The general rule is that once one party to a contract falls into a category of person in whom trust and confidence is reposed he is obliged to show that the contract or sale was fair and freely assented to. This is referred to as the presumption of undue influence. The value of the presumption is that it results in the transaction being set aside if the onus is not discharged ie the onus, on the party seeking to uphold the transaction, of showing the propriety of the transaction. The presumption may arise in two sorts of cases. The evidence may show a particular relationship which, of itself, raises the presumption eg religious adviser and pupil: *Allcard v Skinner (1887)*.

Secondly, there is an indeterminate range of cases in which the whole evidence, when meticulously considered, may disclose facts from which it should be inferred that a relationship is disclosed which justifies a finding that there is a presumption of undue influence: *Re Founds Estate (1979)*. An example of this second class of case may be brother and brother: *Armstrong v Armstrong (1873)*. The simple fact of marriage raises no automatic presumption of undue influence but a relationship of trust may be disclosed on the evidence: *Northern Banking Company v Carpenter (1931)*.

Where the presumption does not arise automatically or by inference from the facts of the case, then the party seeking to impugn the transaction will have to convince the courts that the transaction should not stand. In *Glover v Glover (1951)*, the court stated that certain matters are always regarded as relevant and sometimes conclusive amongst which the following receive special mention:

-   that the transaction in question was a voluntary gift or for manifestly inadequate consideration;

-   a marked disparity in age and position between the parties to the transaction.

Where the presumption does arise, it is for the person trying to uphold the transaction to adduce evidence to show the lack of any influence used to close the deal. Factors to show this would be independent legal advice, *Horry v Tate & Lyle Ltd (1982)*, or evidence that all relevant information about the transaction had been disclosed: *Midland Bank v Cornish (1985)*. If the party seeking to uphold the transaction does not adduce evidence to rebut the presumption then the presumption operates to impugn the transaction at the option of the weaker party.

If a person later approves a bargain, he will be bound by it: *De Montmorency v Devereux (1840)*.

In cases where the presumption operates but there is no evidence of fraud or overbearing conduct, relief must be sought promptly. A delay of five years defeated a claim in: *Allcard v Skinner (1887)*.

7. Both conditions and warranties are terms of the contract. The distinction between them is related to their importance and determines their effect. In deciding whether to classify a term as a condition or a warranty the court must construe the contract taking account of the intention of the parties ie whether they intended a term to be of such importance that it was to be a condition. It is recognised however that they may not in making the contract have been able to assess the importance of a particular term and that this can only be assessed if the term is broken and it then becomes clear whether or not the consequences of breach are serious. In such cases the term is intermediate or innominate until it can be seen whether it should be classified as a condition: *Cehave v Bremer,The Hansa Nord, 1975*.

In the Sale of Goods Act 1893 a warranty is defined as a term breach of which gives rise to a claim for damages but not a right to reject the goods and treat the contract as repudiated.

There is no definition of condition in the Sale of Goods Act 1893 but it is a term which relates to the main purpose of the contract, ie breach of it is likely to frustrate the commercial object of the contract. If it is a condition breach of it entitles the injured party to reject the goods and to treat the contract as repudiated unless he has by accepting the goods or part of them reduced the remedy available to him to a claim for damages for breach of warranty only.

8. (a) The ownership of the goods passed to Ben when the purchase was made since this was a sale of specific goods in a deliverable state: Sale of Goods Act 1893 s18 rule 1. There is no evidence of any contrary intention.

   Bill however retained the car in his possession. If a seller who has possession delivers the goods to a second buyer (Bob) who receives the goods in good faith and without notice of the previous sale, the second buyer obtains good title (although Bill had none): s25. The question does not state whether these conditions, including delivery to Bob, are satisfied though it implies that they were. If that is the position Ben cannot recover the car from Bob. He may however claim damages from Ben.

   (b) In paying by cheque which was dishonoured, Con purchased the car by fraud and Ron is entitled to avoid the sale to Con on that account. In the ordinary way a seller who wishes to avoid a voidable contract must communicate his decision to the buyer. But if he is unable to do so, say because the buyer has disappeared, and he takes other steps such as reporting the matter to the Gardái, that is sufficient: *Car & Universal Finance Co v Caldwell 1965*.

   Con, however, does have voidable title to the car until Ron reports the affair to the Gárdai. A sale by a person who has voidable title before his title is avoided gives good title to the buyer if he buys in good faith and without notice of the seller's defect of title: s23.

   Brian's position therefore depends on the time of his purchase in relation to Ron's report to the Gardái. If Brian's purchase comes before Ron avoids the contract by his report Brian has good title to the car: *Lewis v Averay 1971*. But if the report precedes the purchase Con no longer has any title at all (and as the contract is rescinded he is not a buyer in possession and nor does his sale to Brian appear to be a disposition by a mercantile agent in the course of his business – it is a private treaty sale). In that case Brian gets no title because Con has none: *nemo dat quod non habet* applies.

9. (a) The general principle is that the risk of loss or damage to goods remains with the seller until property in the goods is transferred to the buyer whereupon the risk passes to him whether delivery has been made or not: Sale of Goods Act 1893 s20.

There are however exceptions to the rule. The parties may agree expressly or even by implication that the risk shall pass before or after the transfer of ownership. Thus under a contract for sale of goods cif (cost, insurance, freight) risk passes to the buyer as soon as the goods are loaded on the ship. But ownership does not pass until the shipping documents are delivered to the buyer.

The position may also be affected by trade custom which the parties have by implication adopted as a term of the contract. For example in *Bevington v Dale 1902* furs were delivered 'on approval' and stolen by burglars. It was shown that it was a custom of the fur trade that goods delivered 'on approval' are at the risk of the person who ordered them on these terms even though he is not then and might never become the owner.

S20 is also qualified by two provisos:

(i) If delivery is delayed by the fault of either party the goods are at the risk of the party at fault as regards any loss which would not have occurred but for his fault.

(ii) If seller or buyer is in possession of goods which belong to the other he has the normal duty of a bailee (to take reasonable care) and is liable if he is in breach of his duty.

(b) Sale of Goods Act 1893 s18 rule 5 provides that where there is a contract for the sale of unascertained goods by description, and goods of that description in a deliverable state are unconditionally appropriated to the contract, either by the seller with the assent of the buyer or by the buyer with the assent of the seller, the property in the goods thereupon passes to the buyer. Such assent may be expressed or implied and may be given either before or after the appropriation is made.

In the problem the Co-op has, with the assent of Murphy, unconditionally appropriated five tons of fertiliser and has informed him of the appropriation. Under section 18 the property has been transferred to Murphy who is liable for the loss. The Co-op must be advised that it is entitled to recover the price of the fertiliser unless the warehouse was burnt down owing to negligence. The risk was transferred when the property was transferred.

10. (a) The rights of the seller against the buyer personally are an action for the price or an action for damages for non-acceptance.

By s 49 the seller may sue for the price in either of two situations:

(i) When the property in the goods has passed to the buyer and he wrongfully neglects or refuses to pay for them according to the terms of the contract. The contract may specify that the price is payable at a particular time or stage in the sale. If it says nothing about the date of payment the price is due when the goods are delivered: s28.

(ii) When the contract provides that payment is due on a specified date irrespective of delivery and the buyer wrongfully neglects or refuses to pay it. The seller may in this case sue for the price even though property in the goods has not passed and the goods have not been appropriated to the contract.

Under s 50 the seller has a general right to sue the buyer for damages for non-acceptance where the buyer wrongfully neglects or refuses to accept and pay for the goods. In this case the first head of the rule in *Hadley v Baxendale 1854* applies and the usual measure of damages is the difference between the contract price and the market price (if there is an available market) at the time when the goods ought to have been accepted. If therefore the market price is above the contract price at the relevant time the seller will recover only nominal damages since he suffers no loss.

If he has re-sold to another buyer at the same or a higher price he cannot usually recover damages for loss of profit on the sale which has fallen through since he makes his profit on the sale to the other buyer: *Lazenby Garages v Wright 1976*.

(b) The principle stated above applies. The miller must be advised that the dealer may recover damages of £20 per ton being the difference between the market price (£80) and the contract price (£100) at the date when acceptance was due: s50.

No property in the wheat has passed (the goods are unascertained when the contract is made and have not been appropriated to the contract) nor is there a fixed contractual date for payment irrespective of delivery. The seller could not maintain an action for the price in this case.

11. (a) Michael has rights to terminate the agreement. Section 5 of the 1946 Act provides that a hirer of goods can terminate an HP agreement at any time before the last instalment falls due. This is done by giving notice in writing notifying the owner. Once this is done the hirer must pay all outstanding sums and such further sums, if any, which would bring the total repayments up to one half of the HP price. A hirer may also be liable however for any damage done to the hired goods beyond ordinary wear and tear. Michael must then allow Leisure Finance plc to take possession of the caravan. A clause in an HP agreement excluding or restricting this right will be void.

(b) Looking at the options available to the Leisure Finance plc in the event of Michael defaulting in his repayments, they are as follows:

Where Michael deals as a consumer, then pursuant to ss32 and 35 of the 1980 Act Leisure Finance plc is deemed to be a party to the HP agreement and thus can enforce it as if it was the original owner of the goods.

Section 12 of the Hire Purchase Act 1946 provides that the owner and the finance company may repossess the hired goods provided one third of the HP amount has not been paid and provided there is a provision in the agreement to that effect. To this end Leisure Finance plc cannot enter on to the hirer's premises to repossess the goods. In the event that Michael had paid more than one third of the purchase price then it must apply to the court for repossession. The court would then have discretion to order the return or not. As Michael has not paid more than one third, the finance company need not apply to court.

Had Michael not requested termination then the company could enforce its right to repossess the goods provided there was a term in the agreement to that effect and Michael would in theory also be liable to pay the full amount of instalments payable under the agreement. However, since Michael requested the termination of the agreement, which request the company ignored, a court would support his right to terminate the agreement. Accordingly Michael will only be liable for an amount totalling half of the total HP price and to return the goods.

The Consumer Credit Act 1995 was passed by the Oireachtas in July 1995 but at the time of writing (February 1996) is not yet in operation. This Act, which replaces the Hire Purchase Act 1946, the Hire Purchase (Amendment) Act 1960 and Part III of the Sale of Goods and Supply of Services Act 1980, regulates the form of various credit agreements including HP agreements, conditional sale agreements and other credit arrangements

12. A bill of exchange is defined as an unconditional order in writing, addressed by one person to another, signed by the person giving it, requiring the person to whom it is addressed to pay on demand or at a fixed or determinable future time a sum certain in money to, or to the order of, a specified person or to bearer: Bills of Exchange Act 1882 s3.

   (a) This order to pay is expressly conditional (on Frank passing his driving test). It is a valid order to pay but not a bill of exchange.

   (b) This too is not a bill of exchange because it makes payment conditional on the sale of the goods (they might be destroyed or prove unsaleable).

   (c) The following points arise.

      (i)   Capacity to issue a bill of exchange is determined by the same rules as apply in contract: s22. The best man clearly understands what he is doing in spite of his inebriated state. He has the required capacity to draw a bill.

      (ii) A bill of exchange must be in writing. But it need not be in any particular form – the back of the envelope will do. But as between banker and customer the bank would probably refuse to pay a cheque (which this is) unless written on one of its pre-printed cheque forms.

      (iii) A bill of exchange need not be written in ink or other permanent form. But a customer owes his bank a duty to take usual precautions against alteration of a cheque which he issues: *London Joint Stock Bank v Macmillan & Arthur 1918*. If the order written in pencil is subsequently altered, the drawer could not deny the bank's right to debit his account with the amount paid (unless the alteration was apparent).

      (iv) The order is addressed to a person (the bank) and signed by the drawer. The payee is designated not by his name but by the trade name (Green Dragon) under which he apparently carries on business. This satisfies the requirement that the payee (of an order bill) shall be a 'specified' person indicated 'with reasonable certainty'.

      (v)   The words 'or order' are misplaced. They should follow the designation of the payee to indicate that he may indorse for payment to someone else. But this is immaterial. The words 'or order' would be implied if omitted altogether: s8.

   It is therefore a valid bill of exchange though the drawee bank might raise the points indicated above.

13. (a) (i)   An indorsement in blank is simply the signature of the payee or other current holder on the back of the bill, eg 'J Smith' if the bill is payable to J Smith. An indorsement in blank converts an order bill to a bearer bill.

(ii)   A special indorsement specifies the person to whom the indorser authorises payment to be made in place of himself, eg 'Pay H Brown (sgd) J Smith'. The bill is still an order bill payable to H Brown or any person to whom he in turn may indorse it (or he may indorse it in blank).

(iii)   A restrictive indorsement is one which prohibits further negotiation of the bill, eg 'Pay H Brown only (sgd) J Smith'. A restrictive indorsement may also be one which merely authorises the indorsee to collect payment for a specified purpose or person, eg 'Pay H Brown for the account of C Black, (sgd) J Smith'.

(b)   Declan signs as agent for his employers. It is in fact an unauthorised indorsement which has no legal effect: s24. This is a bill of exchange and presumably not a cheque so that the rules which protect a bank against liability do not apply.

It is not clear how the indorsement comes to be made and for what purpose. Since the indorsement is made on behalf of the employers and the bill is sent to their bank for collection, it seems that the employers were the payee or indorsee of the bill, or the holder when it came into their possession. If that is so, indorsement on their behalf is unnecessary and it does not matter that the indorsement is invalid. The bank in collecting payment is merely acting as agent for a customer. If the customer, Declan's employer, is the true owner payment to him is in order and no problems arise.

In indorsing the bill even in the name of another person Declan assumes personal liability on it unless he indicates expressly that he signs 'for and on behalf of' his principal: s26. The facts here have something in common with those of *Rolfe Lubell v Keith 1979*.

14.   (a)   On B's indorsement of the cheque in blank, it becomes a bearer cheque transferable by delivery and without need of indorsement by C.

C is transferor by delivery to D. As such he is not liable on the cheque but he warrants to his immediate transferee (if the latter is a holder for value) that the cheque is what it purports to be, that he has a right to transfer it and that at the time of transfer he is not aware of any fact which renders it valueless: s58

The question does not state whether value is given at any stage, by B, C or D. If any one of them does give value then D is at least a holder for value to whom the above mentioned warranties are given by C. (If D himself gives value he is likely to be a holder in due course).

If D is a holder for value and C is unaware when he transfers the cheque to D that A is about to stop payment or has done so, C's warranties are true and he is not liable because in fact the bill (unknown to C) is valueless. C warrants merely that he does not know the cheque to be valueless.

Although D has no claim on C (if C's warranties to him are true) D does have claims (if D is at least a holder for value) on A as drawer and B as indorser. Each of them by his signature undertakes that the cheque shall be paid and that he will compensate the holder provided that the requisite proceedings on dishonour are taken: s55. But D's claim is for 'compensation' - he can only recover from A or B what he has paid C. If he paid C nothing, D has no loss for which he can claim compensation.

If D has suffered loss he may claim against B as indorser provided that he first discharges his duty of presenting the cheque to A's bank and then giving notice of dishonour to B within 24 hours (to preserve D's rights against B). If D takes this action, B will claim on A who as drawer undertakes to compensate any indorser who is required to pay.

D may alternatively claim for his loss from A. In this case notice of dishonour need not be given since A himself has countermanded payment: s46.

(b) If at the time of transfer to D, C knew that A had stopped payment, his warranty to D is untrue (the cheque is to his knowledge valueless) and C is liable to compensate D for any loss arising from the breach of warranty.

15. (a) A holder in due course is a holder who has taken a bill, complete and regular on the face of it, under the following conditions.

    (i) He became the holder of it before it was overdue and without notice that it had been previously dishonoured, if such was the fact.

    (ii) He took the bill in good faith and for value, and at the time the bill was negotiated to him he had no notice of any defect of title of the person who negotiated it: s29(1).

This definition excludes an original payee since the bill is not 'negotiated' to him (*Jones v Waring & Gillow 1926*) and it excludes the holder of a bill which bears an irregular indorsement: *Arab Bank v Ross 1952*. If an indorsement is forged he is not the holder at all.

(b) A holder in due course differs from a holder for value in the following respects.

    (i) A holder in due course must have given value for the bill himself. A holder for value is the holder of a bill for which value has at some time been given but not necessarily by him.

    (ii) A holder in due course must satisfy the other conditions set out in (a) above. They do not apply to a holder for value.

    (iii) A holder in due course can enforce the bill against all previous parties. A holder for value has rights against previous parties down the sequence as far as the last to receive value.

    (iv) A holder in due course has various presumptions in his favour, for example s21 (delivery), ss54-55 (liabilities of parties) and s64 (alteration).

    (v) A holder in due course takes the bill 'free of equities', enforceable against previous parties. A holder for value has the same rights as the transferor to him had – he takes subject to equities.

16. In collecting payment of the stolen cheques and paying the proceeds into Peter's account the bank, although innocent of any fraudulent intent, becomes liable to the true owner of the cheques (Trading & Co) for damages (£2,000) for conversion of its property unless the bank is protected by Cheques Act 1959 s4.

S4 protects a collecting bank from liability provided that it obtains payment for a customer, in good faith and without negligence. Peter is a customer, since he has an account and the bank has acted in good faith. But it is likely that the bank has lost the protection of s 4 by its negligence.

When a customer delivers to his bank for collection a cheque which appears to be payable to someone else the bank has a duty to enquire as to the customer's title to the cheque. It should also make further enquiries if the customer's answer or spontaneous explanation does not suffice to remove doubt. The facts of the question are taken from *Baker v Barclays Bank 1955* where the customer presented to his bank for collection cheques payable to a firm, saying that he was shortly to become a partner and had begun to handle the firm's financial affairs. The bank was held to be negligent in failing to make further enquiries to verify this information.

The bank may contend that in modern banking practice it is simply not possible to make the enquiries necessary to determine whether a customer's statement is true or a cunning fraud. This view was the basis of the decision in *Marfani v Midland Bank 1967*. But in *Marfani's Case* there was nothing inherently suspicious. It is clear from other decisions that as soon as something unusual comes to the bank's notice it is negligent if it fails to make some further enquiries about the matter.

In this case if Peter's 'company' is a company registered under the Companies Acts its existence can be verified by a search at the Companies Registry. Even if there is a registered company of that name its cheques should be paid into a bank account in the company's name. If Peter's company is in fact a sole trader's business then Peter is using a 'business name' because he is not trading under his own name. The bank could test the veracity of his explanation by asking to see the letterheads which he would use (with his name as proprietor) if he really is trading as Trading & Co.

Another and simpler procedure would have been a telephone call to the bank on which the cheques were drawn to obtain confirmation from the drawer that he intended Peter to receive payment as Trading & Co.

These points merely illustrate that a bank when told an unlikely story can usually test its veracity without difficulty. In such circumstances it is negligent if it fails to do so.

17. There are various elements of intellectual property law which can be used to protect the commercial investment in this product namely:

Trade mark. Assuming that the product name that has been chosen is capable of distinguishing the product from other similar products the company can seek to have the product name registered as a trade mark, in Part B of the Register of Trade Marks kept under the Trade Marks Act 1963. If the particular name is an invented word or is adapted or graphically rendered in such a way as to be distinctive it may be capable of being registered as a Part A mark under the Act which will afford it a higher degree of protection. The mark can be registered for soft drinks of the type that is being produced. Whichever part of the register the mark is registered in, the company will have the exclusive use of the mark in relation to the classes of goods for which it is registered. The company may also wish to consider the use of a defensive trademark.

The container. While it is probably hoped by the company that the buying public will closely associate the product with the distinctive container it is not possible at this time to register the shape of a container as a trade mark. Coca Cola failed in their attempt to have their distinctive bottle shape registered as a mark.

SUGGESTED SOLUTIONS

Copyright. The designer will probably have made drawings for the new distinctive container. These drawings would be artistic works within the meaning of the Copyright Act, 1963. As the work in designing the container was commissioned the copyright in the artistic works belongs to the company. A rival who would seek to imitate their container could probably not do so without breaching the copyright in the artistic works as the reproduction of a two-dimensional work in a three dimensional form is a restricted act. This applies to the manufacture of goods for which drawings exist. It should be borne in mind that those parts of the design which are purely functional are not protected once the company has had more than 50 containers manufactured and sold *(Copyright (Amendment) Act, 1987)*. However, if you assume that the distinctive shape of the container arises from its design rather than its function the company is protected from anyone who would seek to imitate its container for 50 years.

Passing off. Before the actual market launch of the new product in its container the company does not have any goodwill in the product, such can only come from the presence of the product in the marketplace and the public associating the name and get-up of the product with it.

At this time it would appear from the question that the colour scheme to be used is already associated with the company's products and if a competitor were to launch a rival product which used that colour scheme in such a way as to be likely to cause confusion in the buying public and deceive customers into believing that the rival's product was the company's or was associated with the company then the company could take an action against that rival on the grounds that that rival was passing-off his product as that of the company's.

Passing-off however only protects existing goodwill and prevents others using that goodwill on their own benefit. No goodwill will arise in respect of the new product until it has become familiar to at least some section of the buying public. After the market launch the product will presumably become known to the public and a goodwill will begin to build up in respect of it. If at some future time a rival were to market a product which was through its colour scheme, printing, container, name or however similar to the company's product to the extent that the public could be confused into mistaking it for the company's or associate it with the company then the company may be able to restrain that rival from passing-off its product as theirs. This is so even if there are sufficient differences as to avoid the rival product breaching the company's trademark or copyright. Such goodwill will start with the market launch and will be strengthened by advertising and build up over time. The makers of Jif lemon have a product that was so familiar and distinctive, because of its lemon shaped container, that they were able to stop the marketing of lemon juice in lemon shaped containers which were different in size to theirs *(Reckitt and Colman Ltd v Borden Inc 1990)*.

18. (a) The court may order dissolution of a partnership in any of the following circumstances under the Partnership Act 1890, s 35 (as amended):
    (i) If a partner is found to be a lunatic or if he is shown to be of permanently unsound mind (but not if the partner found lunatic is a limited partner unless his share cannot be ascertained by any method other than dissolution).

    (ii) When a partner, other than the partner suing, becomes in any other way incapable of performing his partnership duties.

    (iii) When a partner other than the partner suing has been guilty of conduct which in the opinion of the court is calculated to prejudice the business.

    (iv) When a partner other than the partner suing wilfully and persistently commits a breach of the partnership agreement or so conducts himself that it is not reasonably practicable for the others to carry on partnership with him.

      (v)   When business can only be carried on at a loss.

      (vi)   When the court considers it just and equitable.

  (b) The circumstances in which dissolution can be effected other than by order of the court are:

      (i)   If the partnership is entered into for a fixed term, on the expiration of that term.

      (ii)   If for a single adventure or undertaking, by termination of such adventure or undertaking.

      (iii)   If for an undefined time, by notice of one partner to the others of his intention to dissolve partnership.

      (iv)   By mutual consent.

      (v)   Subject to agreement, on the death or bankruptcy of any partner.

      (vi)   At the option of the others if one partner allows his share of the partnership property to be charged for his separate debt.

      (vii)   If the object becomes illegal or the partnership becomes an illegal association eg by a change of law.

      (viii) If the firm itself becomes bankrupt.

19. (a) Charles cannot be expelled unless the partnership agreement specifically provides that a majority can expel any partner: Partnership Act 1890, s 25.

    (b) If the partnership is one for an undefined time, then Alex and Brian can give notice of dissolution at any time, but if it is for a fixed term, then dissolution would constitute a breach of contract: Partnership Act 1890, s 26.

    (c) David cannot be admitted unless partners agree: Partnership Act 1890, s 24.

    (d) Every partner may take part in the management of the partnership business, and any restriction on his authority must be with the agreement of all partners including Charles: Partnership Act 1890, s 24.

20. (a) A partnership is considered in law to be a contract *uberrimae fidei*. As a result, each partner owes a duty to his fellow partners to act in the utmost good faith and to disclose all matters relevant to the partnership. Rory is guilty of a breach of this duty.

        Section 28 of the Partnership Act 1890 stipulates that partners are bound to render true accounts and full information of all things affecting the partnership to any partner or his legal representative. Accordingly Brian can require Rory to disclose full information about his rival business.

        Furthermore, every partner must account to the firm for any benefit derived by him without the consent of the other partners from any transaction concerning the partnership or from any use by him of the partnership property, name or business connection (s 29). And if a partner, without the consent of the other partners, carries on any business of the same nature as and competing with that of the firm, he must account for all profits made by him in that business (s 30). Thus Brian can also oblige Rory to pay over all the profits he received from the rival business.

(b) The fact that the partnership assets will be insufficient to repay the partners after paying off the firm's debts and outside liabilities is not, in itself, a ground for applying to the court to have the partnership dissolved. (Under s 35 the court does have power to decree a dissolution if the business of the partnership can only be carried on at a loss; but there is no evidence that that situation applies here.)

However, s 35 provides two other grounds for compulsory dissolution, either of which might be relevant in this case. First, Rory may have so conducted himself in matters relating to the partnership business that it is not reasonably practicable for Brian to carry on the business in partnership with him; and secondly, the circumstances that have arisen might, in the opinion of the court, render it just and equitable that the partnership be dissolved.

The duty of good faith owed to each other by Brian and Rory will continue during the period of dissolution until arrangements for the distribution of the firm's assets have been made. Brian will be entitled to have any surplus assets of the firm applied in payment of what is due to himself and Rory respectively after deducting, in the case of Rory, what Rory himself owes to the firm under ss 29 and 30; and for this purpose Brian may apply to the court to wind up the business and affairs of the firm (s 39). If any losses arise on the dissolution, they will be borne by the partners in their profit-sharing ratio (s 44).

21. (a) The Partnership Act 1890, s 24, sets out the conditions under which a partnership must run, unless there is agreement to the contrary. Section 24(5) says that every partner may take part in the management of the firm. Section 24(6) states that no partner is entitled to remuneration.

However, in Richard and James's agreement they have stated clauses that overrule these implied authorities. In their deed, they 'shall devote their whole time and attention to the business'. It would be a matter for a court to decide whether Richard is devoting such time to the business as he has undertaken, or if he is falling down on his partnership responsibilities. No partner may claim extra payment for work done by him, but breach of the agreement will give rise to James's right to dissolve the firm with a petition under s 35(d).

Section 35(d) gives the court power to dissolve a partnership when it becomes unreasonable to expect partners to carry on in business together. Upon dissolution, the court may award the plaintiff partner such funds as they think fit in the circumstances, in lieu of damages for breach of the agreement, and only through this facility could James gain compensation for his extra work.

(b) If a bank account becomes overdrawn because of the actions of one partner, even if unbeknown to the other partners, and the withdrawal was ostensibly within the powers given to that partner, it is a valid debt of the firm, and all partners are equally liable. James is, therefore, best advised, if Richard refuses to contribute, to petition for a winding-up under s 35(d).

22. The decision in *Garner v Murray* (1904) was to this effect:

    If on a dissolution one partner has a deficiency of capital, and is, moreover, insolvent and unable to make up his deficiency from his private estate, such deficiency is regarded as a debt due to the individual partners rateably, and not to the firm as such. Consequently the loss is borne, not in the proportion in which profits and losses are normally shared, but by the solvent partners in proportion to their respective capitals as last agreed.

    Thus, assume that prior to dissolution the capital of A, B and C (equal partners) are: A Credit balance £1,000, B credit balance £2,000, C debit balance £500. C is insolvent. The realisation of assets results in a loss of £300. This loss will be shared equally by the partners, thus making their respective capital accounts: A Cr £900; B Cr £1,900; C Dr £600. Now if C's debit balance was a debt due to the firm it would be written off as a firm's bad debt and A and B, who share equally, would lose a further £300 each. As, however, the £600 is regarded as being due to A and B personally, the debt is considered as being due to them proportionately to their last agreed capitals. Thus there is due to A, £1,000/£3,000 x £600 = £200, and to B £2,000/£3,000 x £600 = £400. Consequently A and B each loses the amount considered to be owing to *him* by C, ie £200 and £400 respectively.

    Strictly speaking, the solvent partners should bring in their shares of the loss on realisation in cash, ie £100 each, with the result that the assets are divided between them in proportion to their capitals, ie they will receive £800 and £1,600 respectively.

    Note: Observe that the basis of distribution is 'last agreed capitals'. This will normally be the capitals as shown by the last balance sheet. Current account balances are not normally taken into account, so that if A had a credit balance on current account of £200 and B a credit balance of £50, the basis of allocation would remain as stated above.

23. (a) The Committee of Permanent Representatives performs the function of preparing the work of the Council and carrying out orders given by the latter. It is a subsidiary body known often by its French acronym COREPER.

    The Coreper is composed of the diplomatic representatives of the member States to the Community. These permanent representatives hold the rank of ambassador.

    Coreper is divided into two separate parts: Coreper I and Coreper II. The former is composed of the deputy permanent representatives whereas the latter is composed of the permanent representatives themselves. The former deals with such matters as the internal market, the harmonisation of laws, the common transport policy, the social policy, industrial policy, the environment, budgetary problems. The latter deals with such matters as: external relations, development, energy, policy, regional policy, institutional and political issues.

    The working groups of the Coreper are also composed of representatives of the member States. Their role is to enquire into the technical aspects of the matters to be dealt with by the Coreper. The Commission is represented in the working groups, as well as in the Coreper itself. The working groups are made up of representatives from the civil services of the member states who form part of the permanent representation of that member State before the Community, and also by national experts coming directly from national capitals.

    The presidency of the Coreper is occupied by the permanent representative of the member State which holds the presidency of the Council of Ministers.

SUGGESTED SOLUTIONS

Except for the common agricultural policy which has its own special committee, the Coreper has a monopoly of the deliberations concerning the results of the working groups as well as the preparation of all sessions of the Council.

(b) Special procedures are followed when powers are delegated by the Council to the Commission. It is common practice for the Council to lay down general principles governing a certain matter and to delegate the power to deal with the detailed questions. In order to retain some measure of control, the Council may provide for a 'management committee' to be set up. These committees are composed of representatives of the national governments under the chairmanship of a member of the staff of the Commission. The management committees employ the same system of weighted voting as the Council itself and decisions can be adopted only.

In the case of *Meroni v High Authority 1956* the legality of delegatory powers to management committees was considered by the Court. The plaintiff sought the annullment of the defendant's decision confirming the contribution payable by the plaintiff to the Scrap Equalisation Fund. The contribution amount had been assessed by a special committee appointed by the defendants. The plaintiff defected firstly on the grounds that this was an unlawful delegation of power.

It was argued that the management committee procedure constituted an unwarranted restriction on the decision-making power of the Commission and jeopardised its independence. The Court has pointed out that the management committee could not itself take decisions: if it disapproved of the proposed measure, the only consequence was that the Commission was obliged to communicate the measure to the Council, which could then substitute its own measure for that of the Commission. Therefore, the procedure was not contrary to the Treaty.

Only the function of detailed implementation may be delegated, but not that of the laying down of general principles. But the Court interprets the distinction in a wide sense. In the *Rey Soda Case, 1975* the Court said that the concept of implementation must be given a wide interpretation and that in the sphere of agriculture the Council may confer on the Commission's wide powers of discretion and action.

Therefore, extensive discretionary powers may be delegated to the Commission, provided the empowering permission lays down the basic principles governing the matter in question. So delegated power may be exercised by a simple procedure, that applicable under the Treaty.

24. The administrative stage of the proceedings is covered by the first paragraph of Article 169 of the EEC Treaty: if the Commission considers that a member State has failed to fulfil an obligation under the Treaty, it shall deliver a reasoned opinion on the matter after giving the state concerned an opportunity to submit its observations.

The reasoned opinion specifies exactly what the member State has done wrong. If the matter subsequently goes to the European Court, the opinion or decision serves as a definition of the issues before the Court: the Commission cannot raise any violations which are not set out in it.

The statement of reasons should contain sufficient detail to enable the defendant member State to decide whether it would be worthwhile contesting the matter before the Court.

The Commission is also obliged to set a time limit within which the member State must end the violation. The opinion is not binding and if the member State fails to comply, the Commission must bring the matter before the Court. It may only do so if a time limit specified has expired.

The reasoned opinion also specifies what action may be taken by the member State to end its infringement. However, the member State can choose what measure it takes so long as the infringement is terminated.

There is no time limit for the institution of proceedings or for the delivery of the reasoned opinion or decision. There is no deadline for the commencement of an action by the Commission before the European Court after the delivery of its reasoned opinion, but the Commission must wait until after the expiry of the limit given in the reasoned opinion.

The reasoned opinion forms part of the proceedings which may eventually lead in an action before the Court. This means that a separate action for the annulment of a reasoned opinion is not possible.

The Court has full jurisdiction to consider all the issues because the proceedings are not a review of the opinion or decision; the Court considers *de novo* whether the violation has occurred.

Proceedings cannot be brought under the EEC Treaty if the breach is terminated before the deadline laid down in the reasoned opinion: but what happens if it is terminated after the deadline, but before judgment? This occurred in one case and the European Court ruled that it does not constitute a bar to the action. The Commission might want to obtain a ruling to clarify the matter in case the violation is repeated at a later stage. In practice, however, it will usually drop the proceedings once the breach is remedied.

The Wool Import Case 1969 concerned an Italian law which was considered to be contrary to the Treaty because it imposed a tax on imported wool. Italy had replaced the law by a new and different one after the Commission had brought the matter before the Court. The Italian Government pleaded that the Commission should stop its action. The Commission was uncertain whether the new law sufficiently remedied the situation. It had no interest in the matter other than to obtain a termination of the specific breach. Both parties asked the Court to take account of the new law. The Court considered that this meant a change in the action as originally brought. No administrative stage had taken place with regard to the new law. Therefore the Commission's case was held to be inadmissible.

If the Court finds the allegation proved, it will give judgment against the member State in the form of a declaration that the member State has failed to fulfil an obligation under the Treaty.

In the *Second Art Treasures Case 1971*, the Court held that a decision of the Court is a prohibition on the national authorities against applying a national rule recognised as incompatible with the Treaty and an obligation if necessary, to take all appropriate measures to enable EEC law to be fully applied. The Court will specify what act or omission is the source of the violation. The Court has no power specifically to order the member State to do or not to do something, nor, if the violation takes the form of national legislation contrary to Community law, can it declare the legislation invalid. Article 171 of the Treaty lays down that a member State is obliged to comply with the judgment, though it can choose the way in which this will be done. Proceedings are usually directed not against a national law, but the breach of Community law resulting from it. The *Tax Refund in Italy Case 1964*, illustrates why this is so. In Italy there was a law which provided for the refund of taxes on exported steel products. The Commission considered such a refund to be a violation of the EEC Treaty and instituted proceedings against Italy. It issued a reasoned opinion stating that the export refunds were a violation of Article 96 of the Treaty. The Italian Government defended itself on the grounds that it had put amending legislation before the Italian Parliament. The Commission considered that the amending bill would not terminate the violation. It therefore proceeded with the action. The Italian Government pleaded inadmissibility on the grounds that its substance was different from that at the administrative stage. The Court considered that the substance of the

Commission's case concerned the actual application of the system of refunding taxes on exports, rather than the legal provision on which it was based. The Court held the action was admissible and found that Italy had failed to fulfil an obligation under the EEC Treaty.

25. There is no statement in any of the Treaties as to whether Treaty provisions are directly effective.

Direct effect means that a legal provision grants individuals rights which must be upheld by national courts. It is usually the case that an individual wishes to enforce a right against a public authority, but an individual could conceivably wish to enforce a right against another individual.

A legal provision cannot be directly effective unless two requirements are satisfied. Firstly, the provision must be part of the national legal order, and secondly, its terms must be appropriate to confer rights on individuals.

As regard the first requirement, there can be little doubt that in principle all Community law is valid within the national legal order.

The European Court has laid down three criteria for a provision to be directly effective: the provision must be clear and unambiguous; it must be unconditional; its operation must not be dependent on further action being taken by the Community or national authorities.

As regards the first criterion, this refers to generality and lack of precision. If the provision merely lays down a general objective or policy to be pursued, without specifying the appropriate means to attain it, it can hardly be regarded as a legal rule suitable for application by a court of law. Further legislation is necessary before it can become operative in such cases: an example of this would be Article 5 of the Treaty or Article 6(1).

What is meant by the requirement of unconditionality is that the right must not be dependent on something within the control of some independent authority such as a Community institution, or the member State itself. In particular, it must not be dependent on the judgment or discretion of such a body. An example of this is Article 92-4 of the Treaty where the judgment or discretion of a Community institution is involved. These Articles concern state aids which distort competition by favouring certain enterprises or products at the expense of others. Article 93(2) makes provision for the Commission to decide whether any such aid infringes the provisions of Article 92. Article 93(3) allows the Council to authorise any aid which might otherwise be regarded as contrary to the Treaty.

As regards the requirement that there be no necessity for further action, if the Community provision states that the rights will come into effect only when further action is taken by the Community or by a member State, it would seem reasonable to hold that it cannot have direct effect until that action is taken. But the European Court has laid down a rule that if the Community provision gives a time limit for its implementation, it can become directly effective if it is not implemented by the deadline. In such cases, the only consequence of the requirement is that the direct effect of the measure is postponed until the deadline has passed.

The first case in which the Court of Justice had to answer the question whether individual citizens could invoke Treaty provisions imposing obligations on States concerned Article 12 which states that member States shall refrain from introducing new customs duties. This was the *Van Gend en Loos Case 1962*. The facts of the case were that Dutch importers objected to the rate of import duty charged on a chemical product imported from the Federal Republic of Germany, alleging that reclassifying it under a different heading of the Dutch customs tariff had resulted in an increase in duty prohibited by Article 12 of the Treaty. In the case the Dutch

SUGGESTED SOLUTIONS

Government argued that the article was addressed solely to member States and infringements should be remedied by recourse by the Commission to Article 169 (Failure to fulfil an obligation under the Treaty). The Court held that the prohibition contained in Article 12 was clear and unambiguous, and was not conditional on its implementation by national measure. Therefore, it had direct effect.

The Second Lutticke Case (1965) concerned Article 95 which prohibits internal taxation on the products of other member States in excess of that imposed on similar domestic products. Member States were required to repeal or amend any conflicting legislation after the end of the period of transition.

The Court held that Lutticke could invoke this provision before his national court as from the end of the period of transition. The prohibition against discrimination contained in Article 95 was clear and unambiguous. It is unconditional and not subject to any measure of national law to implement it. The prohibition was therefore complete, legally perfect, and capable of producing direct effects, even though it is addressed to the member States.

In the *Van Duyn Case (1974)* the European Court held that Article 48(3) which limits the clear obligation imposed on member States by the Article to permit free movement for workers, by stipulating that the obligation was subject to limitations justified on the grounds of public policy, public security, or public health. This was not such a condition as to prevent Article 48 having direct effect because the application of these limitations was subject to judicial control.

In the *Second Defrenne Case (1975)*, an argument advanced against the direct effect of Article 119 was that the Article contains the phrase 'the principle that men and women should receive equal pay' which indicated a general aim and not a right. The European Court did not accept this argument. The Court ruled that Article 119 entitled workers to undertake proceedings before national courts in order to ensure its observance. Even though the complete implementation of the equal pay principle could not be achieved without legislative elaboration at the community and at national level, the requirement was nevertheless apt for national judicial application in cases of direct and over discrimination which may be identified solely with the aid of the criteria based on equal work and equal pay referred to by the Article in question.

The Court also held that the Article could not be relied upon to support claims in respect of pay periods prior to the date of its judgment, except as regards workers who had already brought legal proceedings. This was because of the principle of legal certainty. The Commission, State authorities and private individuals had relied in good faith on the fact that Article 119 did not have direct effect as of the end of the first stage.

When the obligation imposed upon a member State has direct effect, that member State is no longer entitled to adopt or to apply national legislation contrary to that obligation. National courts should refuse to apply such legislation due to its illegality, therefore giving priority to Community law. Such was the case in *Rutili (1975)*.

The Articles which have no direct effect can usually be recognised from the fact that the texts leave some discretion to member States or Community Institutions.

Direct effect can operate as between individuals as well as between individuals and member States. In the *Walgrave Case (1974)* motor cyclists who earned their living pacing pedal cyclists in international events asked a Dutch court for a declaration that certain rules of the defendant association infringed the Treaty's prohibition of discrimination on the grounds of nationality. The Court held that the prohibition of discrimination on the ground of nationality does not only apply to the actions of public authorities, but extends likewise to private associations and organisations, whose regulations are aimed at regulating in a collective manner gainful employment and the provision of services. Otherwise, the provisions of the Treaty could easily be circumvented.

The Court has observed that the prohibition of Articles 85(1) and 86 tend by their very nature to produce direct effects in relations between individuals, and therefore create direct rights in respect of the individuals concerned which the national courts must safeguard.

In the *Defrenne Case* the Court held that the prohibition on discrimination between men and women contained in Article 119 applies not only to the action of public authorities, but also extends to all agreements which are intended to regulate paid labour collectively, as well as to contracts between individuals. The Treaty's prohibition on discrimination on the grounds of nationality or sex (as far as pay is concerned) may be invoked against natural and legal persons, as well as against member States.

26. Article 189 lists three different kinds of acts of a binding nature that may (if other provisions confer the power) be adopted by the Council or the Commission. These are Regulations, Directives and Decisions.

Article 189 also contains a short statement of the characteristics of each kind of act. A regulation is essential legislative or normative: it lays down general rules which are binding both at Community level and at the national level. Directives and decisions differ from regulations in that they are not binding generally: they are binding only on the person or persons to whom they are addressed. Directives may only be addressed to member States but decisions may also be addressed to private citizens. Under Article 189, another characteristic of Directives is that they are binding only as to the result to be achieved and leave to the national authorities the choice of form and methods. This suggests that Directives lay down a directive and allow each government to achieve it by the means they regard as most suitable. A Decision, on the other hand, is binding in its entirety.

Article 189 states that a Regulation is directly applicable in all member States. This does not mean the same thing as 'directly effective.' It only means that the provision must be part of the national legal system, ie it must be legally valid from the point of view of national law. The second requirement to make a provision directly effective is that its terms must be appropriate to confer rights on individuals. This is not necessary for a provision to be directly applicable. Accordingly, 'directly applicable' means that the provision is automatically part of the national legal system as soon as it is promulgated by the Community authorities: no national measures of incorporation are necessary.

The European Court has gone further than stating merely that directly applicable measures require no implementing measures by the national authorities, by laying down a positive rule that implementing measures are improper. This is because if such national measures were allowed, they would obscure the Community nature of the measure in the public mind. It could lead to the result that the public perception was that they took effect from the date of the national measure, rather than that of the Community measure. This would mean that the provisions would not come into force on the same date in all member States. Secondly, the uniformity of Community law could be jeopardised if national implementing measures were permitted. Thirdly, national implementation could prejudice the European Courts jurisdiction to give a ruling on the interpretation and validity of the measure under the procedure for a preliminary reference under Article 177 because some national courts might be less ready to make a reference to the European Court if the Community provisions were incorporated into a national measure.

Of course, implementing national measures were permissible where the regulation expressly requires the member States to implement it, where the terms of the regulation are vague enough to necessitate a more detailed national implementation measure.

Article 189 does not state that directives are to be directly applicable. The directive lays down an objective and leaves it to the member States to achieve that objective according to such means as they might think fit. One would have thought that a directive would not have direct effect under these circumstances, but the European Court has found otherwise, where member States have failed to enact implementing measures, individuals can seek to enforce rights directly before national courts.

Article 173, second paragraph, lays down the conditions under which an individual litigant can challenge a Community act before the European Court: any person may institute proceedings against a decision addressed to that person or against a decision which although in the former regulation or decision addressed to another person, is of direct and individual concern to the former.

The distinction between decisions and regulations is decisive for the purposes of Article 173, paragraph 2, since only decisions can be challenged by individual litigants. However, neither the form in which the act is adopted, nor the designation which it gives itself, is conclusive as to its essential nature.

In any proceedings brought by an ordinary litigant, it is an essential requirement that the challenged act be shown to be a decision in the material sense. Obviously, it must have legal effects in that it effects the individual's legal rights or obligation.

27. In the *United Brands Case (1976)*, the European Court defined a 'dominant position' as a position of economic power possessed by an undertaking which enables it to prevent the maintenance of an effective degree of competition on the market concerned by giving it the power to behave independently of its competitors, suppliers, and consumers. The tests will be satisfied if the undertaking has a substantial area of discretion in taking major business decisions, especially in fixing prices and determining the level of output (which are really two aspects of the same question).

In the same case, the European Court pointed out that it was not necessary for an enterprise to have eliminated all possibility of competition for it to have a dominant position in the market concerned. It would exist despite occasional bouts of fierce competition and price wars which were limited in duration and occurred in different areas. Indeed, United Brands had actually been suffering losses for several years. However, the competition was ineffective; United Brands were still able to charge higher prices than its competitors without suffering a significant reduction of its market share.

Under Article 86, an infringement occurs if an undertaking abuses its dominant position in a particular market. In order to be able to determine whether an abuse has taken place, one must first determine whether an undertaking has a dominant position in a particular market.

The European Court has said that a large market share can constitute, *prima facie*, proof of a dominant position on a market. This refers to share of turnover, not of production. A large market share means, for example, 70-90% as in the *Continental Can Case*. A 35% share in the *United Brands Case* was not enough in itself to constitute, *prima facie* proof and so other facts had to be taken into account, ie the strength and number of competitors. An undertaking with a relatively low market share may still be in a dominant position.

In certain cases such as *Commercial Solvents Corporation* the Commission and the Court found that the company had in fact a 'world monopoly' of a particular drug which made it easy to establish dominance.

Market share is not in itself enough to prove the existence of a dominant position. In the *United Brands Case* the Court applied a more flexible concept of dominant position, stating that the market share must not be negligible, but also takes into account, as an additional factor, obstacles to market access by third parties. The Court held that in establishing the existence of a dominant position, consideration may similarly be given to the firm's allegedly wrongful acts. The Court also ruled that a firm's economic strength is not to be measured by its profitability when assessing whether it holds a dominant position. A modest profit margin is not incompatible with a dominant position.

The Court will also have regard to the share which other competitors have in the market. In the *United Brands Case* it noted that its next nearest competitor had 16% of the market. In the case of *Hoffman La Roche v The Commission* the small size of its competitors' market shares helped to establish the dominance of Roche in the markets for Vitamins A, C and E.

In assessing dominance it is necessary to carefully analyse the advantages enjoyed by the 'undertaking' under scrutiny. In particular any obstacles in the way of potential market entrants should be taken into account. This might arise where the undertaking controls essential patents or know-how or because it controls the supply of raw materials essential to the manufacture of the product in question. Whether an undertaking enjoys a dominant position in the market is a question which has to be determined irrespective of the means, fair or foul, by which the position was attained.

The Court and Commission will also look at the ability of an undertaking to command finance. In the *Continental Can Case* the Commission pointed out that the company because of its large size was able to resort to the international capital market. The concept of parent companies and their subsidiaries all forming part of the same undertaking is also important in this context.

It will have regard to the fact that legally distinct companies may be regarded as forming a single undertaking if in practice they are subject to common control. In the *Commercial Solvents Case* the company's control over world supplies gave a related company a dominant position on the common market and *Commercial Solvents Corporation* was answerable for the related company's refusal to supply a third party.

Finally the Court and Commission will look at the conduct and performance of the undertaking in assessing its dominance. In *United Brands Case* the Court noted that the public continued to buy more of its goods even though it was the dearest vendor and deduced from that that such a state of affairs was consistent with the impression of overall strength gained by the company from a structural analysis of the relevant market and predatory-like practices.

28. Article 30 of the Treaty of Rome relates only to the movement of goods between member States. Therefore, trade mark rights that have been divided between the Common Market and third countries may be used by the EEC owner to exclude imports from outside the EEC without infringing Article 30, even if there is a free trade agreement in force between the third country and the EEC, since if there is an Article comparable to Article 30 in such an agreement, the European Court has said that such a provision is not to be given the same meaning in a context of a free trade agreement as in the context of a fully integrated Common Market.

However, if, as in the present case, the right-holder in the third country also owned the trade mark in one of the member States and imported the goods via that member State, the situation would, of course be different, because the right-holder would have been able to market his goods lawfully in the member State where he owned the trademark, thereby obtaining entry to the Common Market as a whole. Under Article 9(2) of the Treaty, the provisions of the Treaty referring to the free movement of goods shall apply to products originating in member States and to products coming from third countries which are in free circulation in member States. Therefore, to all intents and purposes, goods, originating in third countries which have been lawfully imported into a member State, and are therefore in free circulation within the EEC are in exactly the same position as goods originating in a member State, and the provisions of the Treaty on the free movement of goods apply to them equally unless the derogation of Article 36 applies.

Therefore, the situation here is the same as if the right-holder in a member State was attempting to prevent the importation of goods with an identical trademark by the right-holder in another member State.

The European Court in the *Centrafarm v Winthrop Case (1974)* has defined the specific subject matter of trademark rights as a guarantee that the owner of the trademark has the exclusive right to use the trademark, for the purpose of putting goods protected by the trademark, into circulation for the first time, and is therefore intended to protect him against competitors wishing to take advantage of its status and reputation by selling products illegally bearing it.

To use a mark to divide up national markets for goods is a mere exercise of the right and does not form part of the substance of the right, and so it cannot be allowed to override the principle of the free movement of goods between member States under Article 36. The substance of the right allows the right holder to put the goods onto the market for the first time and to prevent infringements of the trademark by third parties. He is not entitled to prevent third parties lawfully putting authentic goods onto the market of another member State where he has exhausted his right, by already having put the goods onto the market in another member State. This is the so-called principle of 'exhaustion' which applies throughout the EEC wherever the goods are first marketed in any member State, whereas traditionally some country only gave 'exhaustion' a national meaning, holding that a previous putting onto the market of the goods in another country did not exhaust the right of the national holder, even when it was the same person or a connected person who had done the previous putting of the goods onto another national market.

The court has insisted on applying the same principle even to a case where there was no such link between the two right holders. The *Cafe Hag Case (1973)* concerned the 'Hag' trademark for decaffeinated coffee. Originally acquired in several European states by the German Hag company, the mark for Belgium and Luxembourg was later assigned to its Belgium subsidiary. After the war, the Belgian Government sold the Belgian business to Belgian owners as an act of sequestration by way of war reparation. Thereafter, there was no connection of any kind between the Belgian and the German Hag enterprises. The Court held that it would contravene the free movement of goods principle for the owner of the Belgian mark to use it to stop the importation of German Hag's goods, either by a parallel importer who had bought the goods legitimately in Germany and subsequently attempted to import them into Belgium or by German Hag itself directly. The fact that there was no link between the Belgian and the German enterprises did not matter. It was enough that the mark had the same origin. The Court dismissed the fact that as a result the consumer could be confused as to the source of the product by saying that this problem could be remedied by recourse to adequate labelling.

This decision has been seen as an attack on the very substance of the trademark right and has been severely criticised in many quarters on these grounds. This is because trade marks, although they do not give a legal guarantee of consistency in quality, what they do do is that they afford the right-owner an opportunity to enable the customer to link the product with its source, so that he knows where to return for more if he likes the product. It is then up to the right-holder to maintain the desired standard of quality and consistency. If he varies this to the customer's disliking, the latter will cease to purchase the product.

The same or similar trademarks may be held by different undertakings in different Common Market countries in three circumstances: firstly, where they shared a common origin, but ownership was split up by voluntary assignment; secondly, where the marks shared are of common origin but passed into commercially unconnected hands as a result of government intervention as was the case in the *Cafe Hag Case*; or, thirdly, where the marks were at all times owned and developed by entirely separate enterprises; *Terrapin v Terranova*.

In the first two cases, the *Cafe Hag* judgment means that there is no right to prevent the free movement of goods between member States under these circumstances. However, the *Terrapin v Terranova Case (1975)*, established that there is a right to prevent the free movement of goods in the third case.

In that case, under German law, the owner of the well-known mark 'Terranova' registered for certain building materials, was held entitled to prevent a British firm from using or registering its mark 'Terrapin' for prefabricated buildings; and nothing in Articles 30-36 overrode this. The Court drew the line here, although it is hard to see the justification for treating the second case differently from the third (the Court held that in the Hag Case the guarantee to consumers had already been undermined by the subdivision of the market). The policy of free circulation is not so strong that a bona fide mark owner in one part of the market can use it in another market where a separate enterprise already has conflicting rights: he must instead build up his trade with a new mark system.

Original manufacturers have found ways to hinder parallel imports. Parallel or indirect imports occur when the goods have been put onto the market of the exporting state, and a third party has acquired them and attempts to put them onto the market of another member State. A recent case concerns the export of drugs from a cheaper market (UK) to an expensive one (Germany). In *Hoffman La Roche v Centrapharm Case (1977)*, the pills marked 'Roche Valium' were originally sold in lots of 100 or 250. For commercial reasons the parallel importer had to re-package them in lots of 1,000; this it did, relabelling them with the original mark and an indication that it was the marketeer. The Court said that the essential function of the trademark is to guarantee the identity of the origin of the trademarked product to the consumer by enabling him, without any possibility of confusion, to distinguish that product from products which have other origins. This would be jeopardised if it were possible for a third party to affix the mark even to an authentic product. This was the substance rather then the exercise of the right.

But the European Court altered its position by going on to say that even if the infringement does go to an essential aspect of the mark it still remains to be asked whether the rights are not being used as 'a disguised restriction on trade', under Article 36 of the Treaty.

Article 36 provides that the provisions of Articles 30-34 shall not preclude prohibitions or restrictions on imports, exports or goods in transit justified on the grounds of, *inter alia*, the protection of industrial and commercial property. Article 36 goes on to say that such prohibitions or restrictions shall not, however, constitute a means of arbitrary discrimination or a disguised restriction on trade between member States.

Article 36 is, of course, the basis for all the European Court cases on intellectual property rights.

INDEX

REVIEW FORM

IRISH BUSINESS LAW SUPPLEMENT

Name: _____

How have you used this text?

Home study (book only) ☐

On a course: college _____ ☐   Other _____

How did you obtain this text?

From us by mail order ☐   From us by phone ☐

From a bookshop ☐   From your college ☐

Where did you hear about BPP texts?

At bookshop ☐   Recommended by lecturer ☐

Recommended by friend ☐   Mailshot from BPP ☐

Advertisement in _____ ☐   Other _____

Your comments and suggestions would be appreciated on the following areas.

Introductory section

Content of solutions

Errors (please specify, and refer to a page number, if you've spotted anything!)

Presentation

Other

Please return to BPP(I) Publishing, 3 Rosemount Park, Newtownabbey, BT37 ONL.